Build Your Own 80486 PC and Save a Bundle

Aubrey Pilgrim

NOTICES

IBM®
PC-DOS®
PS/2®

IBM Corp.

1486™

Intel Corp.

Microsoft®
MS-DOS®
Windows®

Microsoft Corp.

FIRST EDITION
THIRD PRINTING

Library of Congress Cataloging-in-Publication Data

Pilgrim, Aubrey.
    Build your own 80486 PC and save a bundle / by Aubrey Pilgrim.
        p.   cm.
    Includes index.
    ISBN 0-8306-8628-2   ISBN 0-8306-7628-7 (pbk.)
    1. Microcomputers—Design and construction—Amateurs manuals.
I. Title.
TK9969.P564   1990
621.39'16—dc20   90-46706
                                                                          CIP

TAB Books offers software for sale. For information and a catalog, please contact TAB Software Department, Blue Ridge Summit, PA 17294-0850.

Questions regarding the content of this book should be addressed to:

Reader Inquiry Branch
Windcrest Books
Blue Ridge Summit, PA 17294-0850

Acquisitions Editor: Ron Powers
Technical Editor: Sandra L. Johnson
Production: Katherine G. Brown
Cover Design: Lori E. Schlosser

Contents

Introduction

You do not have to be an engineer to assemble your own 486. You will not have to do any soldering or wiring, or use any electronic test instruments. The board level components have already been installed and tested. All you will have to do is insert the plug-in boards into the slots on the motherboard, connect some cables, install two screws to hold the motherboard in place, then two more screws for the power supply and five for the case. Once you have purchased all of the components, it should take no more than 20 to 30 minutes to assemble. Anyone can do it. I will show you how easy it is.

Computerphobia

Some of you might still be unconvinced. Some people are still afraid of the computer, standing in awe of its mysterious and fantastic capabilities. If you are a bit reluctant to build your own, you should not worry. A computer is primarily just a bunch of transistors, resistors, capacitors, and other electronic components. I guarantee you that it will not bite you. Computer voltages are only 5 and 12 volts DC, so you cannot even get an electric shock unless you ignore the warnings and remove the cover of the power supply. Then you would have to put your hand in the power supply and touch the bare components while the power was on in order to get a shock. The power supply has an input of 110 volts AC that it transforms into the low DC voltages.

The computer changes data into a form of low voltage electricity that can represent zeroes and ones. Computer programs cause the electronic components to route and shape the small bits of electricity and cause them to perform all sorts of useful data.

   Billions of dollars worth of a large variety of computer boards have been designed and manufactured. A myriad of options are possible by using the different boards. You simply plug them into a motherboard for whatever option you desire. Again, no soldering, wiring, or technical expertise is required.

A short history of electronics

Electricity has been around for some time. In 1800 Alessandro Volta demonstrated the first battery. Basically, a battery is made up of two dissimilar materials or *electrodes*. One has an excess of electrons; the other has a deficiency. All elements have electrons flying around the nucleus of the atom, and some have one or more excess electrons. If a proper medium is present, the excess electrons will flow from one electrode to the other. The electrons continue to flow until a balance between the two materials or electrodes is reached. At this time, the battery is completely dead or discharged.

   It was soon found that if a motor was placed in a circuit between the two poles, the flow of the electrons through the motor would cause it to turn.

   Relatively speaking, the first vacuum tubes were developed only a short time ago. The basic vacuum tube had a cathode and a plate with a grid between them. If a high positive voltage was placed on the plate and the cathode was heated by a filament, electrons were boiled off and flew through the vacuum to the plate because of the high positive voltage. When this happened, current would flow through the tube. A small negative voltage applied to the grid could block electrons and keep them from reaching the plate. In this case, no current would flow through the tube. By varying the small amount of voltage on the grid from positive to negative, the flow of large amounts of current could be controlled.

   Radio and television stations fling high voltage signals out into the atmosphere. Depending on the broadcast power and how far from the broadcast station, the signal voltage might be only a few millionths of a volt when it reaches radio or television antenna. The signals are made up of alternating waves that vary from a positive level to a negative level. When these alternating signals are applied to the grid of a vacuum tube, they cause the current through the tube to be turned on and off. This causes a mirror image or identical alternating copy of the input signal to be created at the plate of the tube. The small input signal applied to the grid can cause the output copy of the signal voltage to be millions of times larger and stronger than the input. This replica of the small input signal is then strong enough to power a loudspeaker or to cause images to be painted on a television screen.

   In the early 1940s, a group of scientists connected several thousand vacuum tubes together and created a primitive computer. It cost millions of dollars and filled a large room. It could do less computing than a modern $5 handheld calculator.

The vacuum tubes were crude and massive and used excessive amounts of power. In the late 1940s, three scientists named Barden, Brattain, and Shockley discovered the transistor. The transistor was relatively small and required only a small amount of voltage and power to operate. Yet it could do almost everything that the vacuum tube could do, and it could do many things that the vacuum tube could not do.

The electrons that cause a lamp to light up or a computer to run are very tiny. You cannot begin to see them, even with the most powerful microscope. Reasonably, developers began to reduce the size of the transistors. Soon it was discovered that several transistors and other components could be placed on a single slab of silicon. This was the birth of integrated circuits.

The integrated circuits were made smaller and smaller and more and more transistors were added. The small integrated circuits made it fairly easy to develop computers.

The *central processing unit* (CPU) is the brains and main chip in computers. The more transistors, the more powerful the computer can be. In the early 1980s, Intel developed the 8088 CPU with 29,000 transistors on a single chip. The 80286 CPU came along a short time later with 125,000, then the 80386 CPU with 275,000. Today the 80486 CPU has 1,200,000 transistors on a silicon chip that is about 0.4″ wide and 0.65″ long. Before the end of this century, CPUs might have over a hundred million transistors.

The photo on the next page shows a fairly modern vacuum tube at the bottom. Above the tube in the center is a single transistor. At the top left is the original 386 chip with 275,000 transistors. Next to it is the newer version of the 386. Note that it is about half the size of the original. At the far right is the 486 chip with 1,200,000 transistors. The chips shown in the photo were defective, so Intel embedded them in plastic and made them into key chains.

The computer's impact

The computer has had a tremendous impact on so much of our lives. It has revolutionized the way research and development is done.

The computer has made it possible to land a man on the moon and have routine space flights. New products are rolling off computerized manufacturing lines. All kinds of things from pacemakers to cameras to automobiles to computer dating now use computers and high-tech electronics.

To say that the computer technology is moving forward in leaps and bounds is an understatement. Electronic technology made some extraordinary advances in just a few short years, but the computer technology advances have been even more dramatic. In the early 1980s, many of the desktop computers had only 16K of memory, while some of the better ones had as much as 64K.

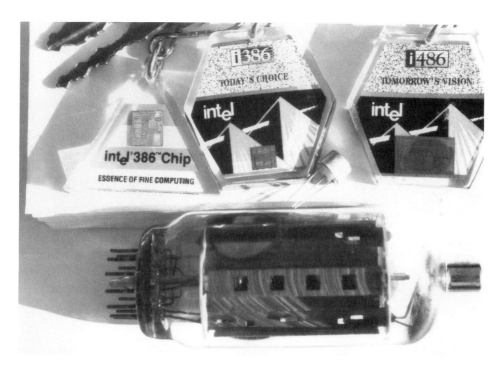

Evolution in electronics. A vacuum tube on the bottom, a transistor above and in the center, the original 386 chip with 275,000 transistors, the new 386 chip and the 486 chip with 1,200,000 transistors.

My first computer was a Morrow Designs with 64K of memory. It had two single-sided floppy drives that could hold only 140K on each diskette. (In those days, single-sided diskettes cost from $5 to $10 each. Double-sided diskettes were even more expensive. Now you can buy them for 25 cents apiece.) I was able to use WordStar on my little Morrow to write my first book. Even with its limitations, this tiny computer was an order of magnitude better than using a typewriter. (One downside to using a computer, according to a psychologist at the University of Pennsylvania, is that using a computer instead of a typewriter can cause a person to gain about seven pounds in a year's time. You do not get as much exercise as you would using a typewriter because most of your files are on the computer disk, so you seldom have to get up and search through a file drawer for information. So that is why I am getting fatter. I thought it was just because I was eating too well.)

Appearing less than ten years after the early Apple, Morrow, Osborne, and other CP/M machines is the fabulous 486 desktop computer. It is about the same size of those early 1980s computers, but the difference between the early computers and the 486 is about as great as that of a biplane from World War I and the space shuttle.

Organization of this book

I go into some detail about the 486 system. I list some of the hundreds of applications of the 486 system. I recommend some standard off-the-shelf software and explore such things as desktop publishing, networks, and other business and personal uses for the 486.

I describe the 486 and give reasons why you should build your own. I give you descriptions of the parts and components needed to assemble an 80486, along with photos and instructions on how to assemble an 80486. I also describe how to upgrade a PC, 286, or 386 to a 486.

I describe operations of floppy disks and hard disks. The importance of backups gets its own chapter, as do monitors, the function and operation of memory, keyboards and other methods of input to the computer, communications software and hardware (including modems, E-Mail, and fax), and printers. I briefly discuss the use of the 486 in business. I review a few accessories and adjuncts for the 486 and some of the most useful software that you will need. I list a few magazines and discuss mail order sources for the materials needed. A few tips on troubleshooting in case something goes wrong wrap up the book.

The author. I hope you enjoy the book.

The Glossary has hundreds of new buzz words and acronyms invented for the computer revolution. This extensive list should help you hold your own in any computer setting.

The subjects covered in each of the chapters are of interest to the newcomer as well as the experienced user of computers, especially if you want to build your own 486 and save a bundle.

1
CHAPTER

The fantastic 486

You can build a fantastic 486. It is the most powerful and fastest desktop computer in existence at this time. You do not have to be an engineer or technician to be able to assembly one. You will not have to do any soldering or wiring. In fact, you do not have to know anything about electronics in order to build a computer. If you know how to use a screwdriver and how to plug a few cables together, then you can do it. Once you have bought all of the parts that are needed, it should take less than an hour to assemble.

To build or not to build

Should you build your own or buy one ready-made? One company is offering a barebones 486 for less than $5000, but most of the larger brand name companies are charging from $7000 up to $20,000, depending on the goodies included. Depending on what you put into it, you should be able to save from $2000 up to $5000 if you build it yourself. In answer to the question above, I would say, by all means build your own. Because it can be assembled in less than an hour, I think it is well worth it. Most of us do not often get the opportunity to save money at the rate of over $2000 an hour.

What to do if you do not have $4000 for the parts

The 486 motherboard is the most expensive item and costs from $2500 and up to $5000. A motherboard for an XT costs about $65 plus the cost of memory. A 286 motherboard costs $200 to $300. A 386SX costs about $500 and a 386DX or standard 386 costs $600 to $800. The motherboard is the main difference in all of these computers. Most of the plug-in boards, disk drives, and other peripherals could all be the same in any of these computers mentioned.

If you do not have a computer, and you really need one now, you can use this book to easily build anything from an XT, 286, 386, or 486. You can purchase your parts as you can afford them. Because all of the components are compatible, you can also buy them from different vendors. If you can get by for a while with something less than a 486 system, you can upgrade it later when the motherboard prices have come down.

The 486 is basically a fast 386 with a built-in coprocessor. Except for the cost of the 486 chip, the motherboards should not cost much more than the 386 motherboards. Prices will come down when the companies have recouped their design and development costs, the 486 buying frenzy has cooled off a bit, and more 486 motherboard vendors enter the market, especially the companies of the East. The prices will come down. I guarantee it.

Lots of photos and easy instructions

It is actually easier to assemble this powerful computer than it is to learn some of the so-called "user friendly" software packages. I have great difficulty in learning some of the software that is supposed to be very easy to learn and use. Some of the problem is my fault. I am like a lot of people; quite often I do not read the instructions all the way through or follow them completely. However, some of the manuals and instructions seem to have been written for those people who already know the product while many other manuals and documentations are almost worthless.

Because I have had so many bad experiences with manuals, I have tried very hard to avoid mistakes made by others. I have tried to make this book as clear and easy to use as possible.

Cost of a 486

Some minicomputers require the space of half a room and cost from $50,000 up to over $100,000. Depending on the application, a desktop 486 might be able to outperform them. You can easily assemble a 486 for less than $5,000. Or you can spend up to $50,000 if you want a lot of extras and goodies.

The price of a 486 will be coming down. At the present time, the CPU alone costs about $1500. A motherboard costs from $2500 up to $5000. At this time, only a few companies have designed new motherboards for the 486. They must recover their design costs, and because they have very little competition, they can charge quite a lot. Eventually there will be lots of vendors and the prices will come down.

CPU

Just a very short time ago, the 386 seemed to be the ultimate desktop PC. The 386 CPU has 275,000 integrated transistors on a silicon chip. The original chip was about 0.375 by 0.4 inches square. Using newer technologies, they have now shrunk it down to about 0.225 by 0.275 inches. The 486 CPU has 1,200,000 transistors on a chip that is about 0.4 inches wide and about 0.65 inches long. It is the first chip ever designed with over one million transistors on it (Fig. 1-1). Figure 1-2 is a diagram of the 486 CPU.

Intel Corp.

1-1   The i486 chip from Intel with 1,200,000 transistors. ·

Inevitably, some circuits or transistors on some of the chips are defective. Intel embedded some of the defective chips in plastic and made them into keychains. The photo in the Introduction shows keychains made with the original 386, the new 386 and the 486 chips along with a transistor and a vacuum tube. The small squares in the plastic keychains are actual 386 and 486 chips. This photo helps to put into perspective the tremendous advances that have been accomplished. It is now possible to integrate an entire computer on chips in less space than the single vacuum tube required.

Processing speed

The fastest 386 today operates at 33 million cycles per second (33 MHz). It provides 25 times the performance of the original IBM PC. The 486 of today operates

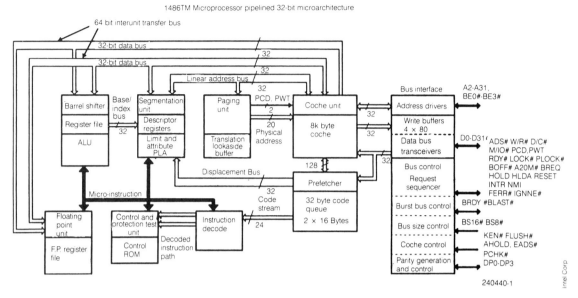

1-2 A block drawing of the functions of the i486 from Intel.

at 25 MHz, but it can process data by several times faster than the fastest 386. Though the 486 operates at a slower clock frequency than the 33 MHz 386, its internal design allows it to process data with a fewer number of clock cycles. The 486 provides performance 50 times greater than the original IBM PC. Later versions of the 486 will operate at 33 MHz and, eventually, all the way up to 50 MHz.

Backward compatibility

Despite all of its speed and power, the 486 is still compatible with the early 16K desktop PCs and can still run the same software. In addition, it can run all of the latest and most sophisticated software available. Actually, software that can take full advantage of the 486 capabilities has not yet been written. (We do not even have software that can fully utilize all of the 386 capabilities at this time.)

You will also be able to use most of the billions of dollars worth of the older boards and peripheral equipment that has been developed over the last ten years. If you or your company has a large investment in PCs, XTs, 286s, or 386s, the 486 will be able to use the plug-in boards, disk drives, printers, and most other equipment.

Built-in on-chip coprocessor

Some other features of the 486 is that it has integrated memory management with paging. It also has floating point and cache memory units and a high performance integer unit. Many software packages such as Lotus 1-2-3, dBASE, AutoCAD, and others have been designed to work best with a coprocessor. The 486 has a coprocessor built into it. Running at 25 MHz, a 486 can process applications two to four times faster than a 386 running at 33 MHz with an external 80387 co-processor.

Built-in on-chip cache

The 486 has 8K of on-chip cache memory in among its 1,200,000 transistors. It is designed so that it has a very high hit-ratio. Because it does not have to traverse the circuits to an external cache memory, it is very fast. The 486 has an external 32-bit data bus that can be used to refill the on-chip cache when a miss occurs. It uses a new burst bus transfer mechanism that can read a double word from external memory each clock cycle, then write it to the on-chip cache. In the burst mode, the 486 can throughput data at a rate of 80 megabytes per second. (*Burst mode* means that the bus is taken over and a packet of data is sent as a single unit. The bus cannot be accessed by other requests until the burst operation is completed. Over 80 megabytes per second can be sent in a burst mode.)

The 486 is capable of directly accessing four gigabytes or four billion (4,000,000,000) bytes of RAM memory. Using one megabyte chip, it takes 9 chips to make one megabyte. It would take 36,000 one megabyte chips to make four gigabytes. Even with the newer 4 megabyte chips, it would take 9000 chips. You probably would not be able to put that many chips into a desktop unit.

IBM and some of the Japanese companies are working on a 16 megabyte chip. It will still take 9 chips to make 16 megabytes, but this will considerably reduce the board real estate needed for memory.

RISC performance

The 486 offers all of the performance associated with the 32-bit *reduced instruction set computing* (RISC) found in many workstations. RISC type computers are usually very expensive and require special software. The 486 is 100% compatible with DOS software, but will also be able to run Unix, Xenix, OS/2, and other engineering software. Most engineers need DOS compatibility because they might spend half their time using software such as word processing, computer-aided software, business software, graphics, and others.

Multiprocessing and multitasking

The 486 supports multiprocessing and is able to communicate with other processors to make efficient use of shared resources. It also retains all of the multitasking features of the 386.

Who needs a 486?

So who needs all that speed and processing power of a 486? The same question might have been asked in the early 1980s when it was decided to go from 16K memory to 64K. You can be sure the question was asked when it was decided to go from 64K to 640K memory. I had no trouble running dBASE II, SuperCalc, Lotus 1-2-3, or WordStar on my little 64K Morrow. So when IBM first came out with a PC that could have as much as 640K, many people never bothered installing more than 128K or 256K at the most.

Today very few programs can run on anything less than 640K. Many of the new programs require up to two or three megabytes of hard disk space just to install them. Many of them cannot run unless you have two or three megabytes of expanded or extended RAM memory.

As I have indicated before, the computer technology continues to grow and expand at a dizzying pace. At this very moment, engineers and programmers are developing and designing hardware and software that will require even more memory and capabilities than you have today. The even more powerful 586 will probably be out shortly. Much of today's fantastic technology will be obsolete tomorrow. That does not mean that the software and hardware of today will not still be useful tomorrow. Many people are still using 64K CP/M machines and running dBASE II and many other useful programs on them. After all, if it satisfies their needs, that is all that matters.

To many people and businesses, time is money. They cannot afford to wait for a computer to go through several billions of iterations. It can be a shameful waste of human labor and valuable resources to have to wait for a complex spreadsheet or database.

So who needs a 486? You do, if you or your business does programming or uses any kind of design software. You should have a 486 on your desk for such things as computer-aided design (CAD), computer-aided software engineering (CASE), or almost any kind of development and design.

If you or your business does a lot of number crunching with spreadsheet programs such as Microsoft Excel, Borland's Quattro, Computer Associates Super-Calc5, or Lotus 1-2-3, then you need a 486.

If you or your business uses programs such as dBASE IV, Paradox, askSAM, FoxBASE, R:Base or any of the other databases, then you need a 486.

If you are a CPA and you use accounting, bookkeeping, or tax programs, then you could make good use of a 486.

If you are in a manufacturing business that uses servers, networks, multitasking, or multiprocessing, then you need a 486.

If you are involved in any one of a thousand other businesses where a fast and powerful computer is needed, then you need a 486.

Why do you need a computer this powerful and fast? If you do not mind waiting, most jobs can be done with an XT or AT. Waiting for a computer is almost as frustrating as waiting in a traffic jam. If you have a lot of money and you want the biggest and best, no law says you cannot have a 486. You only live once, so you might as well enjoy the best if you can afford it. You will be amazed at what a 486 can do for your ego.

Most people do not need all of the power and speed of the fabulous 486. But I suppose it is about like owning a Maserati. A person might never need all of its speed and power and might never be able to find a highway where he could push it up to 150 miles per hour, but I am sure it would be a fantastic feeling to own one. Almost as good as owning a super 486.

You can do it

Considering the power and sophistication of the 486, some of you might still have doubts about being able to build one. Would you have doubts about being able to build a lowly PC or XT? Please believe me, it is no more difficult to assemble a 486 than an XT, 286, or 386. Except for the motherboard, they are all assembled the same way.

The future

The present 486 operates at 25 MHz, but lots of 33 MHz chips should be available soon. (At a premium price, of course.) Eventually it will be tweaked up to where it will operate at about 50 MHz.

Because Intel is the only source for the 386 and the 486, they cannot manufacture enough to satisfy the demand. Already Intel has a few engineers working on the 586. It will probably have twice as many transistors on it as the 486 and will be much faster and more powerful. Intel has stated that they expect to have CPU chips with over 100 million transistors in less than ten years. This will provide you with more goodies than most computer people ever dared dream of. But I am sure that you do not want to wait that long. Lots of goodies are available right now.

Very Large Scale Integration (VLSI) is quite common now. Texas Instruments and Rockwell International, under contract to the Air Force, have developed a chip packaging technique that far surpasses the most densely packaged chip. They have been able to integrate an entire computer in a package about the size of a pack of playing cards. It weighs 75 grams (about $2^1/_2$ ounces), and is capable of up to 500 million operations per second (MOPS). It should not be too long before this technology can be used to build an entire 486 that would fit in the palm of your hand.

In the next chapter, I talk a bit about some of the components that you will need to assemble a 486.

2
CHAPTER

Components and cost

I have been asked many times, "What does it cost to build a computer?" That is almost like asking "How much does a car cost?" When someone asks me about cost, I answer with my own questions, "What do you want your computer to do?" and "How much do you want to spend?"

The cost of a computer

Of course to build a 486 is going to cost considerably more than it costs to build an XT or 286. I have seen ads for XT motherboards, with 0K memory, for about $65. (That 0K means zero K or no memory. You have to pay close attention to the ads. Some are rather misleading.) A 486 motherboard can cost from $2500 up to $5000. The rest of the basic components for an XT or a 486 can cost about the same. In fact you can use most of the same components such as disk drives, plug-in boards, mice, scanners, printers, and other peripherals in both machines.

Again, the main criteria in the cost of a computer is what you want it to do and how fast you want it to do it.

Another cost factor to consider is whether to buy a ready-made computer or build your own. I mentioned earlier that you could save from $2000 to $5000 if you build your own. But believe it or not, some people do not have to worry about money. These people do not mind spending $10,000 or more on a ready-made compatible.

MCA

I hate to admit it, other kinds of computers exist besides the compatibles, including the genuine IBM PS/2 line and the Apple Macintosh. The original 8-bit PC and XT boards and motherboard slot connectors had 31 contacts on each side for a total of 62. This was the bus and was more than sufficient for the power, grounds, refresh cycles, RAM, ROM, and all of the other I/O functions. These machines can only address one megabyte of memory and it only takes 20 lines, or 2^{20}, to address one megabyte.

When IBM introduced the 16-bit AT, it was designed so that it could address 16Mb of memory. So a total of 24 lines, or 2^{24}, were needed. Several other new bus functions were also added to the AT bus. They needed the 62 pins already in use on the bus, plus several more for the new functions. They needed a larger connector, but a new connector could obsolete all of the hardware that was available at that time. Someone at IBM came up with a brilliant design and simply added a second 36-pin connector in front of the standard 62-pin. The new connector readily accepted 8-bit or 16-bit boards.

Later when the 386 and the 486 were developed, they still used the AT standard bus. Many of the 386 and 486 ISA machines have a special 32-bit connector for memory boards, or access to 32-bit memory on the motherboard. However, most of the standard I/O functions are severely limited by the 16-bit AT bus.

In 1987, IBM introduced their new PS/2 line with *micro channel architecture* (MCA). This new system added many new functions to the computer, but it used a new bus system that was completely incompatible with the older hardware. Users were in about the same boat as the Apple users; they had only one vendor and the prices were very high.

To ensure that they remained the only vendor, IBM took out patents on almost every aspect of their PS/2 design. They let it be known that their stable of high-powered attorneys were ready to pounce on anyone who violated any of their patents. IBM had published all of the schematics and documentation for their original PCs, so it was easy for the clone makers to design compatible machines. This time they were very careful not to publish any data. So it is difficult for a cloner to know whether they are violating any of IBM's MCA patents. But IBM said, don't worry, just send us your designs and we will tell you whether you are in violation or not. Not many have done this.

IBM magnanimously offered a license to anyone who wanted to clone their PS/2s. For this, they wanted a rather high fee and a percentage of the price of each unit sold. In addition, they wanted back royalties from anyone who had sold IBM compatibles in the past. The back royalties could have amounted to millions of dollars. Many of the smaller vendors could not possibly pay it.

It was readily admitted that the MCA offered some real advantages over the old original IBM standard. One of the excellent features of the MCA system is the

programmed option select (POS). The MCA plug-in boards have a unique identification or ID. When a board is plugged in, the bus recognizes it by its ID and
automatically configures the board for use with the system interrupts, ports, and
other system configurations. If the board has any switches, it will tell you how
they should be set. I recently spent almost a whole day trying to install a board
that had three dip switches and three different jumpers. The switches and jumpers
had to be set so the board would not conflict with the rest of the system. The three
dip switches alone means that there were eight different possible configurations
(2^3), then add the three different jumpers for another eight different possible configurations or 64 total possible combinations. By the time you turn the computer
off, set the switches, then turn it back on and wait for it to reboot, it can be
awfully time consuming and frustrating. I had a manual, but like many of them, it
was practically worthless. A PS/2 with MCA POS could have saved me all the
time and frustration.

MCA offers several other very good features such as bus arbitration. This is a
system that evaluates bus requests and allocates time on a priority level. This
relieves the CPU of some of its burdens. The MCA bus is also much, much faster
than the old AT bus.

MCA has several other excellent benefits, but IBM is still the single source.
There are a few clones and a few third-party MCA boards, but they must pay a
license fee to IBM so they are rather expensive. IBM is the sole owner of the
design. MCA users are completely at the mercy of the whims of IBM.

Many people do not believe that the advantages of the MCA are great enough
to abandon the large supply of inexpensive IBM compatible hardware that is
readily available.

ISA

Many of the 486s use the *industry standard architecture* (ISA). ISA is what used
to be known as the IBM standard. For the vast majority of applications, the ISA
system is more than adequate. Figure 2-1 shows my standard-size ISA motherboard from Micronics. I have space for 16 megabytes of *single inline memory
modules* (SIMMs), but only 4 megabytes installed. Figure 2-2 shows a baby-size
ISA motherboard from A.I.R. It has 16 megabytes of SIMM memory on a plug-in
board. Figure 2-3 shows a different type of baby-size ISA motherboard from
Monolithic with 8 megabytes of SIMM memory on board.

For high-end workstations and minicomputer tasks, some of the 486s and
newer 386s use the *extended industry standard architecture* (EISA). Figure 2-4
shows a Micronics EISA motherboard. (More about EISA later.)

One of the greatest advantages of the ISA systems is the extraordinary versa-
tility and flexibility that it offers. At least 10 billion dollars worth of IBM compatible, or ISA, computer components exist. One of the reasons why so many ISA
components are available is the open system architecture.

2-1 My standard-size 486 board.

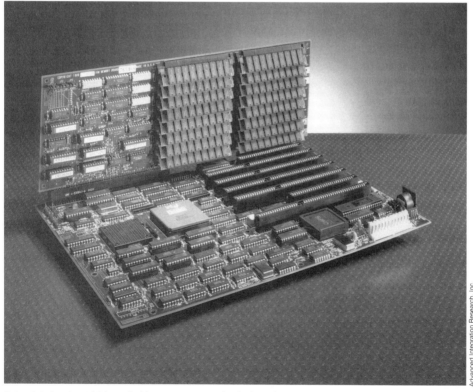

2-2 A baby-size 486 board with memory on a plug-in board.

Monolithic Systems Corp.

2-3 A baby-size 486 with 16Mb of on-board memory.

Micronics Corp.

2-4 An EISA motherboard.

Most of the ISA components are interchangeable. You can take any board or peripheral from a genuine IBM XT or AT and plug it into any of the clones, and it will work. You can also plug any of the components found in a clone into a genuine IBM or another clone, and it will work. Because there are so many clone products and vendors, they are readily available almost anywhere. Because there is so much competition, they are relatively inexpensive.

EISA and the gang

Many of the clone manufacturers were rather unhappy with IBM and their MCA PS/2 systems. IBM had introduced a system that was no longer compatible with a large number of clone manufacturers. IBM was counting on the large users to abandon the clones and jump on their PS/2 bandwagon. Many of them did so. It was clear that the cloners were being hurt.

A group of compatible makers got together. This gang included Advanced Logic Research (ALR), AST Research, Compaq Computer, Epson America, Everex Systems, Hewlett-Packard, Olivetti, Micronics, NEC, Tandy, Wyse Technology, and Zenith. They developed the *extended industry standard architecture* (EISA). This new standard includes the bus speed, arbitration, bus mastering, programmed option select, and other functions found on the MCA. But unlike the MCA, the EISA bus is downward compatible. The new EISA standard is designed so that the older style XT and AT boards can still be used. It does not matter whether your boards are 8, 16 or 32 bit, the EISA bus accepts them.

In some areas, the EISA system will outperform the MCA system. One of the biggest advantages of EISA over the MCA is that it is backwards compatible and allows the use of the billions of dollars worth of earlier hardware.

The EISA connector

I noted earlier that IBM designed the 16-bit AT bus by simply adding an extra 36-pin connector to the 8-bit 62-pin connector. This was an excellent idea because all of the earlier 8-bit boards could still be used.

The AT bus or ISA has 49 contacts per side or 98 total. Each contact is 0.06″ wide with 0.04″ space between them. The total connector contact area of a board is 5.3″ long.

The IBM MCA system needed 116 contacts, but they designed the MCA board by miniaturizing the contacts. Each of the MCA board contacts is 0.03″ wide with 0.02″ between them. This is just half the width of the ISA boards. The total connector contact area of a board is 2.8″ long, making any older ISA boards unusable in the MCA system.

The EISA system also needed more contacts so they added 100 more for a total of 198 contacts, 82 more contacts than the IBM MCA has. This gives EISA an opportunity to add more functions than the MCA system. They added the extra contacts on the plug-in EISA boards below the ISA contacts. They connected the lower EISA contacts with etched lines that interleave the 98 ISA contacts.

Unlike the MCA system, the EISA connector is designed so that it is compatible with all of the previous 8-bit and 16-bit boards, as well as the new 32-bit EISA board. They did this by designing a socket that was twice as deep as the original ISA slot or connector socket. This new socket has two sets of contacts, one set at the bottom of the socket and one at the top portion. At certain locations across the bottom of the socket are narrow tab projections that act as keys. These tabs prevent an 8-bit or 16-bit board to be inserted to the full depth of the socket. The contacts of the 8-bit and 16-bit boards therefore mate with only the upper contacts.

The EISA boards have two sets of contacts, one set directly below the other. They used the 0.04″ space between each ISA contact to connect the EISA contacts. The boards have notches cut in them to coincide with the keys on the floor of the EISA socket. Therefore, the EISA boards can be inserted to the full depth.

Figure 2-5 shows the evolution of connectors. An 8-bit board is shown on top, then a 16-bit board, an MCA board and an EISA board on the bottom. (The EISA board shown is a communications controller, primarily for use on local area networks.)

The ISA boards cannot be inserted deep enough to contact the EISA contacts so they touch only the top ISA contacts, but an EISA board can be inserted into an ISA connector. Because it cannot be inserted to its full depth, the EISA contacts would be touching the ISA contacts. It probably would not cause the computer or board to blow up, but it would not do it any good. There are some things that you just know you should not do.

A special chipset is required to design an EISA motherboard. At this time, Intel is the only manufacturer of the EISA chipset. Intel has designed chipsets for both the 386 and 486. Several companies are producing both 386 and 486 EISA motherboards. There is no reason why there could not be one for the 286, but it appears that they will not design one for the 286.

Intel designed the 286, but later licensed AMD and Harris to also manufacture them. AMD and Harris have improved on the Intel 286 design in several areas and have eroded the Intel 286 market, so Intel has more or less abandoned the 286. Intel is now promoting the 386SX to replace the 286. The 286 is still an excellent machine, and a 286 EISA machine could fill the gap for many low-end needs where the high cost of a 386 or 486 EISA cannot be justified.

As of mid-1990, rumors indicate that IBM is working on an EISA system also. Some people are amazed that IBM might be copying the clones, but it is right and proper that they do so. After all, the clones have copied IBM for many years; turnabout is only fair.

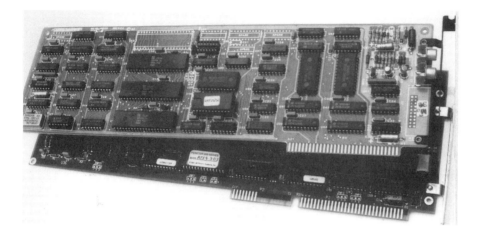

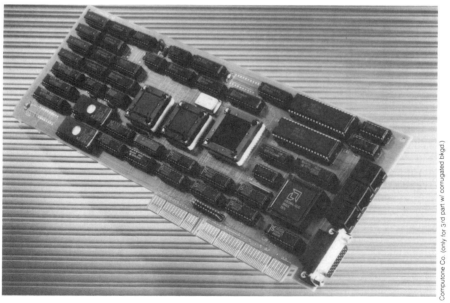

2-5 The evolution of connectors. The board on top is 8 bit, the next one is a 16 bit, the next one is IBM's MCA, and the bottom is the EISA connector.

Do you need an EISA computer

Do you need an EISA motherboard for your 486? That depends on whether you will be using it for high-end applications such as a network server or a workstation. Because the EISA motherboard provides much more functionality than the ISA, it is considerably more expensive. If you have the money, go ahead and buy one, even if you do not need the extras right away because it will make life a little simpler and less frustrating. Figure 2-4 shows a Micronics EISA motherboard.

Components and prices

Except for the motherboard, you will need about the same basic components for a 486 that is needed for an XT, AT, 286, or 386 machine. Here is a list along with approximate prices. Prices vary greatly among the various vendors. Prices also tend to change, usually downward, almost daily.

Component	Price range	
motherboard	$2500	5000
case	30	150
power supply	50	100
keyboard	30	150
monitor	65	3000
monitor adapter	50	600
floppy drive, 1.2Mb	60	125
floppy drive, 1.44Mb	60	125
hard drive	250	1500
hard drive controller	75	300
Total	$3170 − 11,050	

As you can see there can be a wide variation in the cost, depending on the components that you choose. At this time, the motherboard is the most expensive item. I bought a Micronics motherboard. (Micronics was one of the original gang.) It was one of their first production models. It has 4 megabytes of memory and 256K of SRAM. I paid $4450 for it. One reason for the high cost is that the Micronics motherboard was designed and manufactured in Sunnyvale, CA. As more vendors enter the market, especially those with manufacturing facilities off-shore, the competition will force the prices down. By the time you read this, the cost of a 486 motherboard will probably be down to around $2000 or less.

I was a bit disappointed in my Micronics board when I first got it. I had spent this large amount of money for the motherboard, but it had no built-in ports at all. My original 386 motherboard had two serial ports, two parallel ports, a light pen port, and an EGA adapter built into the motherboard. I had to go out and buy a

$15 I/O board in order to run my printer. I did not mind the cost of the I/O board, what I do not like is having to give up one of my slots for it.

I have checked several other motherboards. I don't know why, but it seems that very few of the other manufacturers are adding ports. At this time, the only one that I have found with built-in ports is the baby-size AIR.

One solution to the problem of saving ports might be a multifunction board. Monolithic Systems has the ultimate multifunction board. Their MicroPAQ VGA/multifunction board combines the capabilities of three separate expansion cards. It is a Super VGA adapter for up to 1024-×-768 color resolution, it has two serial ports, a parallel printer/scanner port, a floppy drive controller for all types of floppies, and an IDE hard disk interface.

Tower cases

If you don't have too much desk space you might consider the tower case. This allows your system to sit on the floor by your desk. The standard tower cases are a bit larger than the standard size case and have more bays. It will allow you to install up to seven or more half-height drives. For instance, you might want to install a CD-ROM and a tape backup system along with two floppy drives and two hard drives.

The tower cases are a bit more expensive than the standard or the baby size cases. The three sizes of tower type cases are a minitower for baby sizes, a medium size for baby and standard sizes, and a large standard size. The smaller sizes do not have as many bays for mounting drives. Most of the tower cases include a power supply and are sold for $110 up to $200 each.

Buying a barebones unit vs. components

Many companies offer barebones systems that include the basic components. Some of the prices are very attractive and are difficult to beat. They are fine for people who do not know how easy it is to assemble their own. Some of the components in these preassembled systems might not be what you want. For instance, you might want floppy drives that can read and write to all formats, a good high-resolution monitor and adapter, and a couple of good high-capacity, fast hard drives. It might not seem important, but you should especially try the keyboard before you buy a unit. In most cases, it will be your primary contact with your computer.

If a price seems too good to be true, then the vendor has probably cut a few corners somewhere. Some very good bargains are out there, but you should be careful. Your best protection is to be fairly knowledgeable about the computer business. Computer magazines and books (like the one you are holding) are some of the better sources for this knowledge.

Sources

In later chapters I discuss each of the components listed in detail. If you are fairly new to computing, I recommend that you read the chapters on floppy disk drives, hard disk drives, monitors, keyboards, and the major components before you buy your parts. At the end of each chapter, I list a few companies who provide the components discussed. In some cases, I might suggest or recommend certain components based on my experiences. That will not necessarily mean that you should buy only those products. As I have said before, billions of dollars worth of products are available. Many of them are very similar in functionality and quality. What you buy should depend primarily on what you want your computer to do and how much you can afford to spend.

One of the better ways to find the components and compare prices is to look through the many computer magazines such as *Computer Shopper* or *Computer Monthly*. You will find the addresses of these and other computer magazines in chapter 16. Many of the ads in these magazines are from mail order houses (more on mail order in chapter 16).

Another good source is to visit a computer show or swap meet. If you live near a large city, there will probably be shows every weekend or so. Of course, the local vendors and computer stores will be most happy to help you. They might charge a bit more than a mail order house, but if anything goes wrong, they are usually very quick to help you or make it right.

Sources for 486 motherboards

Here are a few of the companies who are offering the 486 motherboard. I am sure that there will be more and that they will also cost less than mine did.

V.I.P.C.
384 Jackson St., #1
Hayward, CA 94544
(415) 881-1772

MICRONICS
935 Benecia Ave.
Sunnyvale, CA 94086
(800) 234-4386

A.I.R.
528 Weddell Dr., #3
Sunnyvale, CA 94089
(408) 734-1248

WAVE MATE
2341 205th St., #110
Torrance, CA 90501
(213) 533-5940

AMI
1346 Oakbrook Dr., Suite 120
Norcross, GA 30340
(404) 263-8181

FOUNTAIN TECHNOLOGIES
12k World's Fair Dr.
Somerset, NJ 08873
(201) 563-4800

DCM DATA PRODUCTS
610 Tandy Center
Fort Worth, TX 76102
(817) 870-2202

ICC
8 East Lawn Dr.
Holmdel, NJ 07733
(201) 946-3207

SOYO USA
148 8th Ave. #H
City of Industry, CA 91746
(818) 330-1712

CALIBER COMPUTER
1635 McCandless Dr.
Milpitas, CA 95035
(408) 942-1220

ARTEK COMPUTER SYSTEMS
750 Montague Expressway, #203
San Jose, CA 95131
(408) 433-9208

AOX INCORPORATED
486 Totten Pond Rd.
Waltham, MA 02154
(617) 890-4402

INTERPHASE CORP.
2925 Merrell Rd.
Dallas, TX 75229
(214) 350-9000

CUI
1680 Civic Center Dr. #101
Santa Clara, CA 95050
(408) 241-9170

MONOLITHIC SYSTEMS
7050 S. Tucson Way
Englewood, CO 80112
(800) 525-7661

TP USA
46560 Fremont Blvd.
Fremont, CA 94538
(415) 623-9162

ASSOCIATES COMPUTER
3644 Tibbett Ave.
Riverdale, NY 10463
(212) 543-3364

INFORMTECH
Call (800) 624-8999 for nearest office.

AMERICAN DIGICOM
1233 Midas Way
Sunnyvale, CA 94086
(408) 245-1580

DASH COMPUTER
528 Weddel Dr.
Sunnyvale, CA 94089
(408) 734-8879

GST, INC.
6900 Hermosa Circle
Buena Park, CA 90620
(714) 739-0106

JOINDATA SYSTEMS
14838 Valley Blvd. #C
City of Industry, CA 91746
(818) 330-6553

SYNCOMP
1400 W. Lambert Rd. D
Brea, CA 92621
(213) 690-1011

ICC
8 East Lawn Dr.
Holmdel, NJ 07733
(201) 946-3207

AXIK COMPUTER
333 Cobalt Way, #108
Sunnyvale, CA 94086
(408) 735-7241

BABTECH ENTERPRISE
1933 O'Toole Ave. #A-104
San Jose, CA 95131
(408) 954-8828

CHAINTECH
10450 Pioneer Blvd., #8
Santa Fe Springs, CA 90670
(213) 944-2291

DTK COMPUTER
15711 E. Valley Blvd.
City of Industry, CA 91744
(818) 333-7533

EVERLASTING TECHNOLOGY
47517 Seabridge Dr.
Freemont, CA 94538
(415) 226-8888

KEYPOINT
12130 Mora Dr.
Santa Fe Springs, CA 90670
(213) 944-3041

I hope I have convinced you that you can build your own. In the next chapter, photographs and instructions show how easy it is.

3
CHAPTER

Putting it
all together

This chapter covers what you need to assemble your computer and how to do it. You will not have to do any soldering because all of the parts are connected together with cables and screws.

Parts needed

You will need these basic parts for your computer including the motherboard, chassis, power supply, floppy drive, hard drive, floppy and hard drive controllers, cables for disk drives, monitor and adapter card, and keyboard. I recommend that you read the chapters on the basic parts before you buy them.

You should also have a power strip with at least six outlets so that all of your equipment can be plugged into a single source.

Tools needed

You will need a screwdriver, preferably two of them, a Phillips head and a flat blade type. It will be helpful if they are magnetized. You can magnetize them yourself by rubbing them briskly on a strong permanent magnet. Those found on cabinet doors or the voice coil magnet of a loudspeaker will do fine. **Caution!** Do not place a magnet of any kind near or on your floppy disks. It can erase them.

Though not absolutely essential, a pair of longnose pliers comes in handy. If you have to remove or replace any chips, it would be helpful to have a small bent screwdriver for prying them out. The metal fillers on the back of the chassis are an excellent tool for lifting chips (Fig. 3-1). A small flashlight also is very handy for checking in dark places to make sure that everything is plugged in right.

3-1 The back panel cover for unused slots makes a good tool for lifting out chips.

Software needed

You will need a copy of DOS to boot up the system. You can boot up with almost any version of DOS, but I would strongly suggest that you use DOS 4.01, 5.0, or DR DOS 5.0. You must have a boot disk that has been formatted with system files on it.

Benchtop assembly

If you have your parts, you can start putting them together. Before I install a system in the chassis, I usually plug everything together and try it out on a workbench. If you don't have a workbench, just set it up on the kitchen table. Plug all the cables, drives and boards in and make sure it works. If something doesn't work properly, it is much easier to find the problem than if it is mounted in the chassis. Once you are satisfied that everything works, then you can mount it in the chassis.

Caution!

Before you open the plastic bags or handle any sensitive boards, you should ground yourself, especially if you are working on a floor that is carpeted. You can build up a static charge on your body of several thousand volts by just walking across a carpeted floor. This static voltage could possibly damage some of the fragile transistors on the boards. You can discharge yourself by touching the faucet of a kitchen sink, or almost any metal surface.

Instructions for assembly

Figure 3-2 shows the chassis, power supply, floppy disk drives, hard disk drives, cables, and disk drive controllers.

3-2 Some of the basic components that are needed to assemble a computer.

Figure 3-3 shows a Micronics 486 motherboard. The eight plug-in connector slots are shown in the top right portion of the motherboard. Below the plug-in slots are the vertical slots for *single inline memory modules* (SIMM). The four slots near the rear are filled with four megabytes of memory. To the right of the SIMMs is a white connector for the power connection from the power supply. Immediately above the power connector is the round connector for the keyboard cable.

Step 1: Connect the power supply to the motherboard

Plug the power supply cables into the white 12-pin connector on the motherboard. Figure 3-4 shows the power cables being connected.

Caution! It is possible to plug these connectors in backwards. If you do so it could cause severe damage to your motherboard and system. Note that the connectors from the power supply are usually in two parts, one marked P8 and one

3-3   My 486 motherboard.

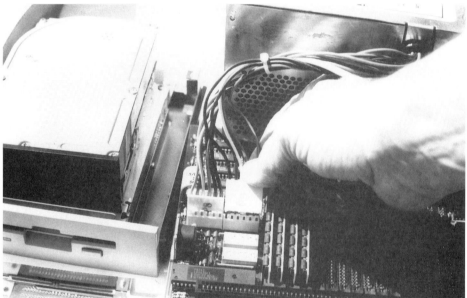

3-4   Plugging in the power supply to the motherboard. The two connectors are usually marked P8 and P9. P8 goes toward the rear. When properly connected, the four black wires are in the center.

P9. P8 plugs in toward the back of the connection and P9 toward the front. Each connector will have two black ground wires. When connected properly, the four black wires will be in the center.

Step 2: Connect floppy drives

Caution! Be very careful when installing drives and cables. Most of them can be plugged in backwards. This could cause severe damage to your drives or to the controllers.

You should have a wide 34-wire ribbon cable with a connector on each end and one near the center. The connector on one end will have a split and several of the wires will be twisted (Fig. 3-5). This connector plugs into the edge connector on the floppy that will be your drive A:, the drive that you boot from. You can hook up any drive as drive A:, but I would recommend that you install a 5¼" 1.2Mb drive.

3-5 Connecting floppy disk drive A:. Note that the cable has a split and some twisted wires. This connector goes to drive A:. The edge connector on the drive should have etched numbers indicating pin 1 and pin 34. The edge connector also has a slot between pins 2 and 3.

Note that this connector can be plugged in backwards or upside down. A different color wire, blue, black, or red, on one side of the cable indicates pin one. The floppy drive edge connector should have the numerals 2 on one side and 34 on the other. There should also be a slot cut into the edge connector between contacts 2 and 3. The colored wire side should be on the same side as the slot.

If you have a second floppy drive B:, the center connector should be plugged onto the edge connector. You can use any drive for drive B:, but I would recommend that you install a 3½" 1.44Mb drive. Again, the edge connector should have a slot cut between contacts 2 and 3, so the colored wire side should go to that side of the connector marked pin one or two (Fig. 3-6).

Step 3: Connecting floppy drives to the controller

The connector on the other end of the cable is connected to the floppy drive controller. If you have a hard disk controller, it can be capable of controlling the two

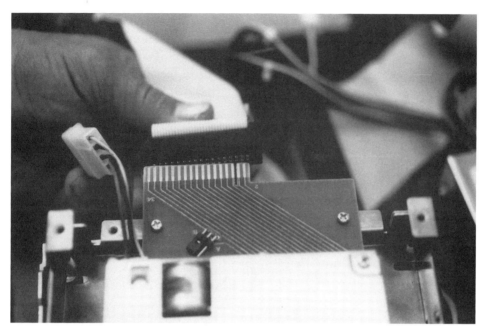

3-6 Connecting the B: drive to the connector in the middle of the cable. Note that the edge connector has a slot between pins 2 and 3. Note that the cable has a different color wire that indicates pin 1.

floppies and two hard drives. Check any documentation that you may have received with your controller. If it has a floppy controller, it will probably have two sets of 34 pins. The set of 34 pins in the center of the board is usually for the hard drive. The floppy connector might be towards the rear. Again, check your documentation. Pin numbers should be on the board indicating pin one (Fig. 3-7).

If you have a separate floppy controller, check for pin one and plug in the connector. Most of the newer floppy controllers have pins but the older ones used an edge connector on the end of the board. Make sure that your controller cable has the proper type of connector for your controller. Figure 3-8 shows a Compaticard floppy controller that has both types of connectors. It will control up to four floppies of any kind.

When connecting a cable to a board with pins, it is very easy to plug the connector in so that it contacts only one row of the pins. Check to make sure that the connectors are installed properly.

Step 4: Connecting hard drives

Caution again! The hard drives and cables can also be plugged in backwards, which could cause severe damage. Check markings carefully.

If you have bought one or more hard drives, they are probably not formatted. If you are not too familiar with the formatting of hard drives, read chapter 6. If you are not too experienced, you might try to get your vendor to format them for you.

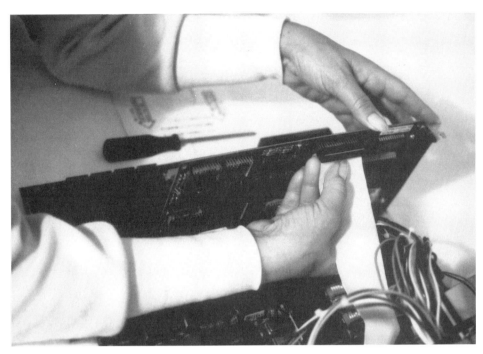

3-7 Connecting the floppy drive cable to a controller board that controls both hard disks and floppies. Check your documentation, but usually the floppy connector goes to the pins at the rear of the board. Make sure that the colored wire side goes to pin 1.

3-8 This is a controller for floppies only. It can control up to four floppies of any kind.

The flat 34-wire ribbon cable for your hard drives might look very much like your floppy cable. If you have only one hard drive, you might have a cable with just a single connector on each end. Or you might have one with three connectors just like your floppy cable, but the connector on one end might or might not have twisted wires like your floppy. If it has twisted wires, they will be at a different location on the hard drive connector than on the floppy, so the cables are not interchangeable.

The hard drive will have two edge connectors at the back, a 34 contact exactly like the floppy and a smaller 20 contact one. These connectors will also have slots cut in the board between pins 2 and 3, so it is fairly easy to determine where pin one is. Plug the end connector of the cable into the edge connector so that the colored wire side is on the pin one side (Fig. 3-9).

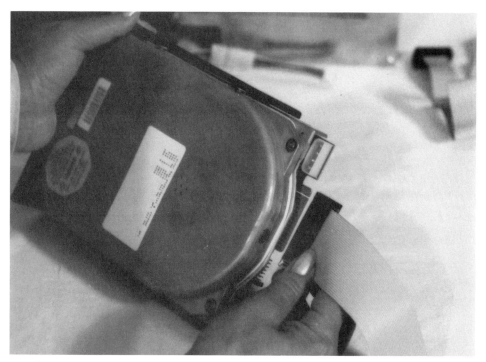

3-9   Connecting a hard disk. It will have a 34-wire cable that is similar to the floppy cable. A colored wire indicates pin 1. Note the slot on the edge connector between pins 2 and 3.

If you are installing a second hard drive, then there are some pins between the two edge connectors that should be jumper configured (Fig. 3-10). The ballpoint pens point to the pins and black jumpers. If you have a straight through cable, with no twisted wires on the end connector, the hard disk on the end connector should have a jumper on the set of pins nearest the 20-pin edge connector. Hard drive number two will have the second set of pins jumpered. If the cable has a twist in it, then the second set of pins on both hard drives are jumpered. Your drives might be different than these Seagate drives, so check your documentation.

A removable inline terminating resistor pack is in the center of the boards in Fig. 3-10. The hard disk at the bottom shows the terminating resistor pack

3-10 A closeup of the edge connectors of two hard drives. Note that they have a 34-pin and a 20-pin connector. The ballpoint pens point to the pins that have to be shorted out when connecting two drives. They also have removable resistor packs. The drive in the middle, or number two, drive should have the resistor pack removed. Check your documentation.

unplugged. The hard disk that is plugged into the center connector should have this resistor pack removed.

Figure 3-11 shows the 34-wire ribbon cable about to be connected to the hard disk controller. Again, be sure to install the connector so that the colored wire lines up with pin one on the board.

Install the 20-wire flat ribbon data cable connector on the hard disk (Fig. 3-12). Look for pin numbers on the edge connector, or for the slot between contacts 2 and 3 and orient the connector so that the colored wire goes to that side.

Connect the 20-wire data cable to the hard disk controller (Fig. 3-13). There will probably be two sets of 20 pin connectors. Usually, the first hard disk will be connected to the set of pins nearest the 34-pin hard disk connector. The 20-wire data cable from the second hard disk will be connected to the other set of 20 pins. Again, check the documentation for your hard disks.

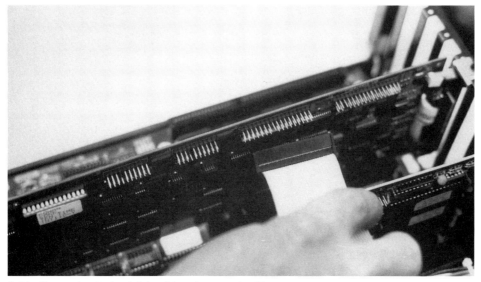

3-11 Connecting the hard disk cable to the controller. Note that the colored wire goes to pin 1.

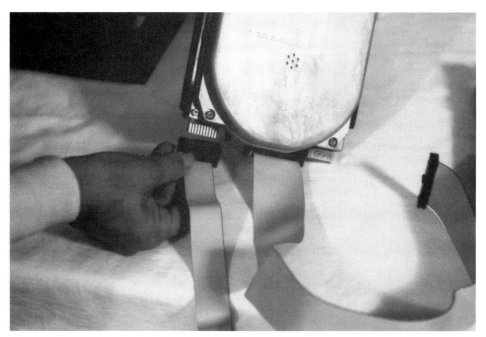

3-12 Connecting the 20 wire data cable to the hard drive. Note the colored wire and the slot between pins 2 and 3.

Step 5: Connecting the power cables to the drives

The power supply should have four cables each with four wires. They should be plugged into the matching connector on each drive. These connectors can only be plugged in one way.

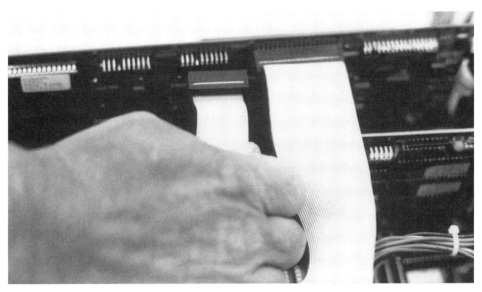

3-13 Connecting the data cable to the controller. The first hard drive connects to the set of pins nearest the 34-wire cable. Note that the colored wire goes to pin 1.

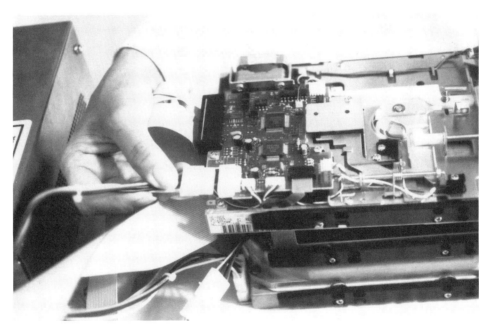

3-14 Connecting the power to the floppy drives. It can only be plugged in one way. The hard drives have the same connectors.

Step 6: Connecting the keyboard, the monitor, and the power

Plug the keyboard into the socket on the back of the motherboard. Then install the monitor adapter plug-in board and connect the monitor cable. Plug the monitor power cord into your power outlet.

Check again to make sure that everything is plugged in properly. Connect the power cord to the power outlet and the power supply.

Figure 3-15 shows the system all connected and ready to go. Put your boot floppy disk in drive A: and turn on the power. You will probably get a message that your computer configuration needs to be set. It will probably give you instructions on how to set the time, date, and number and types of floppies and hard drives that you have installed.

3-15 All connected on the bench top and ready to try it out before installing in the case.

Step 7: Installing the system in the chassis

If you have no problems, then you can install the system in the chassis. Figure 3-16 shows the floor of the chassis. Note the raised portions and the slots in them. Figure 3-17 shows the power supply being installed. Note the raised tongues on the floor of the chassis. The power supply has two recessed cut-outs on the bottom that slip onto the raised tongues. Two screws are then inserted on the back panel of the chassis to secure the power supply.

Figure 3-18 shows the backside of the motherboard. The white objects are stand-offs that will fit in the slots on the floor of the chassis. Figure 3-19 shows the motherboard being installed. Line it up so that the stand-offs drop into the openings of the slots, then slide it forward about a half inch. The stand-offs will lock the motherboard so that it cannot be lifted. A screw should be installed in the center at the rear and one in the front to fasten the motherboard securely.

3-16 The case showing the raised channels with slots for the motherboard standoffs.

3-17 The power supply showing the raised tongues on the floor of the chassis. The power supply has matching slots to accept the tongues. Set the power supply over the raised tongues, slide it toward the rear and install two screws.

3-18   The backside of the motherboard. The white objects are standoffs. The lower photo is a closeup of a standoff that has been removed.

You will see several wires for the small speaker, the switches and light emitting diodes (LEDs) on the front panel. Refer to the documentation that came with your motherboard as to where these wires should be connected. Most of the LEDs will have a black wire and a different colored wire. The colored wire should go to pin one on the motherboard; the black wire will be ground.

3-19 Sliding the motherboard into the chassis. Position it so that the standoffs slide into the openings on the raised channels.

Depending on the type of case that you bought, your drives might have to have plastic slide rails installed (Fig. 3-20). Then small clamps are used to hold the drives in place.

Go back and check all of the cable connections again. Make sure that they are all plugged in properly and securely. Check all of the boards to make sure that they are all seated properly.

You are now ready to install the cover. Slide it on and install a screw in each of the four corners on the back panel and one more in the top center.

Congratulations! You have just saved about $2000.

Computer furniture

If you have assembled your computer on the kitchen table, sooner or later your spouse will probably ask you to remove it. If you are setting up a home office, and you are not very rich or too proud, you might buy some used office furniture. Desks and filing cabinets might get dinged up and the paint might get scratched, but they seldom wear out. You can usually find a used office furniture store in most larger cities. Many of the larger stores such as K-Mart, Sears and Montgomery Wards also carry computer furniture. More about furniture in chapter 14.

User groups

You should not have had any trouble putting your system together, but chances are that you will have some software or hardware problems sooner or later. You will

3-20   Installing the plastic slide rails on the floppy drives. Your system may be different. Some have metal slide rails.

probably need some help. One of the best places to get help is from a *user group*. These are groups of people very much like you who have computers. Most of them have had problems like the ones that you will experience. They are usually happy to help you solve your problems.

Besides being a source of help, many of the groups provide their members with public domain software. Some have vendors come to the meetings and demonstrate their products. Many of them use the combined buying power of the group to arrange for discount prices on software and hardware.

The Pasadena User's Group is one of the largest in the country, primarily due to their president, Steve Bass. He has had speakers and presenters from major companies come to the meetings. Often speakers and presenters give away some of their products at the meeting, which is raffled off to the attending members.

Several of the members have volunteered to be in a skills bank. These members have an expertise in some phase of computing such as an expert in using a particular program, or in troubleshooting and diagnosis. One of the members put all of the volunteers' names and telephone numbers in a FoxBASE database and put it on the user group bulletin board and on floppy diskettes. The members can search the database to find an expert member who can help with a particular problem.

The meetings are enjoyable and we usually have fun. One member told an unusual computer story at one of the meetings. He said a friend had bought a computer and set it up on the kitchen table. But the table had one short leg and the computer started slipping off. His friend looked around for something to put under the table leg, but could not find anything the right size. It only needed about a quarter inch. He noticed that it was about the thickness of a checkbook, so he slid his checkbook under the table leg. It made the table perfect. He was probably the first person ever to use his checkbook to balance his computer.

The *Computer Shopper Magazine* publishes an extensive list of most of the user groups in the country each month. They also publish a list of the bulletin boards which can be very helpful to you. You can pick up a copy of the *Computer Shopper* at most magazine racks, or better yet, subscribe to it at P.O. Box 51020, Boulder, CO 80321-1020. It is one of the largest magazines in circulation and in size with about 800 large pages of articles and ads every month. It is an excellent source for shopping and comparing of prices.

If you have an older computer, you can find out what you can do to upgrade it in the next chapter.

4
CHAPTER

Upgrade by installing a 486 motherboard

If you have an old PC, XT, 286, or 386, you can easily install a new 486 motherboard. This can give you all of the benefits of a new 486 system at a fairly reasonable cost. Just pull out your old motherboard and install a new 486 board. Baby 486 boards will fit in a PC or XT. If you have an older standard 286 or 386, several vendors offer standard 486 motherboards.

486 ISA or EISA

You can install an industry standard architecture (ISA) motherboard or the extended industry standard architecture (EISA) motherboard. The EISA will be a bit more expensive, but it is more versatile and powerful.

386 EISA

Also 386 EISA motherboards offer some benefits that even the 486 ISA does not have. If you do not need all of the power of the 486 at the moment, you might consider installing a 386 EISA. A 386 EISA motherboard with a 387 coprocessor will give you almost all of the benefits of the 486 EISA at a lower cost. Any of the procedures listed here can apply to the 386 EISA upgrade as well as the 486.

Use your old components

Even if you are moving up from an old PC or XT, you will be able to use many of your old components such as the plug-in boards and disk drives. Unless your memory chips are a very fast 70 ns or better, you would not be able to use them. Besides, most of the new motherboards use single inline memory modules (SIMMs). More about memory in chapter 9.

Keyboards

If you are upgrading from an old PC or XT, you might not be able to use your old keyboard. Although the PC, XT, 286, and 386 keyboards look exactly alike and have the same connector, the PC and XT keyboards will not work on the 286 or 386 because they have a different scanner frequency. Some of the keyboards have a small switch on the back side that allows them to be switched from one type to the other. Some of the newer ones can detect what system it is connected to and switch automatically. The 286 and 386 keyboards will work on a 486 with no problems.

Keyboards have come way down in price. I have seen some fairly good ones at swap meets for $30 to $50. Try the keyboard before you buy it. Some require only a very light touch. If you are heavy-handed like me, you might not be happy if it is too light. More about keyboards in chapter 10.

Disk drives

You can use your old floppy disk drives on your new 486, but you might want to install a 1.2Mb and a 1.44Mb. These drives can read and write to 360K and 720K formats as well as the high-density ones. The higher capacity makes them much better for backing up and archiving. More about floppies in chapter 5.

If your old hard drive is less than 30Mb and is fairly slow, you should consider buying a new one, or at least a second one. Most controllers have the ability to control a second hard drive. The new software packages require an enormous amount of disk space. Most of the newer hard drives are much faster than earlier ones and have much greater capacities. More about hard drives in chapter 6.

Monitors

You might have an old monochrome or CGA monitor, and they will work fine with the new 486. But depending on what you want to do with your new baby, you might not be too happy with it. To me, the monitor is one of the more important components of my system. I spend a lot of time looking at it. I like color, so even if I am doing nothing but word processing, I will spend a little extra for good color. More about monitors in chapter 8.

Deciding what to buy and where

One of the first things that you will have to do is decide what you want. Or, if you are like me, decide what you want at a price you can afford.

I subscribe to about 50 computer magazines. These magazines have excellent articles and reviews of software and hardware. They also have lots of ads from stores that sell by mail. The ads give me a good idea of the price I will have to pay for an item. There can be quite large variations in prices from dealer to dealer. Mail order may be one of the better ways to purchase your parts, especially if you do not live near a large city.

Larger cities usually have lots of computer stores. There are hundreds in the San Francisco Bay area and in the Los Angeles area, as well as computer swaps going on every weekend. If I need something, I go to one of the swap meets and compare the prices at the various booths. I often take a pad along, write the prices down, then go back and make the best deal that I can. Sometimes you can haggle with the vendors for a better price, especially if it is near closing time.

Case size

The standard size AT or 286 is a bit larger than the XT. Again, the XT is 5″ high, 19$1/2$″ wide and 16$1/2$″ deep. The AT is 6″ high, 21$1/2$″ wide and 16$1/2$″ deep. By combining several chips into single *very large scale integrated* (VLSI) chips, the clone builders developed a *baby* 286 motherboard. It is about one inch longer than the XT, but it still fits in the XT case. Baby 386 and baby 486 motherboards have also been developed.

Figure 4-1 shows an XT motherboard on the left and the standard size 486 on the right. Several companies manufacture baby 486 motherboards that are about the same size as the XT motherboard, so you could remove the XT motherboard and install a baby 486.

One early problem was that several companies had developed 16-bit plug-in boards for the standard size AT, which are about one inch higher than the 8-bit XT boards. These wider 16-bit boards cannot be used in the smaller XT size case. With the advancing technology, most plug-in boards are now small enough that they will fit in an XT case.

Many people still prefer the original standard size 80286 case, but it has no real advantage over the baby size. The standard size case is only two inches wider than the XT or baby size. That does not sound like much, but if your desk is as cluttered as mine, it is a lot. It uses up an extra 33 square inches of desktop real estate.

Some people like the floor-standing tower-type cases because it frees up some of the desktop. The tower cases are even larger than the standard case and has space for more drives and other goodies. The floor standing case and power supply will cost about $200, whereas the desktop case and power supply might

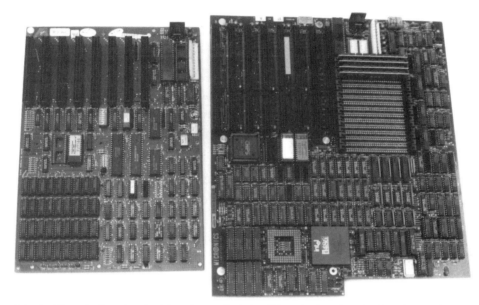

4-1 An XT motherboard on the left and a standard-size 486 motherboard on the right. A baby-size 486 motherboard is about the same size as the XT and can be installed in an XT case.

cost $100 to $125. The tower cases come in three different sizes. Figure 4-2 shows a mini-tower for baby-size motherboards.

Instructions and photos

The basic instructions and photos in chapter 3 apply in most cases to the upgrading of any computer. Refer back to that chapter if you have any problems.

Upgrading a PC or XT to a 486

The original PC and XT uses the 8088 *central processing unit* (CPU). This CPU has about 29,000 transistors and operates at 4.77 megahertz (MHz). Computers perform their operations by moving blocks of data in precise blocks of time. The PC and XT can cycle 8 bit blocks of data at 4.77 million times per second. That sounds fast but it takes 8 bits to make a single byte. It also takes 8 bits to create a single character of the alphabet. It takes a whole lot more bytes if you are using graphics. It can be painfully slow if you have to run a CAD program or a large spreadsheet. The turbo XTs are souped up so that they can operate faster than their normal 4.77 MHz. Most have a "high gear" so that they can be shifted up to 8 MHz or even up to 10 MHz or 12 MHz. However, a 486 can process data 20 to 40 times faster than a PC or XT.

If you have an original true-blue IBM PC, it will only have five slots, so the case or chassis has five openings on the back panel. The XT has eight slots with eight openings in the back panel. Almost all motherboards now have eight slots. If

4-2 A mini tower case with the cover removed.

you have an old PC case with the five openings in the rear panel, it will not accommodate the eight-slot motherboards. Your best bet is to scrap the old case with the five-slot openings and buy a new case. It would only cost about $30 for a new one, or about $100 with a larger power supply. If you are in love with the IBM logo and want to keep the old case, a few companies make special mother-boards for the old five-slot PC. Buying one of these special five-slot motherboards will cost much more than what a new case and an eight-slot motherboard would cost. It would be much better to buy a new case, rip the IBM logo off the old case and tape it to the new one.

If you are upgrading an original PC, you should also buy a new power supply. This PC had a puny 63 watt power supply. The XT and later models had 135 to 150 watt power supplies. Depending on what you install in your 486, you might be able to get by with a 150 watt power supply. You would be better off with a 200 watt supply. The supply will cost from $60 to $100.

Upgrading a 286 to a 486

You can easily upgrade a 286 to a 486. The 286, or IBM AT (for Advanced Technology), uses the 80286 CPU. It has 125,000 transistors and is a 16-bit system. The original IBM AT operated at a very conservative speed of 6 MHz, but many of the 286 clones now run at 12 MHz, 16 MHz and even up to 20 MHz.

An 80286 CPU handles data in 16-bit chunks, just twice that of the 8088. A 286 operating at 10 MHz would be more than four times faster than an XT operating at 4.77 MHz. Because it handles twice as much data per cycle, the 286 is still more than twice as fast as an XT even if the XT is operating at the same 10 MHz. But even the fastest 16-bit 286 is a slowpoke compared to the 32-bit 486.

Upgrading a 386 to a 486

The 386 systems use the Intel 80386 CPU. This CPU has 275,000 transistors and can handle data in 32-bit chunks, the same as the 486. But the 486 has 1,200,000 transistors and can handle data much faster than a 386.

The standard 486 and 386 motherboards are the same size as the original AT motherboards. The baby 386 and baby 486 motherboards are also the same size. It is very easy to pull out a 386 motherboard and install a 486. You should have no problems in using your 386 peripherals and plug-in boards.

Upgrading a 386SX to a 486

The 386SX can also be easily upgraded to a 486. Simply pull out the motherboard and install the same size 486 motherboard.

Intel, the sole developer and manufacturer of the 80386 or 386DX, also developed the 386SX. Like the 386DX, this chip uses 32 bits internally, but only 16-bit lines externally. The 16-bit external operation will cause it to be a bit slower in some applications than the 32-bit 386DX. The chip costs about $150, approximately half of what the 386DX costs. A 386SX motherboard costs from $350 up to $600. Because of the comparatively low cost of the chips and the relative ease of designing a motherboard, many 80386SX systems have been sold.

Upgrading an AT&T 6300 or Zenith-151

These computers have a different type of case. You should be able to use most of your present components, but to add a new motherboard, you will have to buy a new case and power supply.

Installing the motherboard

Now that you have bought a new motherboard, it is easily installed in a few easy steps. The following procedures can be used for installing any motherboard.

Remove the cover

The first thing to do is to remove the cover from your old computer. Unplug the power and remove the screws at each corner on the rear panel and the one at the top center. Slide the cover off.

Remove plug-ins

Make a rough diagram of the cables and the boards where they are connected. You might even take pieces of tape or a marking pen and mark each board and cable with a number. Notice that the ribbon cables have one wire that is a different color. This indicates pin one. Pay close attention as to how the connectors are oriented. On most boards that have vertical connections, pin one will be towards the top. If the connection is horizontal, pin one is usually toward the front of the computer, but this might not always be so. Check the boards for a small number or some indication as to which is pin one. Note the colored wires on the ribbon cables and record their position on your diagram. If possible, leave the cables from the disk drives connected to the plug-in boards when you remove them.

Note that the connectors from the power supply are connected so that the four black wires are in the center. When reconnecting the cables, it is possible to replace the cable connectors upside down or backwards or on the wrong connector. Make sure that your diagram is complete before disconnecting anything.

Remove all of the plug-in boards, the keyboard cable, and the other wires and cables that are connected to the motherboard. If at all possible, leave the cables connected to the disk controllers. Just pull the boards out and lay them across the power supply. It should not be necessary to remove the disk drives or the power supply.

Remove the motherboard

Depending on the type of computer you have, you can have nine standoffs holding the motherboard off the chassis. If so, you should find nine small nuts on the bottom of the chassis. The standoffs that would be inserted in the holes might also be made of plastic. If they are plastic, they will be held in place by flared portions of the body of the standoff. Use a pair of pliers to press the flares together so that the standoff can be removed.

Install memory chips

If you got a motherboard without memory, it might be possible to use the chips from your old 386 motherboard. You probably will not be able to use chips from an older machine. Whether you can use old chips depends primarily on how fast your new board operates and what kind of chips it uses. Most of the 486 motherboards use the SIMM type chips.

For the older 4.77 MHz PCs and XTs, 200 ns was plenty fast enough. You will probably need at least 70 ns for your 486. Some systems use wait states so that you can use slower memory chips. The size and speed of the chips are usually marked on the top along with the vendors name and other information. The zero will be left off, so you might see something like 64-15 or 256-12, which would indicate 64K at 150 ns and 256K at 120 ns.

If you are going to use your old memory chips, you will need a small screwdriver or some other tool to pry them out of their sockets. The blank fillers on the back panel, where there are no boards installed, are a very good tool for lifting chips out of their sockets.

You should have received some kind of diagram or information with your motherboard that tells you where and what kind of memory to install. Be very careful when inserting chips or SIMMs to ensure that they are all oriented in the proper direction and the proper location. Ordinarily, most of the chips on the boards will all be oriented in the same direction. Be careful not to bend the legs, and make sure that all of the legs are inserted.

Some of the baby 486 boards use a separate plug-in board for memory. You will probably have to install memory in it.

Install the new motherboard

Plug all of the components together outside of the case and try them out. If it doesn't work, it is fairly easy to troubleshoot. If there are no problems, install it in the case, try it again, then install the cover.

I use the same procedure to install the motherboard that was detailed in chapter 3. Most of the new boards use a stand-off system that is different than that used in the old PCs and XTs. Most of the new cases have raised channels on the floor of the chassis. The channels have holes with elongated slots. Plastic standoffs with rounded tops and a thin groove fit in the holes. The standoffs are pressed into holes in the motherboard.

The board is then placed so that the standoffs fit into the holes in the raised channels. The board is moved to the right so that the grooves slide into, and are locked, in the narrow elongated slots. Then one screw at the back center of the board and one at the center front locks the board in place.

Replace the boards and cables

You are now ready to start replacing your components. Reconnect the power to the board from the power supply. Make sure that it is oriented so that the four black wires are in the center.

Replace your plug-in boards and any cables that were disconnected. Make sure that they are connected properly with the colored wire going to pin one. If you made a diagram before you removed them, you should not have any problems.

Amaze your friends

I have been told that Paul Newman, the movie actor who loves racing, has a beat-up old Volkswagen. He pulled out the VW engine and replaced it with a powerful V8. With this beatup old VW, he would pull up alongside someone who had a powerful car, then pull away and leave them in his dust. The looks of amazement and disbelief must have been worth all the money and effort he put into the old VW.

You could do about the same thing with an old PC or XT. On the outside it may still look like a lowly PC or XT. But underneath the hood is a veritable powerhouse. If your friends or coworkers do not know that you have upgraded to a 486, you can astonish and amaze them with the speed and power of your new machine.

5
CHAPTER

Floppies

Floppy drives and diskettes are a very important part of the personal computer. It would be very difficult to operate a personal computer without them.

Double-density drives

There are about 40 million 360K floppy drives in existence. They are slow and limited in capacity, but they are reliable and dependable. They have contributed mightily to the personal computer revolution. Almost all software packages sold in the past have been distributed on 360K double-sided double-density (DS/DD) diskettes. Several hundred million 360K diskettes are in existence, most of them filled with software. I have about 500 myself.

The 360K drive has served well, but there are newer, faster drives, with much greater capacity. They will eventually replace the old and faithful 360K.

High-density drives

The 1.2Mb and 1.44Mb drives can read and write to all formats. These drives are selling for as little as $60 apiece at some discount stores and up to as much as $120 at other stores. The 360K and 720K drives may cost five to ten dollars less than the high-density drives. Because you can read and write to all formats with the high-density drives, I do not know why anyone would buy a 360K or 720K drive today.

At one time, some people reported that they occasionally had trouble reading and writing to 360K diskettes with 1.2Mb drives. I have kept one of my old 360K drives around for several years just in case I ever had any trouble. I have never had to use it.

Extended density drives

Several companies are now offering a 3$^1/_2$" *extended-density* (ED) 2.8Mb floppy drive. The 2.8Mb diskettes have a barium ferrite media and use perpendicular recording to achieve the extended density. In standard recording, the particles are magnetized so that they lay horizontally in the media. In perpendicular recording, the particles are stood vertically on end for greater density.

The ED drives are downward compatible and can read and write to the 720K and 1.44Mb diskettes. At the present time, the ED drives are still rather expensive at about $400 each. The diskettes cost about $10 each.

The ED drives require a special controller that costs over $100. You can buy an XT floppy controller for a 360K drive for about $15, but the XT controllers have a transfer rate of only 250 KHz. The controllers for high-density drives have a rate of 500 KHz while the extended-density drives operate at 1 MHz. Figure 5-1 shows a Compaticard IV controller for ED drives.

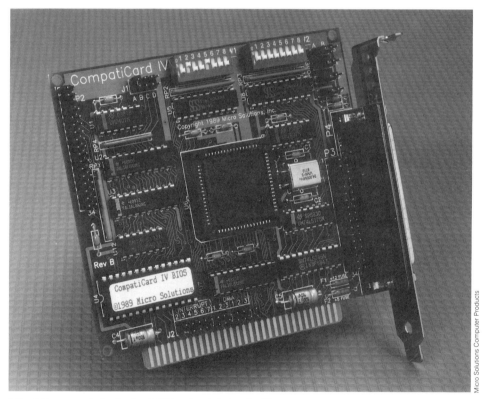

Micro Solutions Computer Products

5-1 A floppy controller for the 2.8Mb extended density drives.

The cost of the extended-density drives and diskettes will come down if more vendors enter the market, but it is questionable as to whether these drives will become widespread. At this time many vendors are waiting to see whether IBM adopts the 2.8Mb. They are also keeping an eye on the very-high-density (VHD) drives discussed below. If the 20Mb drives become the new standard, there will be little need for the 2.8Mb.

Very-high-density drives

Very-high-density drives are $3^1/2''$ drives that can store over 20Mb on a diskette. Companies that have developed these drives are:

Brier Technology	(408) 435-8463
Insite	(408) 946-8080
Citizen Watch	(213) 453-0614

With no standard among the competing systems, they all use different methods to achieve the very high density.

One of the problems that had to be overcome in very-high-density drives was that of tracking. The drives have little trouble reading and writing to the 135 tracks per inch (TPI) of the standard $3^1/2''$ diskette. But 20Mb requires many more tracks that are much closer. Brier Technology's Flextra uses special diskettes that have special magnetic servo tracks embedded beneath the data tracks. The Insite diskettes have optical servo tracks that have been etched into the surface with a laser beam. The heads then lock onto the servo tracks for accurate reading and writing to the data tracks. The Brier drive costs about $800. It is being distributed by the Q'COR Company at (800) 548-3420. The Insite drive is about $1400. The special diskettes for these systems cost about $20 each. Figure 5-2 shows a Brier Flextra (25Mb unformatted, 20Mb formatted) diskette and drive.

5-2 The Brier Technology Flextra 20Mb $3^1/2''$ floppy. It uses a special floppy diskette.

At this time, neither of these systems are downward compatible with the 720K and the 1.44Mb. Both companies are working to make them compatible. Actually, it should not be absolutely necessary that they read the other formats. A person should be more than happy just to be able to store 20Mb on a diskette, but compatibility would save having to install another drive, it would save a bay, and it probably would save a slot.

The Citizen unit will use standard 3½" diskettes. It will use RLL type of recording and have a track density of 542 TPI. It will be downward compatible and should be able to read and write to the 720K and the 1.44Mb formats. It is expected to sell for about $200. Production quantities should be available in early 1991. This seems to be a fantastic system.

Bernoulli drives

The Bernoulli drives use a 5¼" removable flexible floppy disk. These floppies have many of the characteristics of a hard disk. They are able to store from 20Mb to 44Mb of data on a disk. They are discussed more fully in the next chapter on hard drives.

Diskettes

The 360K and 720K diskettes are called *double-sided double-density* (DS/DD). The 1.2Mb and 1.4Mb are called *high-density* (HD).

At one time, high-density diskettes were much more expensive than the 360K or 720K, but all diskettes are now quite reasonable. The 360K DS/DD diskettes are now selling for as low as 21 cents each, and the 720Ks are going for as little as 39 cents each. The 1.2Mb HD diskettes are also selling at discount houses for as little as 39 cents apiece. The 1.44Mb HDs are selling for as little as 89 cents each.

These are real bargains. You can buy ten of the 1.2Mb HDs for only $3.90. You can store 12Mb of data on them at a cost of less than 33 cents per megabyte.

I list some of the discount diskette vendors at the end of this chapter.

Some floppy diskette basics

Floppy diskettes are made from a plastic material called polyethylene terephthalate that is coated on each side with a thin layer of magnetic material. The magnetic coating is made primarily from iron oxide, or powdered rust. Bits of cobalt and other materials are added to give it special magnetic characteristics. The finished product is similar to the tape used in audio cassette and video tape recorders. The next few paragraphs have explanations of a few terms used with disk drives and diskettes.

Tracks A diskette is similar in some respects to a phonograph record. A record has only one track that starts at the outer edge and winds toward the center.

A 360K floppy has 40 single concentric tracks on each side. The 1.2Mb and the 3¹/₂″ floppies have 80 tracks on each side. See Figure 5-3.

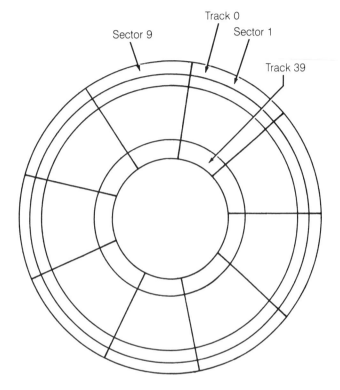

5-3 Showing the relationship between tracks and sectors on a floppy diskette.

Sectors The 360K and the 720K are formatted so that each track is divided into 9 sectors. Figure 5-3 is a representation of the relationship between tracks and sectors. Each of the 80 tracks of the 1.2Mb high density floppy is divided into 15 sectors, and 18 sectors per track on the 1.44Mb. Each sector holds 512 bytes. If you do the math for a 360K diskette, it would be 9 sectors × 512 bytes × 40 tracks × 2 sides = 368,460 bytes. During formatting, 6144 bytes are used to lay out the tracks and sectors so you actually end up with only 362,496 usable bytes.

The math for a 1.4Mb floppy is 18 sectors × 512 bytes × 80 tracks × 2 sides = 1,474,560 bytes. Again, during formatting, 16,896 bytes are used to lay out the tracks and sectors so you end up with 1,457,664 usable bytes.

Cylinders The tracks on each side of the disk are directly opposite of each other; that is track 0 on side 0, or the top side, is exactly opposite track 0 on side 1, or the bottom side. If you could strip away all of the other tracks, the two tracks might look somewhat like a cylinder, even though it would be rather flat.

Heads Two heads read and write on the disk. When head 0 is over track 1, sector 1, on the top of the diskette, head 1 is addressing track 1, sector 1 on the bottom side of the diskette. The heads move from track to track as a single unit.

Data is written to track 1 on the top side, then the heads are electronically switched to the bottom side and writing is continued to track 1 on the bottom side. It is much faster to switch between the heads electronically than to move them to a different track.

FAT When data is recorded, it is written in the first empty sector that it finds. For instance if sectors 5, 6, and 7 on track 2 were not being used, data would be written or recorded in those sectors. The location of the track and sector numbers of that particular data would then be recorded in the *file allocation table* (FAT) section of the diskette. Because each track and sector is numbered, the location of any data on the diskette can be easily found.

TPI The 40 tracks of a 360K is laid down at a rate of 48 *tracks per inch* (TPI) so each of the 40 tracks is $1/48$ of an inch wide. The 80 tracks of the high-density 1.2Mb is laid down at a rate of 96 TPI, so each track is $1/96$ of an inch. The 80 tracks of the $3^1/2''$ disks are laid down at a density 135 per inch or $1/135$ of an inch per track.

Read accuracy The $5^1/4''$ drives have a conical spindle that centers the diskette. The plastic material that the diskette is made from is subject to environmental changes and wear and tear. The conical spindle might not center each diskette exactly so head to track accuracy is difficult with more than 80 tracks.

Most of the 360K diskettes use a reinforcement hub ring, but it probably does not help much. The 1.2Mb floppies do not use a hub ring. Otherwise, the two formats look exactly the same.

The $3^1/2''$ floppies use a metal hub for centering the diskette (Fig. 5-4).

5-4 Some $3^1/2''$ floppy diskettes. Note the metal hubs which helps to ensure head to track accuracy. The diskette at the top right is a 1.44 Mb, the one on the bottom right is a 720K. Note the extra square hole in the 1.44Mb. The square hole on the right corner of the diskettes has a slide that can cover the hole for write-enable, or uncover the hole for write-protect. This system is just the opposite of the $5^1/4''$ write-protect method.

Though the tracks are narrower and greater in density per inch because of the metal hub, the head tracking accuracy is much better than that of the 5¹/₄″ systems. Hard disks have very accurate head tracking systems. Some have a density of well over 1000 tracks per inch so much more data can be stored on a hard disk.

Rotation speed The heads directly contact the floppy diskettes, so they rotate at around 300 RPMs. Hard disks rotate at 3600 RPMs. The heads and disk surface would be severely damaged if they came in contact at this speed. So the heads "fly" over the surface at a few millionths of an inch above it.

Differences in double-density and high-density diskettes

The main difference between the 5¹/₄″ 360K double-density and the 1.2Mb high-density diskette is that the 360K has an Oersted (Oe) of 300 and the 1.2Mb floppy has an Oe of 600. The 3¹/₂″ 720K double-density has an Oe of 600, while the 1.44Mb's Oe is 700. The *Oe* is a measure of resistance to magnetization. It requires a higher head current to write data to the higher Oe media.

Because the particles with the higher Oe require more current to magnetize them, data can be recorded at a higher density than with the 300 Oe of the 360K. With the 600 Oe of the 1.2Mb, you can double the number of tracks and increase the packing density by increasing the number of sectors from 9 to 15. Because the 360K media is so easily magnetized, if data is packed on them at a high density, it places the particles very close together. They can "migrate" toward each other, or magnetize neighboring particles that are supposed to be zeros. This could cause the data to be corrupted.

The Oe of the 720K and the 1.44Mb is fairly close. One of the major differences between them is that the 1.44Mb has two small square holes at the rear of the plastic shell, while the 720K has only one. Compare the diskettes in Fig. 5-4. The diskette on the right top is 1.44Mb, the lower right one is 720K.

The hole on the right rear of the shell has a small slide that can be moved to cover the hole. A small microswitch checks the hole when the diskette is inserted. If the hole is covered, then it can be written on. If it is open, then the diskette is write-protected. The 3¹/₂″ write-protect system is just the opposite of the system used by the 5¹/₄″ diskettes. The 5¹/₄″ diskettes have a square notch that must be covered with opaque tape to prevent writing or unintentionally erasing the diskette. (Incidentally, you must use opaque tape. The 5¹/₄ system uses a light to shine through the square notch. If the detector in the system can see the light through the notch, then it can write on the diskette. Some people have used clear plastic tape to cover the notch with disastrous results.)

On most of the 3¹/₂″ drives capable of 1.44Mb, a small microswitch checks for the hole on the right rear side of the diskette. If you insert a diskette and the drive finds a hole in the right rear area, it will allow you to format, read, and write the diskette as a 1.44Mb.

Table 5-1 Diskette difference summary.

Drive Type	360K	1.2Mb	720K	1.44Mb
Tracks/side	$0-39$	$0-79$	$0-79$	$0-79$
Sectors/track	9	15	9	18
Oersteds (Oe)	300	600	600	700
Pack density BPI	6000	9869	8717	16000

Table 5-1 summarizes some of the differences in diskettes.

Formatting

The tracks and the sectors must be formatted on a diskette before it can be used. If the A: drive is a high-density drive, to format a 360K diskette with the 1.2Mb drive, type FORMAT A: /4. To format to 1.2Mb, you only have to type FORMAT A: or you might have to type FORMAT A: /T:80 /N:15.

A 1.2Mb drive will try to format a 360K diskette to 1.2Mb if you don't use the /4. It will probably format the outer tracks with no problems, but it will usually find and mark several bad sectors on the inner tracks. Even with the bad sectors, you will probably have more than 1 megabyte of usable space on a 360K diskette.

Because of the difference in the media as explained, I advise against using a 360K as a 1.2Mb, especially for critical data. It might be all right if you are just moving a program from one machine to another. As a test, I formatted several 360K diskettes to 1.2Mb over a year ago. I loaded them with data files and have checked them several times. So far they are still good. But I would not recommend this practice except in an emergency. Taking a risk with your data is not worthwhile, especially when you consider the low cost of high-density diskettes.

Although you can format a 360K diskette to 1.2Mb, you cannot format a 1.2Mb as a 360K. The drive uses a higher head current to format and write to the 1.2Mb. When the command to format to 360K is issued, the head current is not strong enough to magnetize the 1.2Mb media.

To format a 720K diskette on a high-density drive, type FORMAT B: /T:80 /N:9.To format a 1.44Mb diskette, just type FORMAT B: or you might have to type FORMAT B: /T:80 /N:18. The drive checks for the hole on the rear right before it will format to the high density. If it does not find the hole, the computer will sit there a minute, then give the message INVALID MEDIA OR TRACK 0 BAD. You will get the same message if you try to format a 1.44Mb diskette as a 720K.

The media in 720K and 1.44Mb diskettes are fairly similar. If you cover the right rear hole in a 1.44Mb, it can be formatted as 720K. Many of the older laptops use the 720K, so you might need to transfer data when all you have are

1.44Mbs. Or you might want to DISKCOPY a software package that is distributed on 720K diskettes, and all of your diskettes are 1.44Mb.

You can also format and use a 720K as a 1.44Mb although diskette manufacturers strongly recommend against it. The Oe of the 720K and the 1.44Mb is fairly close. Several companies have developed tools for punching the extra hole in 720Ks. These companies claim that the 720K works okay. They have sold thousands of the punches at about $40 each. But if you want to convert a 720K to 1.44Mb, you do not need a $40 punch. The diskettes have a plastic cover or shell that is made from two flat pieces that are bonded together around the edges. The plastic is rather soft.

To mark the location, take two diskettes and open the write-protect slide. Place them with the metal hubs facing, then mark the location through the open write-protect hole. You can use a soldering iron to burn a hole, or use a pocket knife to dig out a small dimple. The hole or dimple needs to only penetrate through the bottom layer of the cover. The bottom is the side with the metal hub. The hole does not have to go all the way through both layers. The location or depth of the hole is not too critical. Make the hole, try it. If it does not work, enlarge it a bit.

As a test, I converted several 720K diskettes and formatted them to 1.44Mb then loaded data onto them. It has been over a year, and so far I have not had any trouble. But again, the cost of the high-density diskettes are now very reasonable, so I would not recommend taking a chance with your data.

Format BAT files

Here are some batch files that save me a lot of time in formatting diskettes. Here is how I made my batch files:

```
COPY CON FMT 36.BAT
C: FORMAT A: /4
^Z
COPY CON FMT12.BAT
C: FORMAT A: /T:80 /N:15
^Z
COPY CON FMT72.BAT
C: FORMAT B: /T:80 /N:9
^Z
COPY CON FMT14.BAT
C: FORMAT B: /T:80 /N:18
^Z
```

The ^Z is made by pressing F6 or you may use the ^ (caret) over numeral 6 and the Z. With the batch files, I only have to type fmt36 for a 360K, fmt12 for a 1.2Mb, fmt72 for a 720K, or fmt14 to format a 1.44Mb.

Where to buy the drives

If you live near a large city, lots of stores should be nearby, as well as computer shows and swap meets. If you do not live near a good source, then next best source would be a mail order house.

Lots of computer magazines are full of ads. Space for these ads is rather expensive, so quite often the vendors use abbreviations. Floppy disk drives are usually listed as FDD, and a floppy drive controller is FDC.

Before I go to a computer show or to a store to buy something, I usually check out the ad prices in the magazines to get an idea of what the price should be. In some cases, the store price might be even lower than the magazine price. The magazine ads have to be made up a month or so before it is published. The computer business is so volatile that often the prices change in the meantime. The computer business is about the only business where the prices of components tend to go down. If you are ordering something by mail, you might call first to see if the price is still the same.

I mentioned earlier that the 360K and the 720K drives are obsolete. However, many people are still buying them. You will see ads for the 360K and 720K drives for almost the same price as that for the 1.2Mb and the 1.44Mb drives.

Several large companies manufacture floppy drives such as Sony, Toshiba, Fuji, Teac, and others. Each company's prices are within a few dollars of the others. Most of them are fairly close in quality, but there might be minor differences. I have two 1.2Mb drives made by Toshiba, one slightly newer than the other. The older one is much quieter and operates much smoother than the new one.

Disk drives have two motors. One motor drives the spindle that rotates the diskette. Then a *stepping motor*, or *actuator*, moves the heads to the various tracks. On my older Toshiba drive, a fairly large stepping motor is used to position the heads. A very small stepping motor is used on the newer one, so it is very noisy when it searches for tracks. But otherwise, they have both worked perfectly.

Floppy disk drive controllers

You may have to buy a floppy disk controller (FDC) for your drives. A FDC may cost from $40 up to $95 or more. If you are installing hard drives, and by all means you should, your hard drive controller might have the ability to control floppies.

Sources for diskettes

Again, the cost of high-density 1.2Mb diskettes is about 39 cents each. The cost of 360K diskettes, in 100 lots, is about 21 cents each. The 3½ " high-density floppies at this time cost as little as 89 cents each. The double-density 720K are selling for about 39 cents each.

Here are just a few companies that sell diskettes at a discount. There are several others; check computer magazines for ads.

MEI/Micro Center	(800) 634-3478
The Disk Barn	(800) 727-3475
American Group	(800) 288-8025
MidWest Micro	(800) 423-8215

6
CHAPTER

Choosing and installing a hard disk

If you are completely new to computing, a hard drive is an assembly of platters with a magnetic plating. Depending on the capacity, there might be several platters on a common spindle. They will have a read/write head on the top and bottom of each platter. The head "flies" just a few millionths of an inch from the platter. Figure 6-1 shows a hard disk with its cover removed.

The need for a hard drive

It would be possible to run your 486 with only floppy disk drives. But that would be like buying a 400 horsepower Cadillac, then using a couple of horses to tow it around. The two horses would get you to your destination, but it would sure waste a lot of time and the power of about 398 horses. I can't imagine anyone running a 486 without a good hard drive.

Factors to consider

You need to choose what type and size of disk to buy. Of course that will depend on what you need to do with your computer and how much you want to spend. We will briefly review some of the factors that should influence your decision.

Seagate Technology

6-1 A hard disk with the cover removed.

Capacity

Buy the biggest you can afford.

You might have heard of Mr. C. Northcote Parkinson. After observing business organizations for some time, he formulated several laws. One law says, "Work expands to fill up available employee time." A parallel law that paraphrases Mr. Parkinson's immutable law says, "Data expands to fill up available hard disk space." It is almost as if those little bytes on the hard disk were reproducing themselves.

Do not even think of buying anything less than 40Mb. Better yet would be 80 Mb minimum. New software programs have become more and more friendly and offer more and more options. Most of the basic application programs that you will need such as spreadsheets, databases, CAD programs, word processors and many others, will each require two to three megabytes of disk storage space.

Over the years I have accumulated hundreds of small programs on 5¼" diskettes. I might never have a use for many of them, but I copy them onto my hard disk. If I ever do need them, they are right at my fingertips, just a keystroke away. This is very convenient but it uses a lot of valuable real estate on my hard disk.

Some day I hope to find time to reorganize by hard disks and delete a lot of the junk that I have accumulated. Deciding what to keep and what to erase can be a real chore. The way disk prices keep coming down, I think it would be easier to buy a bigger hard disk than to reorganize.

Speed or access time

This is the time it takes a hard disk to locate and retrieve a sector of data. This includes the time that it takes to move the head to the track, settle down and read the data. For a high-end, very fast disk, this might be as little as 9 milliseconds (ms). Some of the older drives and systems required as much as 100 ms. An 85 ms hard drive might be fine for a slow XT. A 28 ms drive may not be fast enough for a 386. For disk intensive uses on a 486, a 15 ms ESDI or SCSI system would be advisable.

Of course, the faster the hard disk, the more expensive it will be. A lot will depend on what you want your computer to do and how much you want to spend.

Type of drive, stepper or voice coil

Most of the less expensive hard drives use a *stepper motor*. It moves the heads in discrete increments across the disk until they are over the track to be read or written.

The *voice coil* type hard drives are quieter, a bit faster, more reliable, and, of course, more expensive. Voice coil drives can be recognized because their spec sheets will show that they have an odd number of heads. Actually they do have an even number of heads, one on the top and bottom of each platter. But one head and platter surface is used only as a servo control for the heads. By using calibrated voltages and the servo tracks, a voice coil system can smoothly, quietly and quickly move the heads to the desired track.

Most of the ESDI and high-end SCSI drives use the voice coil technology. More about voice coil technology under "Hard disk basics."

Types of drives

MFM The *modified frequency modulation* (MFM) is an early standard method for disk recording. In the early 1980s, Seagate Technology developed the ST506/412 interface for MFM, and it became the standard. This method formats several concentric tracks on a disk like those laid down on a floppy diskette. The MFM systems divide the tracks into 17 sectors per track, with 512 bytes in each sector. They usually have a transfer rate of five megabits per second. The MFM method can be used with drives from 5Mb up to several hundred megabytes.

Cost will vary, but a current ad for a Seagate ST251 40Mb, 28 ms drive shows a price of $329. A Western Digital combination hard and floppy disk controller (HDC/FDC) is advertised for $106. So two ST251 drives would cost $658 plus $106 for the controller for a total of $764 for 80Mb. So $764 divided by 80Mb would be $9.55 per megabyte. A Seagate ST4096 80Mb 28 ms drive is listed for $539. Including the $106 cost of the controller would give a total of $645 divided by 80Mb equals $8.06 per megabyte.

RLL The *run length limited* (RLL) system is a modification of the MFM system. The RLL drives, when used with an RLL controller, formats 26 sectors per track, which allows 50% more data than on an MFM drive. For instance, a 20Mb could store 30Mb, a 40Mb could store 60Mb. They have a transfer rate of 7.5 megabits, 50% faster than MFM. Not all drives are capable of running RLL. Seagate uses an *R* after the model number to denote the RLL drives.

An RLL drive of similar capacity and speed might cost a bit more than an equivalent MFM. The Seagate ST4144R is similar to the ST4096 MFM 80Mb drive. However, with an RLL controller, the ST4144R formats to 120Mb. It is advertised for $599. A Western Digital RLL HDC/FDC controller is advertised for $124. So drive plus controller would be $723 divided by 120Mb equals $6.02 per megabyte. The ST4096 cost per megabyte is $8.06, or $2.00 per megabyte more than the RLL drive.

Not many people will ever do it, but the ST4144R, or any of the RLL drives, can be used with an MFM controller. However, MFM will only format to 17 sectors per track, or 50% less than the 26 sectors laid down with an RLL controller.

ESDI The *enhanced small device interface* (ESDI, pronounced "ezdy"), is another modification of the MFM system. Most of the ESDI drives are large capacity, usually over 100Mb.

ESDI drives can be formatted to 34 sectors per track so they can store twice as much data as the 17 sectors of standard MFM. They have a very fast access speed, usually 15 to 18 ms and a data transfer rate of 10 to 15 megabits or more per second. These systems are ideal for high-end 386 and 486 systems.

A Seagate Wren ESDI ST2383E 337Mb, 16 ms, is advertised for $1750. A Western Digital ESDI HDC/FDC is advertised for $177 for a total of $1927, divided by 337Mb equals $5.71 per megabyte.

SCSI Most drive manufacturers do not manufacture controllers. In many cases, you buy a drive from one manufacturer, then buy a controller from another manufacturer. The *small computer system interface* (SCSI, pronounced "scuzzy") drives have most of the disk controlling functions integrated onto the drive. This makes a lot of sense because the control electronics can be optimally matched to the drive. The electronics still require an interface card to transmit the data in 8-bit parallel back and forth to the disk, much like a parallel printer port. Because it can handle 8 bits of data at a time, it can have very fast transfer rates. The MFM, RLL, and ESDI drives are serial systems and transfer data one bit at a time over the lines.

As many as eight SCSI devices, such as two or more hard drives, tape drives, CD-ROMs, and WORM drives can be attached to one host adapter. Because each of these devices have their own controller on board, all they require is the data.

SCSI devices can also do multitasking or concurrent processing. A write command can be sent to a drive, and while the drive is writing, it can disconnect from the bus. Because the bus is free, a command can be sent to a second device while the first drive is still busy. With a SCSI system, a second drive can make a mirror image of data for backup. This is not possible with ESDI drives.

SCSI systems allow recording of up to 36 sectors per track compared to 17 sectors of the MFM system, so more than twice as much data can be stored on a disk that is the same size as the MFM. They can also be more than twice as fast as MFM.

Some SCSI drives cost about the same as MFM; for instance, a Seagate ST1096N 80Mb 24 ms is listed at $525. A host adapter would cost about $55 for a total of $580, divided by 80Mb equals $7.25 per megabyte. Seagate uses an *N* after the model number to denote SCSI.

A high capacity SCSI drive such as a ST1201N 117Mb, 15 ms, is currently advertised at $1100. Two of these drives would give you 354Mb for a cost $2200 plus $150 for the host adapter. This would be $6.63 per megabyte.

Also advertised is a ST41200N, 1050Mb, 16.5 ms, for $4170. Add $150 for a host adapter for a total of $4320, of $4.11 per megabyte. Two of these disks would give you 2100Mb (2,100,000,000 bytes of 2.1 gigabytes), for a cost of $8490, or $4.04 per megabyte.

Many companies are also making smaller capacity low-end SCSI drives. Seagate has several such models. The low-end models format each track to 26 sectors, the same as the RLL. An ad for a Seagate ST277N shows basically the same 65Mb, 28 ms drive as the ST277R. The ad price for the ST277N is $426, the ST277R is $350. If you add $54 for a host adapter for the ST277N, the cost is $480 divided by 65Mb is $7.38 per megabyte. An HDC/FDC controller for the ST277R costs $124 for a total of $474 divided by 65 is $7.29, just a few pennies less than the cost per megabyte of the SCSI.

I recently bought a low-end SCSI system, a Seagate ST138N, 30Mb, 28 ms drive for $249. The SCSI systems need a *host adapter*, or interface card, to drive them. A Seagate ST02 host adapter with a built-in floppy controller cost me $54 for a total of only $303 for the system. This seems like a good deal, but it is over $10 per megabyte. The ST277R is about half this price per megabyte.

The ST02 can control all standard floppy drives, but I had lots of trouble installing it. Figure 6-2 shows the 50-wire flat ribbon cable being installed on the drive. Figure 6-3 shows the small $3^1/_2''$ ST138N SCSI hard disk.

The ST02 interface has a very brief installation guide. Several jumpers on the board can configure it to your system's interrupts, BIOS address, and the type of floppy drives you have.

After several hours of frustration, I called Seagate. Their representative asked me if I had any other hard drives installed and if there was another floppy drive controller in the system. I said, "Yes, I have two ST251s and a Konan controller. This controller has a floppy controller on board, but I disabled it according to the Konan manual."

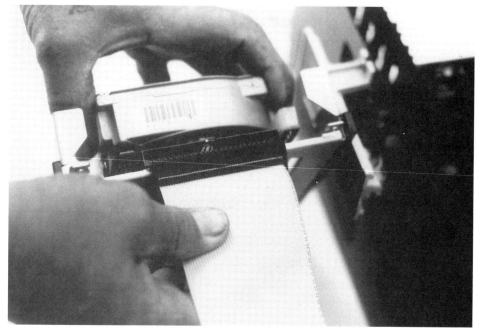

6-2 Connecting the 50-wire cable to the SCSI hard disk.

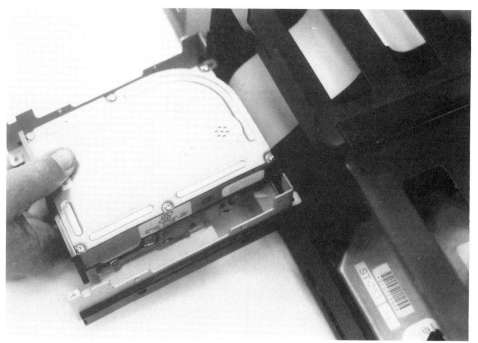

6-3 Sliding the SCSI drive into one of the bays.

He said, "That is not good enough. You cannot run a ST02 in a system where there is another floppy controller, even if it is disabled." Nowhere in their brief installation guide does it mention this fact.

I bought a ST01 host adapter, which has no floppy controller, for $39. The system now works fine.

Figure 6-4 shows the $54 ST02 host adapter. In contrast, Fig. 6-5 shows a high-end EISA SCSI controller from the Interphase Corporation. It sells for $2490 at this time.

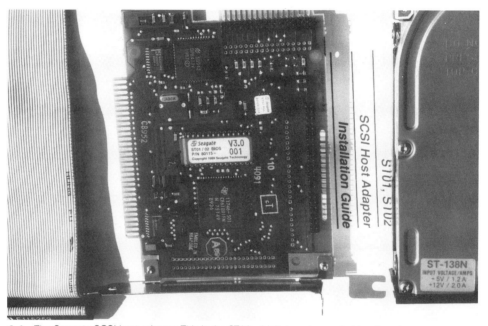

6-4 The Seagate SCSI host adapter. This is the ST02 which can also control two floppies.

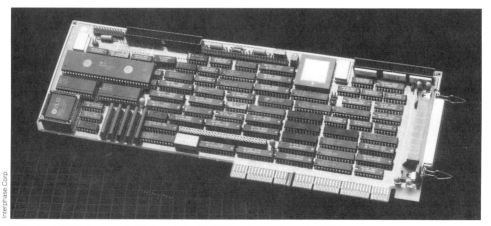

6-5 An E/4810 Barracuda high end dual SCSI host bus adapter for EISA systems.

IDE Several companies have developed drives with *integrated drive electronics* (IDE). The drives are similar to the ESDI drives and were originally developed as a low-cost, low-end alternative for ESDI. They did not have the speed or capacity of the ESDI, but the technology has advanced. Some of them are now equivalent to the ESDI in capacity and speed. Seagate makes a Wren IDE version of their ST2383A with 338Mb, 16 ms, identical to their ESDI ST2383E version, except that the IDE cost is $1840 as compared to the ESDI cost of $1750. You need an HDC/FDC controller that costs about $200 for the ESDI drive. The adapter interface for the IDE costs about $39 plus $1840 equals $1879 divided by 338Mb is $5.55 per megabyte. Figure 6-6 shows an IDE interface that can control two hard disks.

6-6 An interface board for IDE systems.

Some vendors have designed motherboards with a built-in interface and connector for the IDE. A single cable can be used to control two IDE drives. This saves the cost of a controller and also saves one of your slots. For other motherboards, a simple interface is needed to transfer data back and forth to the disk.

Prices The prices of drives from other companies might be a bit more expensive that the ones I have quoted from Seagate. The Seagate 338Mb ESDI ST2383E mentioned above is advertised at $1750. A Core International HC310D2-5 is a 328Mb ESDI drive. Its list price is $4490. The Core International HC380 is a 380Mb ESDI. It lists for $5490. (In all fairness, the street price

Table 6-1 Cost per megabyte summary.

Model	Type	Capacity	Cost+Ctrlr	Cost/MB
ST251	MFM	40	$ 435	$10.87
ST4096	MFM	80	645	8.06
ST4144R	RLL	120	723	6.02
ST2383E	ESDI	337	1927	5.71
ST138N	SCSI	30	303	10.10
ST277N	SCSI	65	474	7.29
ST41200N	SCSI	1050	4320	4.04
ST2383A	IDE	338	1879	5.55
ST4096 w/	Perstor Ctrlr	146	789	5.40

will be a bit less than the list price. In most cases, you should not ever have to pay list price for computer goods.) I used Seagate as an example because they sell more drives than any other company. Also, there are usually more ads for Seagate in magazines so it is easy to compare prices and availability of drives. I list some other companies and their drive models at the end of the chapter.

Controllers

Hard disks need a controller card that plugs into one of the slots in the computer. In the past, very few of the hard disk companies made controllers for their disks, but many of them are now making controllers for their high-end ESDI and SCSI drives. The controllers and drives are then tested and sold as a pair.

Many types of hard disk controllers (HDC) are available. Some were developed specifically for 8-bit systems and others for the 16-bit AT type systems, which includes the 286 and 386. An 8-bit controller can also be used on a 16-bit machine, but a 16-bit cannot be used on an 8-bit. Many of the companies who make 16-bit controllers have integrated floppy disk controllers (FDC) onto the same board. This saves space and is very convenient. These FDC/HDC boards will control 360K, 1.2Mb, 720K, and 1.44Mb disk drives as well as two hard disks.

Several companies manufacture controllers. Some of the major ones are:

Western Digital	(714) 863-0102
Adaptec	(408) 945-8600
Scientific MicroSystems	(415) 964-5700
DTK	(818) 383-7533

and several others. Most of them also manufacture interface boards for the ESDI and SCSI systems and other computer components. Western Digital also manufactures drives.

The MFM controllers are generally less expensive than the specialized ones such as SCSI and ESDI. When they were first introduced, the RLL controllers were significantly more expensive than the MFM, but now there is very little difference.

Perstor Systems manufactures a controller that allows a disk to be formatted to 31 sectors per track (Fig. 6-7). Perstor has both 8-bit and 16-bit controllers. The 16-bit unit has a built-in floppy disk controller for all types of floppy drives. I have used both the 8-bit and the 16-bit for almost two years. I have used them on different drives and have not had any problems.

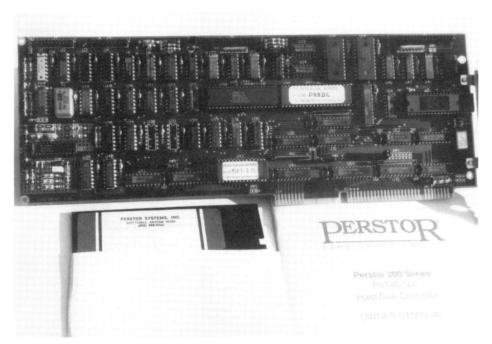

6-7   A Perstor controller. It formats a hard disk to 31 sectors per track instead of the normal 17 of MFM systems. This almost doubles the amount of data that can be stored on a hard disk.

The drives operate at 7.5 megabits per second, the same as the RLL systems, but it is a bit slower than the 10 megabits of the ESDI or SCSI systems. If you can afford to waste a few milliseconds and do not have a lot of money, they offer one of the better megabytes per buck bargains.

For instance, a Seagate ST4096 80Mb, 28 ms drive is advertised for $539. With the Perstor controller, it formats to 146Mb. The Perstor controller is selling for about $250, but it can control two hard disks and two floppies. So if you bought two of the ST4096 for $1078, plus $250 for the Perstor controller, you could have 292Mb for $1328, or $4.55 per megabyte.

Most controllers are not able to control two different drives. Perstor will control two drives that are different in capacity or from different manufacturers. The

Perstor controller might not work with some drives. But they are constantly testing drives. Write them or call them for a list of tested drives and for the prices of their controllers. Their address is:

Perstor Systems
7631 E. Greenway
Scottsdale, AZ 85260
(602) 991-5451

Several companies are now manufacturing controllers and interfaces for high-end drives. STB Systems at (214) 234-8750 offers several hard disk controllers and also adapters for high-resolution monitors. Figure 6-8 shows a hard disk controller and two adapters. Distributing Processing Technology Corporation (DPT) has a very fast and sophisticated SCSI controller for both the ISA and EISA systems. Call them at (407) 830-5522 for specifications and latest prices.

Figure 6-5 shows the Interphase Corporation's E/SCSI 4810 Barracuda, another high-end EISA controller for SCSI hard disks. It is also very fast and can handle up to 14 different devices. You can reach them at (214) 919-9000 for specifications and prices.

STB Systems

6-8 A hard disk controller on the lower left and two different high-resolution monitor adapters.

Note that the advertised price of most disk drives does not include the controller or the necessary cables. An 8-bit controller for hard drives only might cost as little as $40 for a no-name clone. A brand name 16-bit FDC/HDC may cost from $120 to $250.

Physical size

At one time, floppy and hard drives were full height, or $3^1/2$″ high and $5^1/4$″ wide. Only a few very high capacity drives are full height today. The most common size today is the half height, which is $1^3/4$″ high and $5^1/4$″ wide. The smaller size generally uses less power, has less mass, and is faster, so many companies are now making $3^1/2$″ drives with up to 150Mb or more.

Hard cards

Some companies have developed hard disks on plug-in cards. These cards have the disk on one end of the card and the controller on the other. They make it very easy to add a second hard disk to your system. You simply remove the cover of your computer and plug the card in.

The original hard cards were 20Mb, but soon there were 30Mb, then 40Mb, now many companies are manufacturing 80Mb. Because they are small, many of them are rated at 28 ms and less. The Plus Development Company of Milpitas developed the hard cards, and they have remained in the forefront. They have an excellent 80Mb hard card drive (Fig. 6-9). Hard cards are an excellent tool for backups.

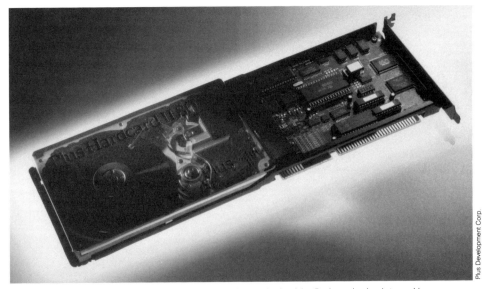

Plus Development Corp.

6-9   The Plus Development Hard Card II 80. It is only one inch wide, fits in a single slot, and is very easy to install.

Removable media

The IOMEGA Corporation has a high-capacity Bernoulli floppy diskette system. Their system allows the recording of up to 44Mb on a special floppy disk. The Bernoulli disks spin much faster than a standard floppy which forces the flexible diskette to bend around the heads without actually touching them. This is in accordance with the principle discovered by the Swiss scientist, Jakob Bernoulli (1654 – 1705).

The average seek time for the Bernoulli systems is 32 ms, which is faster than some hard drives. They are ideal for areas where the data might be confidential. Each person in an office can have their own 44Mb floppy, which can be removed and locked up. This system is also great for backing up a hard disk system.

Iomega has had the field to themselves for several years, so the Bernoulli box has always been a bit expensive at about $1500 for a drive and about $70 for each diskette. Brier Technology, Insite, and several other companies are now giving them some competition with new very-high-density systems. You should soon see prices that are quite reasonable on the very-high-density floppy disk systems.

The Plus Development Corporation, who developed the first hard disk on a card, has developed a removable 40Mb hard disk. The disk and drive motor are all one slim unit which plugs into a fixed housing. The housing can be mounted internally in a floppy disk drive bay or externally. It is very quiet and fast. The list price is about $1200 for the total system. Additional 40Mb hard disk cartridges are about $600 each.

Mean time before failure (MTBF)

Every disk drive will fail sooner or later. Manufacturers test their drives and assign them an average life time that ranges from 40,000 up to 200,000 hours. Of course, the larger the figure, the longer they should last (and the more they cost). These are average figures, much like the figures quoted for a human lifespan. The average man should live to be about 73 years old. But some babies die very young, and some men live to be over 100. Likewise, some hard disks die very young, some older ones become obsolete before they wear out. But be assured that they will all fail eventually. You can never know when they will fail so you should always have them backed up.

Adding a second hard drive

Believe me, you will need a second hard drive. I mentioned earlier that hard drives fail. It is as inevitable as death and taxes. So they should be backed up. A hard drive can be backed up to another hard drive in just seconds. The probability that both drives would fail at the same time is quite small.

I also mentioned the fact that the need for storage is seldom satisfied. Even if you have a disk with a gigabyte of storage, you will soon be trying to store two gigabytes of data on it.

We mentioned earlier that the Perstor and Konan controllers will control different types and sizes of drives. Most controllers will not let you do this. Most of them will only control drives that are the same type, capacity, and from the same manufacturer. So if you can afford it, you should buy two drives of the same type.

If you can't afford it at this time, buy a well-known brand drive. Several drive manufacturers have gone out of business. If you buy an off-brand drive, you might not be able to get a second one later to match your first one.

Sources

Local computer stores and computer swap meets are a good place to find a disk. You can at least look them over and get some idea of the prices and what you want. Mail order is a very good way to buy a hard disk. Hundreds of ads are in the many computer magazines. Check the list of magazines in chapter 16.

Formatting

Formatting organizes the disk so that data can be stored and accessed easily and quickly. If the way the data is recorded was not organized, it would be very difficult to find an item on a large hard disk. I have about 3000 files on my two hard disks. Those files are on tracks and sectors that are numbered. The location of each track and sector is recorded in the *file allocation table* or FAT so any file can be easily located. (Incidentally, I forget what is in each of those 3000 files, and where I may have stored something. I use the Magellan program from Lotus to instantly tell me where any of my data is stored. It is great.)

A brief analogy of a disk organization would be similar to that of a developer of a piece of land. He would lay out the streets and create blocks. He would then partition each block into lots and build a house on each lot. Each house would have a unique address. A map of these streets and house addresses would be filed with the city. A track would be analogous to a street, and a sector number would be similar to a house number.

Each time data is recorded on a disk, the location of that data, by track and sector number, is recorded in the FAT. If the data needs to be retrieved, the computer goes to FAT and reads the data location, then directs the head to the exact track and sector where the data is written.

Formatting is not something that is done every day, and can be rather difficult in some cases. Very little literature on the subject is available. Unless you are fairly knowledgeable, try to have your vendor format your hard disk for you.

One reason the disks do not come from the manufacturer preformatted is that there are so many options. There are also many different controller cards. The controller cards are usually designed so that they will operate with several different types of hard disks, so most have DIP switches that must be set to configure your particular hard disk. Usually some documentation comes with the hard disk controller. Like most other manuals and documentation, the instructions are sometimes difficult to understand, especially if you are a beginner.

Low-level format

A floppy diskette is formatted in a single procedure but a hard disk requires two levels of format, a low level and then a high level.

You should have received some sort of documentation with your hard disk and controller. Some hard disks have the low-level format already performed at the factory. Ask your vendor. If it has been low-level formatted, you can type FDISK, and it will allow you to partition the disk. If it does not allow you do FDISK, or if you are using a controller other than MFM, then you must do a low-level format. If it has not been formatted, use whatever software or instructions that you might have received with the disk.

Using the debug command

With many controllers, you can use the DOS DEBUG command. Type DEBUG and when the hyphen - comes up, type G = C800:5. It would look like this:

```
A > DEBUG
-G = C800:5
```

This message will be displayed: This is a FORMAT routine. It will DESTROY any existing data on your disk! Press < RET > if you wish to continue or < ESC > to abort.

Bad sector data

If you press Return, it will ask you several questions. One question it asks is if you want to input any bad sector data. It is almost impossible to manufacture a perfect hard disk. The disk usually comes with a list of bad sectors that the manufacturer discovered during his testing. If they are very bad, your controller might detect them, but if they are marginal it may not. When you input the list of bad sectors, DOS marks them so that they are not used. As much as 100K or more space might be in bad sectors. But that will be a small percentage compared to the disk's capacity.

Utility programs for low-level format

Some controllers will not let you use the DEBUG command to do a low-level format. Several utility programs can do it for you such as:

Check-It	(800) 531-0450
Disk Technician	(619) 274-5000
SpinRite	(714) 830-2200
DOSUTILS	(800) 752-1333
QAPlus	(408) 438-8247

Some of these programs will also let you set or reset your interleave factor without removing your data.

Interleave factor

You must also choose the interleave factor that you want to use. This is an important item, so I go into a bit of detail about it.

The interleave factor determines to a great extent the speed at which data can be read from a hard disk. You might have the fastest disk in the world, but if the interleave is not set properly, you would have to sit there and twiddle your thumbs while waiting for data. The interleave factor depends on the electronics of the controller, the disk, and the system that it is plugged into.

With the hard disk spinning at 3600 RPMs, data can be read much faster than many systems can handle. For instance, it takes a finite amount of time to read the data from track one, sector one. After it is read, it must be assembled and transmitted to the system. Unless you have a very fast system, by the time sector one is read and transmitted, the disk has spun around past sector two, so it has to wait for a complete revolution in order to read sector two. Again, once sector two is read, sector three has already passed, so again it must wait for the disk to spin around. Because a standard track has 17 sectors, the disk would have to spin around 17 times to read one track. Most files would be spread over several tracks. A long file could take a considerable amount of time to read.

In this example, by the time sector one is read, assembled and sent to the system, the disk might have spun around to where it is over sector four. So if you move sector two over to where sector four normally would be on the track, then you could skip over the next two sectors, and then read sector two immediately after you have read sector one. You could then skip the next two sectors and read sector three and so on around the track. With this arrangement, you could read six sectors in one revolution. This is a 600% increase over the example where you could only read one sector per revolution. Figure 6-10 shows how various interleave settings would be arranged. Of course, a system that can handle a 1:1 interleave would be the fastest.

Interleave factors should be set to match the speed of the system. The interleave factor is set during the low-level format of the hard disk. Normally, the only way to change it, or to experiment with different settings, is to completely reformat the disk, both low level and high level, and then try it. Several utility packages discussed later determine the optimum value and can change it for you without destroying your data.

Perstor controllers

The Perstor controller lets you almost double your disk capacity, and it comes with software that allows you to easily low-level format your drive. It also has a built-in feature to automatically check for the optimum interleave factor. It will

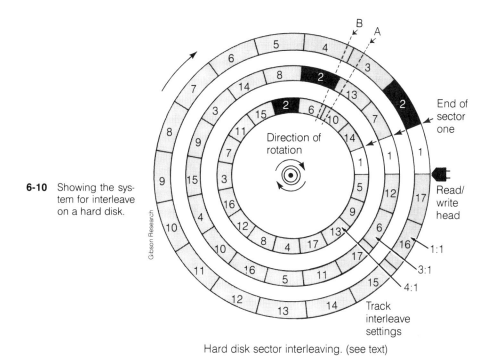

6-10 Showing the system for interleave on a hard disk.

Hard disk sector interleaving. (see text)

test the disk and display the data transfer rate at interleaves of 1:1 up to 6:1. It will then be obvious which factor allows the fastest transfer.

Utility packages

Several hard disk utility packages check the interleave factor for the optimum value for your system. They will even let you change the value without having to reformat your disk. These programs copy a track into memory, reformat that track, copy the information back to the track from memory, then proceed to the next track. Here are a few of the products and companies that provide this type of software:

Spinrite II	Gibson Research	(714) 830-2200
Optune	Gazelle Systems	(800) 233-0383
Disk Technician	Prime Solutions	(619) 274-5000
Mace Utilities	Fifth Generation Systems	(504) 291-7221

These utilities can scan your hard disk and find any marginal areas that might be defective. If data is in the area, it will be moved and the area will be marked so that it will not be used.

If the disk has been used for awhile, the magnetic markers of the original formatting might be getting weak. These programs can reformat the disk and refresh it.

These programs are all a bit different and have several other essential utilities such as data recovery and defragmentation. Everyone who has a hard disk should have at least one of these programs on hand.

New 1:1 controllers

Several improvements and advances have been made so that it is now possible to buy low cost HD/FD controllers that allow 1:1 interleave. These controllers can even be used with some of the low-cost, low-end slow drives. Western Digital, Magitronic, and several other companies, now offer these controllers for prices around $100 or less.

High-level format

After you have completed the low-level format, you can proceed to the high level. Boot up from your floppy disk drive with a copy of DOS and type DIR C:. If the message comes up, Invalid drive specification, put a copy of DOS that has the FDISK command on it in drive A:.

When you type FDISK, this message will be displayed if you are using MS-DOS 4.0:

Fixed Disk Setup Program Version 3.30
©Copyright Microsoft Corp. 1983, 1988

FDISK Options

Current Fixed Disk Drive: 1

Choose one of the following:

1. Create DOS partition or Logical DOS Drive
2. Set active partition
3. Delete DOS Partition or Logical DOS Drive
4. Display partition information

Enter choice: [1]

Press ESC to exit FDISK

If you choose 1, and the disk has not been prepared, a screen like this comes up:

Create DOS Partition

Current Fixed Drive: 1
1. Create Primary DOS partition
2. Create Extended DOS partition
3. Create logical DOS drive(s) in the Extended DOS partition

Enter choice: [1]

Press ESC to return to FDISK Options

If you want to boot from your hard drive (I can't think of any reason why you would not want to), then you must create a primary DOS partition and make it active. DOS 3.3 and earlier versions can only handle 32Mb, but 4.0 allows very large size partitions up to 2 gigabytes. The majority of software programs seem to want to be installed on drive C:. Some will not even run on a drive with a different letter. I usually make the entire first drive my C: drive.

After the FDISK options have been completed, return to drive A: and high-level format drive C:. Because you want to boot off this drive, you must also transfer the system and hidden files to the disk as it is being formatted so you must use a /S to transfer the files. Type FORMAT C: /S. DOS will display a message that says:

> WARNING! ALL DATA ON NON-REMOVABLE DISK DRIVE C: WILL BE LOST!
> Proceed with Format (Y/N)

If you press Y the disk light should come on, and you might hear the drive stepping through each track. After a few minutes, it will display:

> Format complete
> System transferred
> Volume label (11 characters, ENTER for none)?

You can give each partition a unique name, or volume label if you wish to.

You can test your drive by doing a *warm* boot by pressing Ctrl, Alt, and Del at the same time. The computer should reboot.

Now that drive C: is completed, if you have a second disk, perform the low-level format, the FDISK options, and high-level format on it.

Some hard disk basics

Just as it is not necessary to be an engineer to be able to drive a car, you don't have to know too much about a hard disk in order to use one. For those who might be interested, here are some details.

Tracks and sectors

Basically the hard disk is similar to the floppy. It is a spinning disk that has a coating that can be magnetized. The hard disks also have tracks that are similar to the floppy. The 360K floppy disk has only 40 tracks per inch (tpi); the hard disks might have from 300 up to 2400 tpi. Each of the 40 tracks of the 360K floppy is divided into 9 sectors per track; the standard hard disk has 17 sectors per track and some have up to 36.

Speed of rotation and density

Another major difference between the floppy and hard disk is the speed of rotation. A floppy disk spins at about 300 RPM. A hard disk spins at 3600 RPM. As the disk spins beneath the head, a pulse of voltage through the head will cause the area of the track that is beneath the head at that time to become magnetized. If this pulse of voltage is turned on for a certain amount of time, then turned off for some amount of time, it can represent the writing or recording of 1s and 0s. The hard disk spins much faster than a floppy so the duration of the magnetizing pulses can be much shorter at a higher frequency. This allows much more data to be recorded in the same amount of space.

Everything that a computer does depends on precise timing. Crystals and oscillators are set up so that certain circuits perform a task at a specific time. These oscillating circuits are usually called *clock circuits*. The clock frequency for the standard modified frequency modulation (MFM) method of reading and writing to a hard disk is 10 MHz per second. To write on the disk during one second, the voltage might turn on for a fraction of a second, then turn off for the next period of time, then back on for a certain length of time. The head sits over a track that is moving at a constant speed. Blocks of data are written or read during the precise timing of the system clock. Because the voltage must go plus or zero, that is two states, in order to write 1s and 0s, the maximum data transfer rate is only 5 megabits per second for MFM, just half of the clock frequency. The RLL systems transfer data at a rate of 7.5 megabits per second. The SCSI and ESDI systems have a transfer rate as high as 10 to 15 megabits or more.

You have probably seen representations of magnetic lines of force around a magnet. The magnetized spot on a disk track has similar lines of force. To read the data on the disk, the head is positioned over the track and the lines of force from each magnetized area causes a pulse of voltage to be induced in the head. During a precise block of time, an induced pulse of voltage can represent a 1, the lack of a pulse can represent a 0.

The amount of magnetism that is induced on a diskette when it is recorded is very small. It must be small so that it will not affect other recorded bits or tracks near it. Magnetic lines of force decrease as you move away from a magnet by the square of the distance. So it is desirable to have the heads as close to the disk as possible.

On a floppy disk drive, the heads actually contact the diskette. This causes some wear, but not very much because the rotation is fairly slow and the plastic diskettes have a special lubricant and are fairly slippery. However, heads of the hard disk systems never touch the disk. The fragile heads and the disk would be severely damaged if they make contact at the fast speed of 3600 RPMs. The heads "fly" over the spinning disk, just microinches above it. The air must be pure because the smallest speck of dust or dirt can cause the head to "crash" so most hard disks are sealed. You should never open one.

The surface of the hard disk platters must be very smooth. Because the heads are only a few millionths of an inch, or microinches, away from the surface, any unevenness could cause a head crash. The hard disk platters are usually made from aluminum, which is nonmagnetic, and lapped to a mirror finish. They are then coated or plated with a magnetic material. Some companies are now using glass as a substrate for the platters.

The platters must also be very rigid so that the close distance between the head and the platter surface is maintained. You should avoid any sudden movement of the computer or any jarring while the disk is spinning because it could cause the head to crash onto the disk and damage it. Most of the newer hard disk systems automatically move the heads away from the read/write surface to a parking area when the power is turned off.

Another difference in the hard disk and the floppy is that the floppy comes on only when it is needed. Because of its mass, the hard disk takes quite a while to get up to speed and to stabilize. So it comes on whenever the computer is turned on and spins as long as the computer is on. This means that it is drawing power from the power supply all the time. This could possibly cause some problems if your system is fully loaded with boards and has a small power supply.

Clusters

A sector is only 512 bytes, but most files are much longer than that. Many systems lump two or more sectors together and call it a cluster. If an empty cluster is on track 5, the system will record as much of the file as it can there, then move to the next empty cluster, which could be on track 20. The location of each part of the file is recorded in the FAT so the computer has no trouble finding it.

Cylinders

If you could strip away all of the tracks except tracks number one, top and bottom, on all of the platters, it would look somewhat like a cylinder. *Cylinder* refers to each of those tracks with the same number on a stack of platters or on a double-sided diskette.

Multiple platters

So that more recording surfaces can be crammed into a hard disk, it can have from two platters up to as many as 10 or more. All the platters are stacked on a single shaft with just enough spacing between them for the heads. Each disk has a head for the top surface and one for the bottom. If the system has four disks, then it will have eight heads. All heads are controlled by the same positioner, and they will all move together. If head number one is over track one, sector one, then all the other heads will be over track one, sector one on each disk surface.

Head positioners

There are several different types of head positioners, or *actuators*. Some use stepper motors to move the heads in discrete steps to a certain track. Some use a worm gear or screw type shaft that moves the heads in and out. Others use voice coil technology.

The voice coil of a loudspeaker is made up of a coil of wire that is wound on a hollow tube that is attached to the material of the speaker cone. Permanent magnets are then placed inside the coil and around the outside. Whenever a voltage is passed through the coil of wire, it will cause magnetic lines of force to be built up around the coil. Depending on the polarity of the input voltage, these lines of magnetic flux will be either the same or opposite of the lines of force of the permanent magnets. If the polarity of the voltage, for instance a plus voltage, causes the lines of force to be the same as the permanent magnet, then they will repel each other and the voice coil might move forward. If they are opposite, they will attract each other and the coil will move backwards.

Some of the better and faster hard disks use voice coil technology with a closed loop servo control. They usually use one surface of one of the disks to store data and track locations. Most specification sheets give the number of heads on a drive. If you see one that has an odd number of heads such as 5, 7, or 9, it probably uses the other head for servo information. The voice coil moves the heads quickly and smoothly to the track area. Feedback information from the closed loop positions the head to the exact track very accurately.

The voice coil drives may cost 30% to 40% more than the stepper motor types with an equivalent capacity.

Setup routine

When you install a hard disk, your BIOS must be told what kind it is. The BIOS also must know the time, the number and type of floppies you have, and other information. It also needs to set or reset the clock on the motherboard. The diagnostic routine asks several questions, then configures the BIOS for that configuration. This part of the BIOS configuration is in low power CMOS semiconductors and is on all the time, even when the computer is turned off.

One of the questions that the routine asks is what type of hard disk do you have. There were only 15 different types when the AT was introduced in 1984. There are now hundreds. Most new BIOS ROMs list 46 types. If yours is not among the 46 listed, the BIOS usually allows you to input the parameters of any that is not listed. You must tell it what type you have installed. You should have received some information from your vendor that tells you the number of heads, cylinders and other specifications.

CAUTION! Never boot up with a floppy disk version that is different from the version used to format the hard disk. There is a short boot record on the hard disk. If a different version is used to boot up, you might lose all of your data on the disk.

Sources

Some hard disk sources are listed here:

Seagate Technology   (408) 438-6550
Micropolis Corporation   (818) 709-3300

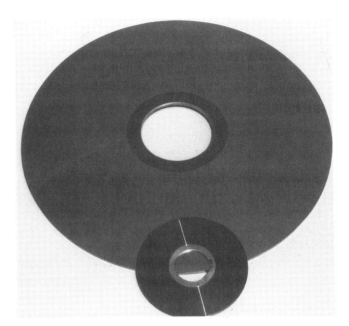

6-11 Hard disk evolution. An early hard disk platter that is 16¹/₄″ in diameter and ¹/₄″ thick. It had a capacity of 1.5Mb on each side. The smaller disk is 5¹/₄″ in diameter and ¹/₁₆″ thick. It can store about 50Mb on each side.

Rodime Systems	(407) 994-5585
Plus Development	(408) 434-6900
Iomega Bernoulli	(800) 465-5522
Microscience	(408) 730-5965
Maxtor Corporation	(408) 432-1700
Western Digital	(714) 863-0102

Progress

Figure 6-11 shows two hard disk platters. The large platter was developed by Ampex Corporation in the early 1970s. It is 16¹/₄″ in diameter and ¹/₄″ thick. It had the ability to store 1.5Mb of data on each side, for a total of 3Mb. This was an enormous amount at that time. The smaller platter is 5¹/₄″ in diameter and is ¹/₁₆″ thick. It can store about 50Mb on each side for a total of 100Mb.

7
CHAPTER

Backup

You probably have several very expensive programs and data on floppy diskettes to load onto your hard disk. Before you do anything, you should write-protect your floppies. If you are using 5¼″ floppies, you should cover the write-protect notch with a piece of opaque tape. If you are using 3½″ diskettes, you should move the small slide on the left side so that the square hole is open. It is very easy to become distracted and wipe out a three or four hundred dollar program. It only takes a minute to cover the write-protect notch, while it can take weeks to get a replacement for the original diskette that has been inadvertently erased.

You should then use DISKCOPY to make exact copies of your original diskettes. The originals should be stored away. Only the copies should be used. If you damage one of them, you can always make another copy.

Accidents and errors

I have been working with computers for several years, but I still make mistakes. One thing that I have learned is that computers do not forgive. Just recently, I copied some files from a floppy disk to my hard disk. I then decided to erase the files on the floppy diskette so I could use it for something else. I typed DEL *.* and the message came up Are you sure? (Y/N). I thought that I was on the A: drive, so I pressed the Y key. I sat there horrified as a whole directory on my hard drive was wiped out.

Luckily, I had backed the directory up recently, but a couple of recent files had not been backed up. Before doing anything else, I got out my copy of Norton Utilities and used the Unerase program to restore the files. When a file is erased, DOS goes to the FAT table and deletes the first letter of each file name. All of the data remains on the disk unless a new file is written over it. Norton Utilities allows you to restore the files by replacing the missing first letter of the file name.

Several others have data recovery utilities:

Norton Utilities	(213) 319-2000
Mace Utilities	(504) 291-7221
PC Tools	(503) 690-8090
DOSUTILS	(612) 937-1107

The early versions of DOS made it very easy to format your hard disk in error. If you happened to be on your hard disk and typed FORMAT, it would immediately begin to format your hard disk and wipe out everything. Later versions will not format unless you specify a drive letter. These versions also allow you to include a volume label, or name, on the drive when you format it by including the /v. You could add a label name later by using the command LABEL. If the drive has a volume label, it cannot be formatted unless the drive letter and correct volume name is specified. (You can display the name of a volume by running CHKDSK, LABEL, or DIR.)

Many people have erased files in error in the past. They are only human, so they will do it again. Some people will not have backups and unerase software. In a fraction of a second, some people will wipe out data that might be worth thousands of dollars. It might have taken hundreds of hours to accumulate and it might be impossible to duplicate it. Yet many of these unfortunate people have not backed up their precious data. Most of these people are those who have been fortunate enough not to have had a major catastrophe. Just as sure as California has earthquakes, if you use a computer long enough, you can look forward to at least one unfortunate disaster. There are thousands of ways to make mistakes. You cannot prevent them all. But if your data is backed up, it does not have to be a disaster. It is a lot better to be backed up than sorry.

Some reasons why they do not and why they should back up

Some of the excuses, and why they are only excuses, follow.

Do not have the time

This is not a good excuse. If your data is worth anything at all, it is worth backing up. It takes only a few minutes to back up a large hard disk with some of the newer software. The Norton Backup is one of the newest and fastest backup programs on the market. It is also one of the easiest to use. It compresses the data so that fewer diskettes are needed.

Fastback, one of the premier backup software programs, is also very fast. It also compresses the data so that fewer floppy diskettes are needed.

Back-It is not quite as fast as the new Norton Backup, but it is very easy to use. It has several verification options to make sure that your backups are true copies. It backs up your data in a DOS-like format. Unlike some of the other backup software, Back-It lets you read the directory to determine what files are on a backup diskette.

The phone numbers are:

Norton Backup	(213) 319-2000
Fastback	(504) 291-7221
Back-It	(800) 233-0383

Several other good backup programs are on the market. If you cannot afford any of these programs, you have a fairly good backup program with your DOS. DOS BACKUP is not as fast or sophisticated as some of the commercial programs, but it does get the job done.

Once the first backup is made, all subsequent backups need only to be made of any data that has been changed or updated. Most backup programs can recognize whether a file has been changed since the last backup. Most of them can also look at the date that is stamped on each file and back up only those within a specified date range. It might take only a few minutes to make a copy of only those files that are new or have been changed. Of course, it is usually not necessary to back up your program software. You do have the original software diskettes safely tucked away, do you not?

Too much trouble

It is a bit of trouble unless you have an expensive tape automated backup system. Backup can require a bit of disk swapping, labeling, and storing. With a little organizing, it can be done easily. If you keep all of the diskettes together, you do not have to label each one. Just stack them in order, put a rubber band around them and use one label for the first one of the lot.

Yes, it is a bit of trouble to make backups. But if you do not have a backup, consider the trouble it would take to redo the files from a disk that has crashed. The trouble that it takes to make a backup is infinitesimal.

Do not have the necessary diskettes, software, or tools

Depending on the amount of data to be backed up and the software used, it might require 50 to 100 360K diskettes, a lot fewer if the high-density diskettes are used. Again, it takes only a few minutes and a few diskettes to make a backup of only the data that has been changed or altered. In most cases, the same diskettes can be reused the next day to update the files. Several discount mail order houses sell 360K diskettes for as little as 21 cents apiece, 39 cents each for 1.2Mb and 720K, and 89 cents for 1.44Mb. Several discount companies are listed at the end of chapter 5.

Failures and disasters only happen to other people

People who believe this way are those who have never experienced a disaster. You can say nothing to convince them. They just have to learn the hard way.

A few other reasons why you should back up

The technology of the hard disk systems has improved tremendously over the last couple of years, but they are still mechanical devices. As such, you can be sure that eventually they will wear out, fail, or crash.

The head crash

Most hard disks are now relatively bug free. Manufacturers quote figures of several thousand hours *mean time before failure* (MTBF). Theses figures are only an average. There is no guarantee that a disk will not fail in the next few minutes. A hard disk is made up of several mechanical parts. If it is used long enough, it will wear out or fail.

A failure can be frustrating, time consuming and make you feel utterly helpless. In the unhappy event of a crash, depending on its severity, it is possible that some of your data can be recovered, one way or another. Several disk repair service companies specialize in recovering and repairing failed disks. Here are a couple who have helped me:

California Disk Drive Repair   (408) 727-2475
Rotating Memory Service   (408) 988-2334

General failure

Outside of ordinary care, you can do little to prevent a general failure. It could be a component on the hard disk electronics or in the controller system or any one of a thousand other things. Even things such as a power failure during a read/write operation can cause data corruption.

Theft and burglary

Computers are easy to sell so they are favorite targets for burglars. It would be bad enough to lose a computer, but many computers have hard disks that are filled with data that is even more valuable than the computer.

In a recent report, a person tried to pawn an expensive computer. The pawnbroker asked to try out the computer. When he turned it on and opened a file, it had a name and address. He asked the person what his address was, and he gave one different than the one shown in the computer. He kept the person busy while he secretly called the police. The computer had been stolen. Fortunately, the owner got it back.

It is a good idea to put your name and address on several of the files on your hard disk. It would also be a good idea to scratch identifying marks on the back and bottom of the case. You should also write down the serial numbers of your monitor and drives.

Another good idea is to store your backup files in an area away from your computer. This way there would be less chance of losing both computer and backups in a burglary or fire.

Archival

Another reason to back up is for archival purposes. No matter how large the hard disk is, it will eventually fill up with data. Quite often, there will be files that are no longer used or only be used once in a great while. I keep copies of all the letters that I write on disk. I have hundreds of them. Rather than erase the old files or old letters, I put them on a diskette and store them away.

Fragmentation

After a hard disk has been used for some time, files begin to be fragmented. The data is recorded on concentric tracks in separate sectors. If part of a file is erased or changed, some of the data might be in a sector on track 20 and another part on track 40. There might be open sectors on several tracks because portions of data have been erased. Hunting all over the disk can slow the disk down. If the disk is backed up completely, then erased, the files can be restored so that they will again be recorded in contiguous sectors. The utility programs mentioned on page 77 can unfragment a hard disk by copying portions of the disk to memory and rearranging the data in contiguous files.

Data transfer

Often it is necessary to transfer a large amount of data from one hard disk on a computer to another. This is quite easy and fast if you use a good backup program. It is easy to make several copies that can be distributed to others in the company. This method could be used to distribute data, company policies and procedures, sales figures, and other information to several people in a large office or company. The data could also be easily shipped or mailed to branch offices, customers, or to others almost anywhere.

Methods of backup

Today you have many choices in backup media and methods. You can use one of several different kinds of disk or tape backups, or for extra safety, you can use more than one method.

Backup.Com

One of the least expensive methods of backup is to use the BACKUP.COM and RESTORE.COM that comes with MS-DOS. A price to pay is that it is slow, time-consuming, and rather difficult to use. It will do the job if nothing else is available.

Tape

Several tape backup systems are on the market. Tape backup is easy, but it can be relatively expensive at $600 to over $1500 for a drive unit and $10 to $30 for the tape cartridges. Most of them require the use of a controller that is similar to the disk controller, so the tape backup system will use one of your precious slots. Unless they are used externally, they will also require the use of one of the disk mounting areas. Because the system is only used for backup, it will be idle most of the time.

If you have several computers in an office that must be backed up every day, you could possibly install a controller in each machine with an external connector. Then one external tape drive could be used to back up each of the computers at the end of the day. With this system, you would need a controller in each machine, but you would only have to buy one tape drive.

One of the biggest problems with tape is that no standards have been established for tape size, cartridges, reels, or format. Quite often a tape that is recorded on one tape machine, even from the same vendor, will not restore on another.

The most common type drives use a $1/4''$ tape that is similar to that used in audio cassettes. The data from a hard disk can be much more critical than music, so the tapes are manufactured to very strict standards. Even so, it is possible that this tape will stretch and could cause the loss of data.

Also $1/2$ drives systems are available for high-end use. They will cost from $3000 to as much as $10,000 or more.

DAT

The audio record and tape industry has fought to keep the digital audio tape (DAT) systems out of the country. They are worried that people will buy compact audio discs, then freely copy them onto DAT systems. But these tape systems are finally making their way into the country, although they are still very expensive.

Several companies are offering the DAT systems for backing up large computer hard disk systems. DAT systems offer storage capacities as high as 1.3 gigabytes on a very small cartridge.

Four companies who are currently offering DAT systems are:

Bi-Tech Enterprises	(516) 567-8155
Identica	(408) 727-2600
Tallgrass Technologies	(913) 492-6002
Tecmar	(216) 349-1009

Videotape

Another tape system uses videotape and a standard home videotape recorder to make backups. This system requires that an interface board be installed in the computer. From 60Mb to 120Mb of data can be stored on a standard videotape that costs from $3 to $5.

This type of system is ideal for the home user. Two leads from the interface easily connect to the VCR. After the backup is completed, the machine can be moved back to the living room for home entertainment.

This low-cost system is also sophisticated enough to be used in large businesses and offices. The Alpha Micro VIDEOTRAX system has an option that will even do an automatic backup.

Besides being used for backup, these videotapes can be used to distribute large amounts of data. For instance, the contents of a hard disk could be copied and sent to another computer within the company or across the country.

Alpha Micro has also demonstrated that it is possible to broadcast software over the TV channels. A VCR can record the software as easily as it does an old movie. The software can then be installed on any computer system that is equipped with an interface board.

Two companies are foremost in this type of backup:

AUTOFAX   (408) 438-6861
Alpha Micro VIDEOTRAX   (714) 641-6381

Their boards cost about $300 to $500.

High-density disk drive

Several companies are now making high-density floppy disk drives. The Bernoulli drive can now put 44Mb on a $5^1/4''$ floppy diskette. Brier Technology and several others have developed $3^1/2''$ floppy drives that can store 20Mb or more.

Even if they cost a bit more, a high-density floppy drive can be more advantageous than a tape. The tape drives would only be used for backup. A high-density floppy would have much more utility, possibly even obviating the need for a hard disk.

Second hard disk

The easiest and the fastest of all methods of backup is to have a second hard disk. It is very easy to install a second hard disk because most controllers have the capability of controlling a second hard disk. You would have to make sure that the second hard disk would work with your first disk, but that should be easy to determine. It would not have to be a large one, a 20Mb or 30Mb would do fine. With a second hard disk as a backup, you would not need a backup software package. A good backup software package can cost $200 or more. You could probably buy a second hard disk for this amount.

An average hard disk will have an access speed of about 40 ms. Floppy disks operate at about 300 ms speed, which can seem like an eternity compared to the speed of even the slowest hard disk. Depending on the number of files, how fragmented the data is on the disk, and the access speed, a second hard disk can back up 20Mb in a matter of seconds. To back up 20Mb using even the fastest software will require 15 to 20 minutes. It will also require that you do a lot of diskette swapping in and out. Depending on the type of diskettes that you use for backup, it can require 50 to 60 360K, about 17 1.2Mb, or about 14 1.44Mb diskettes.

Another problem with using software backup is that it is often difficult to find a particular file. Most backup software stores the data in a system that is not the same as DOS files. Usually there is no directory like that provided by DOS. Even the DOS BACKUP files show only a control number when you check the directory.

Hard cards

It is now possible to buy a hard disk on a card for $300 to $600, depending on capacity and company. At this low price, it would be worthwhile to install a card in an empty slot and dedicate it to backup.

If you have no empty slots, you might even consider just plugging in the card once a week or so to make a backup, then removing the card until needed again. This would entail removing the cover from the machine each time. I remove the cover to my computer so often that I only use one screw on it to provide grounding. I can remove and replace my cover in a very short time.

Software

Several very good software programs on the market let you use a $5^{1}/_{4}$" or $3^{1}/_{2}$" disk drive to back up your data. Again, you should have backups of all your master software, so you do not have to worry about backing up that software every day. Because DOS stamps each file with the date and time it was created, it is easy to back up only those files that were created after a certain date and time.

DOS also stores backup information about the file in the directory entry. One of the bits of information is the archive flag, either a 1 or 0. When the DOS BACKUP command has been used to back up the file, the flag is changed. Several commercial software packages make use of this flag so that only files that have not been backed up can be copied.

One of the most popular backup software programs in Fastback. It has lots of utilities, pull-down menus, and a well written manual. The manual explains just about everything you need to know about backups, such as the difference in an image backup and a file-oriented backup. An *image* backup is an exact bit-for-bit copy of the hard disk copied as a continuous stream of data. This type of backup is rather inflexible and does not allow for a separate file backup or restoration. The *file-oriented* type of backup identifies and indexes each file separately. A separate file or directory can be backed up and restored easily. It can be very time consuming to have to back up an entire 20Mb or more each day. With a file-oriented type system, once a full backup has been made, it is necessary only to make incremental backups of those files that have been changed or altered. The manual is written in plain language that should be easy for anyone to understand.

Several more very good backup software packages are available. Check through the computer magazines for their ads and for reviews.

No matter what type of system or method is used, you should be using something to back up your data. You might be one of the lucky ones and never need it. But, better safe that sorry.

8
CHAPTER

Monitors

The monitor is your primary link with your computer. Most of the time you spend working on a computer will be spent looking at the monitor. You can buy a monochrome monitor for as little as $65. But life is so very short. Life can be a lot more enjoyable if you have a good high-resolution color monitor. Even if you do nothing but word processing, color makes the job a lot easier and more pleasant.

But alas, like so many other things in life, the better the color and the higher the resolution, the higher the cost. Also the larger the screen, or size of the monitor, the higher the cost. You will need a large-size pocket book to buy a large-size monitor.

Several improvements in the design and development of the monitor electronics, such as new chipsets and VLSI integration, have helped reduce the cost of manufacture in the electronic area. Not much can be done to reduce the cost of manufacture of the main component, the cathode ray tube (CRT). A good color CRT requires a tremendous amount of labor-intensive, precision work. The larger the screen, the more costly it is to manufacture.

Many manufacturers make many, many different types, sizes, and kinds of monitors. Lots of competition among the manufacturers helps to keep the prices fairly reasonable.

Many options available

Due to the many types of monitors and many options, you will have some difficult decisions to make when you buy your system. You will have a very wide choice as to price, resolution, color, size, and shape. As we mentioned before, you can buy a 12″ monochrome for as little as $65. You can buy a CGA for about $100, and I have seen good EGA monitors for $250. VGA and Super VGA can cost from $400 and up to $10,000.

The monitor is a very critical part of your system, and it can represent a large percentage of the cost of a system. You should make sure that you get the best that you can afford.

If you are buying by mail, or even at a store, try to get a copy of the manufacturer's specifications and study them. Look at the ads in magazines like the *Computer Shopper*, the *Computer Monthly*, and others to get an idea of the cost of a monitor. Be aware that ads cost a lot of money, so a lot of good information is sometimes left out. So ask questions.

Monitors are usually long lived. I have an early NEC Multiscan model that is about four years old. I have gone through several computers and hard disks, but this monitor is still going strong. (I have probably put a hex on it by saying this. It will probably die in the next few minutes.)

Incidentally, this NEC monitor was one of the more expensive types on the market when I bought it. At that time the VGA system was still just a gleam in IBM's eye. The NEC is digital, but they had used great foresight and built in analog capability as well. I ran the monitor as a digital EGA for a couple of years. When the price of VGA adapters became reasonable. I bought one. I have never been sorry that I had to pay a little extra for this monitor.

What to buy if you can afford it

Buy the biggest and best multisync color Super VGA that you can afford. A 14" NEC 2A will cost about $500 and will have 800 × 600 resolution. An adapter to drive it will cost from $100 to $200. You can buy off-brand monitors and adapters for a little less. For instance, a Goldstar 16" 1610, 1024 × 768 resolution, is advertised for $899 including an adapter. The ad does not say so, but it uses interlacing for vertical scanning. Interlaced scanning can cause flickering. (More about interlacing later.)

It might cost a few dollars more, but you would probably be much happier with a noninterlaced unit. A Princeton Ultrasync 16 is advertised for $799, an adapter would cost about $175. If you use Windows 3.0, a larger screen will let you see several applications at the same time.

If you decide to buy an off-brand system, you should try to check it out first. Check for dot pitch, for multiscanning, for bandwidth, for controls, for noninterlaced, special drivers, glare, swivel, cables, and connectors. Get the vendor spec sheets and read them carefully.

Monitor basics

Here are a few of the monitor specifications, terms, and acronyms so that you can make a more informed decision as to which monitor to buy.

In IBM language, a monitor is a display device. This is probably a better term, since the work *monitor* is Latin for *to warn*. But despite IBM, most people still call it a monitor.

Basically, a monitor is similar to a television set. The face of a TV set or a monitor is the end of a cathode ray tube (CRT). They are vacuum tubes and have many of the same elements that made up the old vacuum tubes that were used before the advent of the semiconductor age. The CRTs have a filament that boils off a stream of electrons. These electrons have a potential of about 25,000 volts. They are "shot" from an electron gun toward the front of the CRT where they slam into the phosphor on the back side of the face and cause it to light up. Depending on the type of phosphor used, once the dot is lit up, it continues to glow for a period of time. The electron beam moves rapidly across the screen, but since the phosphor continues to glow for awhile, you see the images that are created.

When you watch a movie, you are seeing a series of still photos, flashed one after the other. Due to the persistence of vision, it appears to be continuous motion. It is this same persistence of vision phenomenon that allows you to see motion and images on your television and video screens.

In a magnetic field, a beam of electrons acts very much like a piece of iron. Just like iron, a stream of electrons can be attracted or repelled by the polarity of a magnet. In a CRT, a beam of electrons must pass between a system of electromagnets before it reaches the back side of the CRT face. In a basic system, an electromagnet is on the left, one on the right, one at the top, and one at the bottom. Voltage through the electromagnets can be varied so that the beam of electrons is repulsed by one side and attracted by the other, or pulled to the top or forced to the bottom. With this electromagnetic system, a stream of electrons can be bent and directed to any spot on the screen. It is much like holding a hose and directing a high pressure stream of water to an area. You could use the stream to write or draw lines or whatever.

Scan rates

When you look at the screen of a TV set or a monitor, you see a full screen only because of the persistence of vision and the type of phosphor used on the back of the screen. Actually, the beam of electrons starts at the top left corner of the screen, then under the influence of the electromagnets, it is pulled across to the right hand top corner. It lights up the pixels as it sweeps across. It is then returned to the left-hand side, dropped down one line and swept across again. On a TV set, this is repeated so that 525 lines are written on the screen in about $1/60$ of a second. This would be one frame, so 60 frames are written to the screen in one second.

The time that it takes to fill a screen with lines from top to bottom is the *vertical scan rate*. Some of the newer multiscan, or multifrequency, monitors can have variable vertical scan rates from $1/40$ up to $1/1000$ of a second to paint the screen from top to bottom.

The horizontal scanning frequency of a standard television set is 15.75 kHz. This is also the frequency used by the CGA systems. The EGA is about 22 kHz, the VGA is 31.5 kHz and up. The higher resolutions require higher frequencies. The multiscan monitors can vary from 15.5 kHz up to 100 kHz.

Controlling the beam

The CRT has *control grids*, much like the old vacuum tubes, for controlling the signal. The control grid, along with the electromagnetic system, controls the electron stream somewhat as if the stream were a pencil. The grid causes the stream to copy the input signal and write it on the screen. As the beam sweeps across the screen, if the input signal is tracing the outline of a figure, the control grid will turn the beam on to light up a dot of phosphor for the light areas. If the input signal is of a dark area, the beam is shut off so that a portion of the screen will be dark for that area of the image.

Resolution

If you look closely at a black-and-white photo in a newspaper, you can see that the photo is made up of small dots. Darker areas have more dots, and light areas have fewer. The text or image on a monitor or a television screen is also make up of dots very similar to the newspaper photo. You can easily see these dots with a magnifying glass. If you look closely, you can see spaces between the dots. These are much like the dots of a dot matrix printer. The more dots and the closer together they are, the better the resolution. A good high-resolution monitor will have solid, sharply defined characters and images.

An ideal resolution would look very much like a high quality photograph. It will be some time before we reach the resolution of film.

Pixels

Resolution is also determined by the number of *picture elements* (pixels) that can be displayed. The following figures relate primarily to text, but the graphics resolution is similar to the text. A standard color graphics monitor (CGA) can display 640×200 pixels. It can display 80 characters in one line with 25 lines from top to bottom. If you divide 640 by 80, you find that one character will be 8 pixels wide. There can be 25 lines of characters, so 200 divided by 25 is 8 pixels high. The entire screen will be 640×200 or 180,000 pixels.

Most monitor adapters have text character generators built onto the board. When you send an A to the screen, the adapter goes to its library and sends the signal for the preformed A to the screen. Each character occupies a cell made up of the number of pixels depending on the resolution of the screen and the adapter. In the case of the CGA, if all the dots within a cell were lit up, you would have a solid block of dots 8 pixels or dots wide and 8 pixels high. When the A is placed in a cell, only the dots necessary to form an outline of an A will be lit up. It is very similar to the dots formed by the dot matrix printers when it prints a character.

A graphics adapter, along with the proper software, allows you to place lines, images, photos, normal and various text fonts, and almost anything you can imagine on the screen.

An enhanced graphics system (EGA) can display 640 × 350, or 8 (640/80) pixels wide and 14 (350/25) pixels high. The screen can display 640 × 350 (or 224,000 total) pixels. Enhanced EGA and VGA can display 640 × 480 (307,200 total) pixels; each character will be 8 pixels wide and 19 pixels high.

The Video Electronics Standards Association (VESA) has chosen 800 × 600 to be the Super VGA standard, which is 10 (800/80) wide and 24 (600/25) high. Many of the newer systems are now capable of 1024 × 768, 1280 × 1024, 1664 × 1200 and more. With a resolution of 1664 × 1200, you would have 1,996,800 pixels that could be lit up. We have come a long way from the 128,000 pixels possible with CGA.

Interlaced vs. noninterlaced

For CGA, the horizontal system will sweep the electron beam across the screen from top to bottom 200 times in 1/60 of a second to make one frame, or 60 frames in one second. For VGA it would sweep from top to bottom 480 times in 1/60 of a second. For Super VGA it would be 600 times, and for 1024 × 768 it would be 768 times in 1/60 of a second. As you can see, the higher the resolution, the more lines, the closer they are together and the faster they have to be painted on the screen. The higher resolution also causes the electron beam to light up more pixels on each line as it sweeps across.

The higher horizontal frequencies demand more precise and higher quality electronics. These higher quality electronics of course, require higher costs to manufacture. To avoid this higher cost, IBM designed some of their VGA systems with an interlaced horizontal system. Instead of increasing the horizontal frequency, they merely painted every other line across the screen from top to bottom, then returned to the top and painted the lines that were skipped. Theoretically, this sounds like a great idea. But practically, it does not work too well because it causes a flicker. It can be very irritating to some people who have to work with this type of monitor for very long.

This flicker is not readily apparent, but some people have complained of eyestrain, headaches, and fatigue after prolonged use of an interlaced monitor. If the monitor is only used for short periods of time, by different persons, then the interlaced type would probably be okay.

Some companies make models that use interlacing in certain modes. But the same model may be noninterlacing in other modes. Most companies do not advertise the fact that their monitors use interlacing. The interlace models are usually a bit lower in price than the noninterlaced. Many of them also use the IBM standard 8514 chipset. You might have to ask the vendor what system is used.

Other companies besides IBM make interlaced monitors. If you get a chance, compare the interlaced and noninterlaced. You might not be able to tell the difference. If cost is a prime consideration, the interlaced is usually a bit less expensive.

The adapter that you buy should match your monitor. Use an interlaced adapter with an interlaced monitor. An adapter that can send only interlaced signals might not work with a noninterlaced monitor. Some of the high-end adapters might be able to adjust and operate with both interlaced and noninterlaced monitors.

Figure 8-1 shows an unusual adapter, the 8514 Ultra from the ATI Technologies. This adapter will operate in both ISA type systems and MCA. The MCA connector is on one side and the ISA on the other.

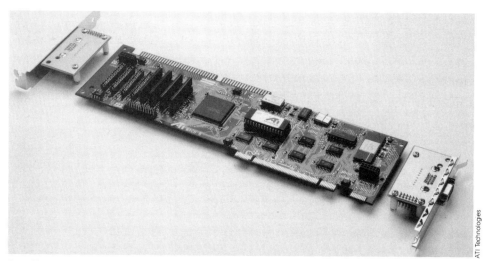

8-1 The 8514/Ultra from ATI Technologies. A very unusual adapter for high resolution monitors. It has a connector on one side for the IBM PS/2 MCA system. It also has a connector on the other side so that it can be used in the standard AT or ISA type systems.

Figure 8-2 shows the high-resolution Princeton Ultra X monitor. It operates in some modes as interlaced and others as noninterlaced.

For more information call:

| Ultra ATI Technologies | (416) 756-0718 |
| Princeton | (800) 221-1490 |

Landscape vs. portrait

Most monitors are wider than they are tall. These are called *landscape* styles. Some others that are taller than they are wide are called *portrait* styles. You will find many of this style used for desktop publishing and other special applications.

Princeton Graphic Systems

8-2   The Ultra X, a high-resolution monitor.

Monochrome

A monochrome monitor has a single electron beam gun and a single color phosphor. It writes directly on the phosphor and can provide very high resolution for text and graphics. It is even possible to get monochrome analog VGA, which can display in as many as 64 different shades. Large monochrome monitors might be ideal for some desktop publishing systems (DTP) and even some computer-aided design (CAD) systems. These large monochrome monitors can be almost expensive as the equivalent size color.

Colorgraphics

Color TVs and color monitors are much more complicated than monochrome systems. During the manufacture of the color monitors, three different phosphors, red, green and blue, are deposited on the back of the screen. Usually a very small dot of each color is placed in a triangular shape. They have three electron beam guns, one for each color. By lighting up the three different colored phosphors selectively, all the colors of the rainbow can be generated.

The guns are called red, green, and blue (RGB), but the electrons they emit are all the same. They are called RGB because each gun is aimed so that it hits a red, a green, or a blue color on the back of the monitor screen. They are very accurately aimed so that they will converge or impinge only on their assigned color.

Dot pitch

To make sure that the guns hit their own color only, a metal shadow mask with very tiny holes is laid over the deposited phosphors. The more holes in the shadow mask, and the closer together the color dots of phosphor, the higher the possible resolution of a monitor.

The distance between the holes or perforations in the shadow mask is called the *dot pitch*. The dots per inch determines the resolution. A high resolution monitor might have a dot pitch of 0.31 millimeter. (One mm is 0.0394 inches, 0.31 mm is 0.0122 inches or about the thickness of an average business card.) A typical medium resolution monitor might have a dot pitch of 0.39 mm. One with very high resolution might have a dot pitch of 0.26 mm or even less. The smaller the dot pitch, the more precise and more difficult they are to manufacture.

Some of the low cost monitors have a dot pitch of 0.42 mm and some as great as 0.52 mm. The 0.52 mm might be suitable for playing some games, but it would be difficult to do any productive computing on such a system.

Adapter basics

It won't do you much good to buy a high-resolution monitor unless you buy a good adapter to drive it. You cannot just plug a monitor into your computer and expect it to function. Just as a hard disk needs a controller, a monitor needs an adapter to interface with the computer. Also, like the hard disk manufacturers, many of the monitor manufacturers do not make adapter boards. Just as a hard disk can operate with several different types of controllers, most monitors can operate with several different types of adapters.

The original IBM PC came with a green monochrome monitor with a monochrome display adapter (MDA) that could display text only. The Hercules Company immediately saw the folly of this limitation, so they developed the Hercules monographic adapter (HMGA) and set a new standard. It was not long before IBM and a lot of other companies were selling similar MGA cards that could display both graphics and text. These adapters provide a high resolution of 720 × 350 on monochrome monitors.

IBM then introduced their color monitor and *color graphics adapter* (CGA). It provides only 640 × 200 resolution.

The CGA is a digital system that allows a mix of the red, green, and blue. The cables have four lines, one each for red, green and blue, and one for intensity. This allows two different intensities, for each color, on for bright or off for dim. So there are four objects, each of which can be in either of two states, or two to the fourth power (2^4). Therefore CGA has a limit of 16 colors.

The CGA monitors have very large spaces between the pixels so that the resolution and color is terrible. It is similar to the nine-pin dot matrix printer.

An *enhanced graphics adapter* (EGA) can drive a high resolution monitor to display 640 × 350 resolution. The EGA system has six lines and allows each of the primary colors to be mixed together in any of four different intensities. So there are 2^6 or 64 different colors that they can display.

The EGA boards are downward compatible so that they will also display older programs that were developed for the CGA or MGA. A couple of years ago, EGA boards cost from $400 to $600. EGA boards sell today for less than $100.

Analog vs. digital

Up until the introduction of the PS/2 with VGA, most displays used the digital system. However, the digital systems have severe limitations. The digital signals are of two states, either fully on or completely off. The signals for color and intensity require separate lines in the cables. As mentioned, it takes six lines for the EGA to be able to display 16 colors out of a palette of 64.

The analog signals that drive the color guns are voltages that are continuously variable. Only a few lines are needed for the three primary colors. The intensity voltage for each color can then be varied almost infinitely to create as many as 256 colors out of a possible 262,144.

The digital systems are sometimes called TTL for transistor-to-transistor logic. Some monitors that can handle both digital and analog have a switch that says TTL for the digital mode.

Low-cost EGA

Just a couple of years ago, EGA monitors cost from $600 up to $800. I have recently seen some fairly good monitors selling today for as little as $250, and EGA boards for less than $100. You can buy a system that might have cost $1000 a couple of years ago for about $350 today. Depending on what you want to do with your computer, this may be all you need.

Very-high-resolution graphics adapters

Many of the high-resolution adapters have up to one megabyte or more of Video RAM (VRAM) memory on board. A single complex graphics drawing can require this much memory or more to store just one image. By having the memory on the adapter board, it saves having to go through the bus to the conventional RAM. Some adapter boards even have a separate plug-in daughterboard. Many of them have their own coprocessor on board, as does the Texas Instruments 34010 or the Hitachi HD63483.

Depending on the resolution capabilities and the goodies that it has, a very-high-resolution adapter board can cost from $350 up to $3400.

The high-resolution adapters are downward compatible. If you run a program that was designed for CGA, it will display it in CGA, even though you have a very-high-resolution monitor, but it will look a lot better than it would on a CGA monitor.

VGA to video adapters

Several companies have developed special VGA adapters that can transform VGA output to a television signal. This National Television Standards Committee

(NTSC) signal can then be recorded on a VCR or displayed on a TV screen. These adapters can be used to create excellent presentations or for computerized special effects.

The US Video Company has several adapters. Their TVGA card can drive a monitor up to 1024 × 768 and also output NTSC signals. They also have several other cards for special effects. Other companies have similar products:

US Video Company	(203) 964-9000
Jovian Logic Corp.	(415) 651-4823
Willow Peripherals	(212) 402-0010

Multiscan

The multiscan monitors can accept a wide range of vertical and horizontal frequencies, making them quite versatile and flexible. Most of the early multiscans could accept both digital and analog signals. If you had an older EGA, or even a CGA adapter card, it would work with it. Many of the new monitors will only accept the VGA analog signals.

The VGA introduced by IBM on their PS/2 systems in 1987 was not a multiscan monitor. It operated at a fixed frequency. A multiscan design costs more to build, so many VGAs are designed to operate at a single fixed frequency. They are not as versatile or flexible as the multiscan, but the resolution can be as good as the multiscan.

Many companies are manufacturing monitors with multi-fixed frequencies with two or more fixed frequencies. Again, they are not quite as flexible as the true multiscan, but they can cost less.

The multiscan monitors may sell for as little as $300 and up to as much as $5000 for some of the large 19″ to 30″ sizes.

What you should buy

The primary determining factor for choosing a monitor should be what it is going to be used for and the amount of money you have to spend. If money is no object, buy a large 19″ analog monitor with super high resolution and a good VGA board to drive it for about $2500.

If you expect to do any kind of graphics, CAD/CAM design work, you will definitely need a good large-screen color monitor, with very high resolution. A large screen is almost essential for some types of design drawings so that as much of the drawing as possible can be viewed on the screen. It takes a lot of time for the computer to redraw an image on the screen. In a large company, it can cost up to $100 or more an hour for an engineer to use a computer. With a small monitor, the engineer might have to spend a large amount of time just staring into space while the computer redraws a portion of the image. With a large screen, more of the drawing will be displayed and less time will be spent on redrawing. At $100 or more an hour, it would not take long to recover the extra cost of a large screen monitor.

You will also need a high-resolution monitor for close tolerance designs. For instance, if you draw two lines to meet on a low-resolution monitor, they might look as if they are perfectly lined up. When the drawing is magnified or printed out, the lines might not be anywhere close to one another.

For desktop publishing (DTP), the very-high-resolution monochrome monitors are ideal. They can usually display several shades of gray. Many of these monitors are the portrait type (they are higher than they are wide). Many of them have a display area of $8^{1}/_{2}'' \times 11''$. Instead of 25 lines, they will have 66 lines, which is the standard for an 11″ sheet of paper. Many have a phosphor that will let you have black text on a white background so that the screen looks very much like the finished text. Some of the newer color monitors have a mode that will let you switch to pure white with black type.

Some of the 19″ and larger landscape type monitors (wider than they are high) can display two pages of text side by side.

For databases, spreadsheets, accounting, or for word processing, a monochrome monitor would probably be sufficient, but not nearly as pleasant as with color.

What to look for

If possible, go to several stores and compare various models. Turn the brightness up and check the center of the screen and the outer edges. Is the intensity the same in the center and the outer edges? Check the focus, brightness, and contrast with text and graphics. There can be vast differences even in the same models from the same manufacturer. I have seen monitors that displayed demo graphics programs beautifully, but were not worth a damn when displaying text in various colors. If possible, try it out with both text and graphics.

Ask the vendor for a copy of the specs. Check the dot pitch. For good high-resolution, it should be no greater than 0.31 mm, even better would be 0.28 mm or 0.25 mm.

Check the horizontal and vertical scan frequency specs. For a multiscan, the wider the range, the better. A good system could have a horizontal range from 30 kHz to 40 kHz or better. The vertical range could be from 45 Hz to 70 Hz or better.

Bandwidth

The bandwidth of a monitor is the range of frequencies that its circuits can handle. A multiscan monitor can accept horizontal frequencies from 15.75 KHz up to about 40 KHz and vertical frequencies from 40 Hz up to about 90 Hz. To get a rough estimate of the bandwidth required, multiply the resolution pixels times the vertical scan or frame rate. For instance, a Super VGA or VESA standard monitor should have $800 \times 600 \times 60$ Hz = 28.8 MHz. The systems require a certain amount of overhead, such as *retrace*, the time needed to move back to the left side of the screen, drop it down one line and start a new line. So the bandwidth should be at least 30 MHz. If the vertical scan rate is 90 Hz, then it is $800 \times 600 \times 90$ = 43.2 MHz or at least 45 MHz bandwidth. A very high resolution would require a bandwidth of $1600 \times 1200 \times 90$ = 172.8 MHz or about 180 MHz counting the overhead. Many of the very-high-resolution units are specified at 200 MHz video bandwidth. Of course, the higher the bandwidth, the more costly and difficult to manufacture.

Drivers

Most of the new software being developed today has built-in hooks that will allow it to take advantage of the high-resolution goodies. The older software programs that were written before EGA and VGA were developed cannot normally take advantage of the higher resolution and extended graphics.

Some manufacturers supply software drivers with their adapters for older programs such as Windows, Lotus, AutoCAD, GEM, Ventura, WordStar, and others. Some vendors supply as many as two or three diskettes full of drivers.

Depending on what software you intend to use, the drivers supplied with the adapter you purchase might be an important consideration.

Screen size

The stated screen size is very misleading and almost fraudulent. The size is supposed to be a diagonal measurement. But on my NEC 14 inch Multisync, it only measures about 13 ". I suppose it would measure 14 " if I took it out of the case and measured the face of the bottle. There is also a border on all four sides of the screen. The usuable viewing area is about 9.75 " wide and about 7.75 " high on this 14 " monitor. One reason is because the screen is markedly curved near the edges on all sides. This curve can cause distortion so the areas are masked off and not used.

This is plenty big enough for most of the things that I do. But for some types of CAD work or desktop publishing, it would be helpful to have a bigger screen. However, prices go up almost at a logarithmic rate for sizes above 14 ". A 14 " might cost less than $500, a 16 " about $1200, a 19 " or 20 " one might cost $2500 or more.

Again the size monitor that you should buy depends on what you want to do with your computer and how much money you want to spend.

Controls

You might also check for available controls to adjust the brightness, contrast, and vertical/horizontal lines. Some manufacturers place them on the back or some other difficult area to get at. It is much better if they are accessible from the front so that you can see what the effect is as you adjust them.

Glare

If a monitor reflects too much light, it can be like a mirror and be very distracting. Some manufacturers have coated the screen with a silicon formulation to cut down on the reflectance. Some have etched the screen for the same purpose. Some screens are tinted to help cut down on glare. If possible, you should try the monitor under various lighting conditions.

If you have a glare problem, several supply companies and mail order houses offer glare shields that cost from $20 up to $100.

Cleaning the screens

Because about 25,000 volts of electricity hit the back side of the monitor face, it creates a static attraction for dust. This can distort and make the screen difficult to read.

Most manufacturers should have an instruction booklet that suggests how the screen should be cleaned. If you have a screen that has been coated with silicon to reduce glare, you should not use any harsh cleaners on it. In most cases, plain water and a soft paper towel will do fine.

Tilt-and-swivel base

Most people sit their monitor on top of the computer. If you are short or tall, have a low or high chair, or a nonstandard desk, the monitor might not be at eye level. A tilt-and-swivel base can allow you to position the monitor to best suit you. Many monitors now come with this base. If yours does not have one, many specialty stores and mail order houses sell them for $15 to $40.

Several supply and mail order houses also offer an adjustable arm that clamps to the desk. Most have a small platform for the monitor to sit on. The arm can swing up and down and from side to side. It can free up a lot of desk space. They may cost from $50 up to $150.

Cables

Some of the monitors come without cables. The vendors may sell them separately for $25 to $75 extra. Even those that have cables might not have the type of connectors that will fit your adapter. At this time, there is little or no standardization for cable and adapter connectors. Make sure that you get the proper cables to match your adapter and monitor.

Monitor and adapter sources

Note: I have only bought a half dozen monitors in my lifetime, so I have not personally had a chance to evaluate the following products. I subscribe to *PC Magazine*, *PC Week*, *Byte*, *PC Sources*, *InfoWorld*, *PC World*, *Computer Shopper*,

Computer Monthly, and about 50 other computer magazines. Most of these magazines have test labs and do extensive tests of products for their excellent reviews. Because I cannot personally test all of these products, I rely heavily on their reviews.

I cannot possibly list all of the monitor and adapter vendors. I suggest that you subscribe to some of the magazines listed here and in chapter 16. Check the reviews and advertisements in these magazines for other vendors.

List price vs. street price

Note that the prices quoted from manufacturers in most magazine reviews are list prices. Often the street price of the products will be less. For instance, here are some list prices from a recent magazine review, and ad prices for the same units from a current *Computer Shopper*:

Model	List price	Ad price
NEC 2A	$ 799	$ 499
NEC 3D	$1049	$ 629
NEC 5D	$3699	$2350

You can see a tremendous difference in the list price and the actual price you should pay. Besides, in this volatile market, the prices change almost daily. Call first if ordering from a magazine ad.

Multisync monitor sources

Listed here are some of the companies who manufacture multisync monitors. They have received excellent reviews in the computer magazines I mentioned. If you call them, they will send you spec sheets on their products:

Acer America Corp.	(408) 922-0333
Amstrad	(214) 518-0668
Cordata	(213) 603-2901
Cornerstone Technology	(408) 435-8900
Dell Computer Corp.	(512) 338-4400
Goldstar Technology	(408) 432-1331
Hitachi America	(201) 825-8000
Idek North America	(714) 661-0409
JVC Information Products	(201) 794-3900
Microvitec, Inc.	(404) 991-2246
Mitsubishi Electronics	(213) 515-3993
Moniterm Corp.	(612) 935-4151
Nanao USA	(213) 325-5202
NEC Home Electronics	(312) 860-9500
Panasonic	(201) 348-7000

Princeton Graphic Systems   (404) 664-1010
Relisys   (408) 945-9000
Samsung Information Systems   (408) 922-5900
Tatung Co.   (213) 979-7055
Taxan USA Corp.   (408) 262-9059
Toshiba America   (312) 945-1500
TW Casper Corp.   (415) 770-8500
Wyse Technology   (408) 433-1200
Sony Corp. of America   (201) 930-7669

Adapter sources

Here are some companies who manufacture high-resolution graphics adapters:

Ahead Systems   (408) 435-0707
AST Research   (714) 863-1333
ATI Technologies   (416) 756-0718
Boca Research   (407) 997-6227
Cardinal Technologies   (717) 293-3000
Dell Computers   (800) 426-5150
Everex Systems   (415) 498-1111
Genoa Systems   (408) 432-9090
Headland (Video Seven)   (415) 623-7857
NEC Technologies   (708) 860-9500
Orchid Technology   (415) 683-0300
Personal Computer Graphics   (213) 216-0055
Renaissance   (206) 454-8086
STB Systems   (214) 234-8750
Tecmar   (800) 624-8560
Trident Microsystems   (408) 738-3194
Western Digital Paradise   (714) 424-2033

9
CHAPTER

Memory

Memory is one of the most critical elements of the computer. If you open a file from a hard disk, the files and data are read from the disk and placed in RAM. When you load in a program, be it word processing, a spreadsheet, database, or whatever, you will be working in the system RAM. If you are writing, programming, or creating another program, you will be working in RAM.

RAM

RAM is an acronym for *random access memory*. Being able to randomly access the memory allows you to read and write to it. It is somewhat like an electronic blackboard. Here you can manipulate the data, do calculations, enter more data, edit, search databases, or do any of the thousands of things that software programs allow you to do. You can access and change the data in RAM very quickly.

Need for more memory

Depending on what you intend to use your computer for, you might need to buy more memory. For some applications, you might need to buy several megabytes more. In the old days, people got by fine with just 64K of memory. Your new 486 will need a minimum of at least 2 megabytes, and even better would be 4 megabytes. Many of the new software programs such as the spreadsheets, databases, and accounting programs require a lot of memory. The Lotus 1-2-3 Release 3 requires about 2Mb of RAM in order to run.

If you bought your new 486 motherboard through mail order, you might have received it with 0K memory. (You probably know that 0K does not mean okay, it means zero K memory.) The price of memory fluctuates quite a lot. Ads are sometimes made up and placed two or three months before the magazine comes out. Because of the fluctuating prices, some vendors will not advertise a firm price for memory. Besides, if they included the price of the memory, it might frighten you away. They usually invite you to call them for the latest price.

Things to consider before you buy memory

Memory comes in several different types, sizes, and speeds, and you must also consider other factors before buying memory. You should buy the type that is best for your computer.

Dynamic RAM or DRAM

Dynamic RAM (DRAM) is the most common type of memory used today. Each memory cell has a small etched transistor that is kept in its memory state, either on or off by a very small capacitor. Capacitors are similar to small rechargeable batteries. Units can be charged up with a voltage to represent 1s or left uncharged to represent 0s. Those that are charged up immediately start to lose their charge, so they must be constantly "refreshed" with a new charge. A computer may spend 7% or more of its time just refreshing the DRAM chips. Also, each time a cell is accessed, it must be refreshed and it cannot be immediately accessed again. If it is 70 nanosecond (ns), it might take 70 ns, plus the time to recycle, or maybe 105 ns or more, before that cell can again be accessed.

The speed of the DRAM chips in your system should be 70 ns or less. You might be able to install slower chips, but your system would have to work with wait states. Wait states could deprive your system of one of its greatest benefits, speed. If the DRAM is too slow, the CPU and the rest of the system would have to sit and wait while it was being accessed and refreshed which would be a terrible waste of time.

Caution!

RAM is easily erased. If there is the slightest power interruption, even for a fraction of a second, all of the charges on the DRAMs, and therefore any data in memory, any work that you have done, is lost. If the computer is turned off, the data in RAM is gone forever. You should get in the habit of saving your files to disk frequently, especially if you live in an area where there are power failures due to storms or other reasons. One of the excellent features of WordStar is that it can be set up so that it will automatically save open files to disk at frequent intervals.

Static RAM or SRAM

Static RAM (SRAM) is made up of actual transistors. They can be turned on to represent 1s or left off to represent 0s and will stay in that way until changed. They do not need to be refreshed. They are very fast and can operate at speeds of 25 ns or less. SRAM is much more expensive than DRAM. A DRAM memory cell needs only one transistor and a small capacitor. Each SRAM cell requires four to six transistors and other components.

Besides being more expensive, the SRAM chips are physically larger and require more space than the DRAM chips. SRAM and DRAM chips are not interchangeable.

The speed and static characteristics of SRAM make them an excellent tool for cache systems. The 486 chip has an on-board built-in 8K cache system. It is very fast, but fairly small. Many of the 486 motherboard designers have included sockets for up to 256K of static RAM cache.

My 486 motherboard cache system allows SRAM to be installed in 32K increments. If you are short of money, or you do not need a lot of cache at this time, you could leave the cache off, or just install a minimum.

A cache system can speed up operations quite a lot. Some programs might require a very lot of accesses to RAM. The computer could be slowed down considerably if it has to search the entire memory each time it has to fetch some data. The data that is used most frequently can be stored in the fast cache memory and speed can be increased by several magnitudes. Of course, your system would have to be designed to accept static RAM in order to use it.

Many laptops use SRAM because it can be kept alive with a small amount of current from a battery. Because DRAM needs to be constantly refreshed, it takes a lot of circuitry and power to keep them alive.

Intel has developed *flash memory*, a type of static memory that requires even less current than SRAMs to keep it alive. It is being used in several new laptops.

Single inline memory module (SIMM)

Your computer motherboard will probably have sockets for SIMMs. This is an assembly for miniature DRAM chips. Usually, nine chips on a small board are plugged slantwise into a special connector. They require a very small amount of board real estate. Figure 9-1 shows my 486 motherboard with 4Mb of SIMM RAM installed. The 12 empty slots would allow me to install another 12Mb. The 4Mb chips are becoming more available on the market. With 4Mb SIMMs I could have up to 64Mb on my motherboard.

IBM and several other companies are now working on 16Mb chips. That seems like a lot of memory, but just a few years ago, 640K seemed like a lot.

Electrostatic voltage

You might have bought memory chips or SIMMs to install on your motherboard or on a plug-in memory board. One of the first things that you should do is to discharge any electrostatic charge that might have been built up on you. If you have ever walked across a carpet and got a shock when you touched the door knob, then you know that you can build up static electricity. It is quite possible to

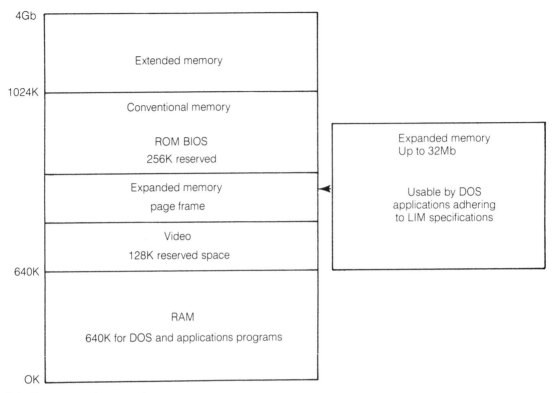

9-1 How memory is arranged.

build up 3000 to 5000 volts of static electricity in your body. So if you touch a fragile piece of electronics that normally operates at 5 to 12 volts, you can severely damage it. You can discharge this static electricity from your body by touching any metal that goes to ground. The metal case of the power supply in your computer is a good ground if it is still plugged into the wall socket. The power does not have to be on for it to connect to ground. You could also touch an unpainted metal part of a lamp or other appliance that was plugged into a socket. You should always discharge yourself before you touch any plug-in board or other equipment where electronic semiconductors are exposed.

Read-only memory

Read-only memory (ROM) is another kind of memory. You can write to or read RAM memory, but ROM is firmware that can only be read, usually only by the computer. ROM usually contains instructions and rules, such as those contained in the BIOS ROM, that control the operation of the computer. Ordinarily, you do not have to worry about ROM except to update your BIOS chips.

The 640K DOS barrier

At one time, one megabyte of RAM was believed to be more than sufficient for any eventuality. So DOS was designed for that limit. How little they knew.

The 8088 CPUs found in all PCs and XTs can access one megabyte of RAM. Only 640K is available for applications, the other 384K is reserved for internal use of the BIOS, the display, and other functions.

The PCs and XTs use an 8-bit bus that has 20 lines for memory access. These 20 lines limit them to 2^{20} or 1,048,576 bytes. The 16-bit 80286 systems have 24 bus lines for memory access. They can address 2^{24} or 16,777,216 bytes (16Mb). The 80386 and 80486 32-bit systems can address 2^{32} or 4,294,967,296 bytes (4 gigabytes).

The 486 can address 4 gigabytes of RAM, but DOS will not let you access more than 640K. (Incidentally, 4 gigabytes of DRAM, in 1Mb SIMM packages, would require 4096 modules. You would need a fairly large board to install that much memory.) Several software programs will let you break the 640K barrier. But first a few basics about the different types of memory.

Types of memory

The main types of memory are *real* or *conventional*, *extended*, and *expanded*.

Real memory

Real or conventional memory is the one megabyte of memory that the 8088 and 8086 systems are able to directly address. Each one of those million bytes have a unique address, much like the individual addresses of streets and houses in a city. The CPU can go to any one of those addresses in the lower 640K and read the data that might be there or write data to that address.

Extended memory

Extended memory is the 4 gigabytes of memory that can be installed above one megabyte. If it were not for the DOS 640K limitation, it would be a seamless continuation of memory. OS/2, Xenix, and Unix regard it as such and will let you address it.

Expanded memory

Some large spreadsheets require an enormous amount of memory. A few years ago in a rare instance of cooperation among corporations, Lotus, Intel, Microsoft, and some other large corporations got together and devised a system and standard specification called *LIM EMS 4.0*. It allows a computer, even a PC or XT, to address up to 32Mb of expanded memory.

The memory is divided into pages of 16K each. Expanded memory finds a 64K window that is not being used above the 640K of the one megabyte conventional memory. Pages of 16K expanded memory can be switched in and out of this window.

Several of the OS/2 functions can be run with DOS and LIM EMS 4. It is now possible to load terminate-and-stay-resident (TSR) programs such as Side-Kick, in memory outside of your precious 640K. LIM EMS also includes functions to allow multitasking so that several programs can be run simultaneously.

The LIM EMS system treats extra memory on the 286, 386, and 486 as extended memory with the proper software and drivers.

OS/2 vs. DOS

MS-DOS 4.01 is fairly good. But DR DOS 5.0 from Digital Research is vastly superior. By the time you read this, DOS 5.0 should be available.

OS/2 costs $325 and Presentation Manager portion costs over $700. (Incidentally, OS/2 1.0 requires about 2.5Mb to 3Mb of hard disk space. Presentation Manager adds considerably more to that amount of required disk space. DOS 3.3 requires about 500K.)

You probably know DOS fairly well already. You might not need all of the multitasking and other exotic functions of OS/2. Depending on what you need to do with your computer, you might be able to get by with an expanded memory specification (EMS) board and the DESQview software package.

DESQview is an excellent program that lets you take advantage of the 486 virtual 8086 and 32-bit protected modes. It lets you run multiple DOS programs simultaneously, switch between them, run programs in the background, and transfer data between them. DESQview is very inexpensive, and no 486 system should be without a copy. For more details, call (213) 392-9701.

Windows 3.0 also lets you go beyond the 640K barrier. It lets you do multitasking and lets you take advantage of the 486 virtual and protected modes. It works with a mouse and performs even better than a Macintosh. Windows is also very inexpensive. It does everything as well or better than OS/2. Every 486 should have Windows 3.0. The 486 does Windows very well.

If you have an older copy of Windows, you can easily upgrade to Windows 3.0. You can get more details by calling (800) 323-3577.

10
CHAPTER

Input devices

Before you can do anything with a computer, you must input data to it. Several ways to input data include from a disk, by modem, by a mouse, by scanner, by barcode readers, by voice data input, by FAX, or on-line from a main frame or a network. By far the most common way to get data into the computer is by way of the keyboard. For most common applications, it is impossible to operate the computer without a keyboard.

Keyboards

The keyboard is a very important part of your system. It is a most personal connection with your computer. If you do a lot of typing, it is very important that you get a keyboard that suits you. Not all keyboards are the same. Some have a light mushy touch, some heavy. Some have noisy keys, others are silent with very little feedback. I have a very heavy hand. I bought a computer once that had a keyboard with very soft keys. If I just barely touched a key, it would take off. I finally took the keyboard to a swap meet and sold it for about half of what it cost me. I then went around to all the booths at the show and tried several keyboards until I found one that had a tactile feel that I liked.

That keyboard lasted for quite some time. But one night I decided to do some more work before going to bed. I had poured myself a glass of wine before bed, so I set the wine glass on the desk near the keyboard. You can guess the rest. One thing I can tell you, keyboards cannot hold their wine. I took it apart and cleaned it, but I could never get it to work again.

Keyboard covers

Special plastic covers can protect against spills, dust, or harsh environments. In some areas a cover is absolutely essential. Most of the covers are made from soft plastic that is molded to fit over the keys. They are pliable, but it would slow down any serious typist.

My dentist has installed a computer right by the treatment chair. He can review the patient's past history, immediately enter any procedures that are done, and enter the billing. My dentist is quite proud of his new computer, so he covered the keyboard with plastic wrap. Because he only uses a two-finger hunt and peck input, it works for him.

My dentist would be much better off with one of the custom made covers. Several companies make them, including:

CompuCover   (800) 874-6391
Tech-Cessories   (800) 736-0909

Well over 400 different keyboards are used in the U.S. If you count the foreign type of keyboards, there are probably over 4000 in existence. These companies claim that they can provide a cover for most of them. The average cover costs about $25.

A need for standards

Typewriter keyboards are fairly standard. With only 26 letters in the alphabet and a few symbols, most QWERTY typewriters have about 50 keys. I have had several computers over the last few years, and every one of them have had a different keyboard. The main typewriter characters are not changed or moved very often, but some of the very important control keys like the Esc, the Ctrl, the PrtSc, the (backslash), and several others are moved all over the keyboard. IBM decided to move the function keys to the top of the keyboard above the numeric keys. Many people have bought programs that use the function keys intensively. Anyone who buys a copy of those programs usually gets a cut-out plastic overlay that describes the uses of the function keys. These overlays usually come in both 84-key and 101-key styles. Those overlays issued before the introduction of 101-key keyboards will not fit on the 101-key keyboards.

The 101-key keyboards are 20″ long and take up about 30% more desk space than the 18″ 84-key keyboards. If you have a large desk, that might not be important. One of my desks has a section in the middle that is lower than the rest of the desk. This makes the keyboard just the right height for comfortable typing. It is great with an 84-key keyboard, but there is just not enough room for a 101-key keyboard in this space.

Several companies have taken note of the complaints about wasted desk space and are producing a 101-key keyboard that is the same size as the 84-key. Many of them also offer an option to change the Ctrl key back to where it was, by the A. I would only buy a keyboard that had a good tactile feel and had an option to change the Ctrl key to where it was. I would suggest that you go to a store, or better yet to a swap meet, and try out several keyboards before you buy one. Figure 10-1 shows the 84-key keyboard on the bottom and the 101 at the top.

10-1 An 84-key keyboard on the bottom and a 101-key keyboard at the top.

Model switch

You should note that the PC, XT, AT, 80286, 80386, and 80486 keyboards all have the same connectors. Any keyboard will plug into any one of those machines, but the PC and XT keyboards have different electronics and scan frequencies. An older PC or XT keyboard can be plugged into an 80286 or 80386 machine, but they will not operate.

The keyboard is actually a computer in itself, with a small microprocessor with its own ROM. It eliminates the bounce of the keys, can determine when you hold a key down for repeat, can store up to 20 or more keystrokes, and can determine which key was pressed first if you press two at a time. The newer microprocessors for the AT type machines are more complex and sophisticated than the early PC types.

Most keyboards now have a small switch on the back side that allows them to be switched so that they can be used on a PC or XT or on the AT type 286, 386, or 486 machines. Some of the newer keyboards can electronically sense the type of computer it is attached to and automatically switch.

Sources

Keyboard preference is strictly a matter of individual taste. I think the Northgate Omni Key/102 that I have used for the last couple of years is one of the best on the market. You can call Northgate at (800) 526-2446. The list price is $99. It has the function keys along the left-hand side, where they were originally. And they give you the option of swapping the location of the CapsLock and Ctrl key back to where it is supposed to be. They give you extra key caps, and by changing a small switch, the keys can be moved.

If you prefer the position of the function keys in a row above the number keys, Northgate has developed the Omnikey Plus. It has an option that will let you add an extra set of function keys along the top. The list price is $119 plus $25 for the extra function key option.

The Key Tronic Company also makes some excellent keyboards. They can even let you change the little springs under the keys to a different tension. The standard is 2 ounces, but you can configure the key tension to whatever you like. You can install 1, 1.5, 2.5, or 3 ounce springs for an extra $15. They also let you exchange the positions of the CapsLock and Ctrl keys. Their keyboards have several other functions that are clearly described in their large manual, the most detailed of any company. You can reach them at (800) 262-6006.

Hundreds of clone makers offer keyboards that are very good for $35 to $90. Look through any computer magazine. If at all possible, try them out and compare. If you are buying a system through the mails, ask about the keyboard options.

Specialized keyboards

Several companies have developed specialized keyboards. I have listed only a few of them here.

Several programs such as SideKick, Windows and WordStar can be used for minor calculations. A keyboard that is available from the Shamrock Company at (800) 722-2898 and also from Jameco at (415) 592-8097 has a built-in solar powered calculator where the number pad is located. The calculator can be used whether the computer is on or not.

Trackballs are devices that are similar to a mouse. A mouse can require quite a bit of desk space. It can also get in the way of papers, the phone, junk, and other items usually found on a working person's desk. The Amtac Company at (718) 392-1703 offers the Keycat keyboard with a trackball built into the right-hand area of the keyboard. This gives a person the mouse benefits and capabilities, without using up any desk real estate. The trackball is compatible with the standard Microsoft and Mouse Systems. The list price for the keyboard/trackball system is $99. The street price should be a bit less. That would seem to be a real bargain when you consider that a stand-alone trackball can cost $75 or more. Several other companies also make combination keyboard systems. Look in the computer magazines for ads.

Just as IBM set the standard for the PC, Key Tronic of Spokane has been the leader in keyboard design. Most of the clone keyboards are copied from the Key

Tronic designs. Besides the standard keyboards, they have developed a large number of specialized ones. Instead of a key pad, one has a touch pad. This pad can operate in several different modes. One mode lets it act like a cursor pad. By using your finger or a stylus, the cursor can be moved much the same as with a mouse. It comes with templates for several popular programs such as WordStar, WordPerfect, DOS, and Lotus 1-2-3.

Another Key Tronic model has a bar code reader attached to it. This can be extremely handy if you have a small business that uses bar codes. This keyboard would be ideal for a computer in a point of sale (POS) system.

Call Key Tronic at (509) 928-8000.

Mouse systems

One of the biggest reasons for the success of the Macintosh is that it is easy to use. With a mouse and icons, all you have to do is point and click. You do not have to learn a lot of commands and rules. A person who knows nothing about computers can become productive in a very short time.

The people in the DOS world finally took note of this and began developing programs and applications for the IBM and compatibles. Dozens of companies are now manufacturing mice. Many software programs have been developed that can be used without a mouse, but operate much faster and better with a mouse. To be productive, a mouse is essential for programs such as Windows 3.0, CAD programs, paint and graphics programs, and many others.

You cannot just plug in a mouse and start using it. The software, whether Windows, WordStar, or a CAD program, must recognize and interface with the mouse. So mouse companies develop software drivers that allow their mouse to operate with various programs. The drivers are usually supplied on a diskette. The Microsoft Mouse is the closest to a standard, so most other companies emulate the Microsoft driver.

Types of mice

The types of mice are not standardized. Some use optics with an LED that shines on a reflective grid. As the mouse is moved across the grid, reflected light is picked up by a detector and sent to the computer to move the cursor.

For a design that demands very close tolerances the spacings of the grid for an optical mouse might not provide sufficient resolution. You might be better off in this case with a high-resolution mouse that utilizes a ball.

The ball mouse has a small round rubber ball on the underside that contacts the desktop. As the mouse is moved, the ball turns. Inside the mouse, two flywheels contact the ball, one for horizontal and one for vertical movements. You do need about a square foot of clear desk space to move the mouse about. The ball picks up dirt, so it should be cleaned often.

Some of the less expensive mice have a resolution capability of only 100 to 200 *dots per inch* (dpi). Logitech has developed a HiREZ mouse that has a resolution of 320 dpi.

The IMCS Company has put a mouse in a penlike configuration. Their Mouse-Pen has a barrel about 6″ long and about ¹/₂″ square. The foot of the pen has a small ball that functions exactly like a mouse. It has two buttons on the barrel. It can be moved just as if you were writing. Call (805) 239-8976 for more information.

Number of buttons

The Macintosh mouse has only one button, which does not give you much choice except to point and click. Almost all of the PC mice have at least two buttons, which gives the user the three choices of click the left button, click the right button, or click both buttons at the same time. Some of the mice have three control buttons. With three buttons the user has a possible seven choices: click left, click middle, click right, click left and middle, click middle and right, click left and right, and click all three. Despite all these choices, most software requires that only two of the buttons be used, one at a time.

Interfaces

Most of the mice require a voltage, usually 5 volts. Some come with a small plug-in transformer that should be plugged into your power strip. Some of them let you insert an adapter between the keyboard cable connector and the motherboard connector.

Some of the mice require the use of one of your serial ports for their input to the computer. This can cause a problem if you already have a serial printer using COM1 and a modem on COM2. Some of the motherboards have ports built into the board so that you do not have to use a slot and install a board for a port. However, you will still need a cable from the on-board COM ports to the outside world.

Microsoft, Logitech, and several other mouse companies have developed a *bus* mouse. It interfaces directly with the bus and does not require the use of one of your COM ports. However, the systems come with a board that requires the use of one of your slots.

Figure 10-2 shows my Logitech bus mouse. It came with two floppy disks full of software and five different manuals for the mouse operation and different programs—all of this for only $69.

Cost

You can buy a fairly good mouse for $50 to $100. One factor in the cost is that some companies include options of software packages and other goodies with their products.

10-2 A Logitech bus mouse. Shown is the bus plug-in card, the mouse, and the five different manuals that come with the mouse.

Another cost factor is the resolution. Some have only 100 dpi, the better ones have a resolution of 200 and up to 350 dots. The higher resolution is necessary for some CAD and critical design work that requires close tolerances.

Some mouse systems are advertised for as little as $30. These would probably be perfectly all right for point and click type work with icons. The higher-resolution systems are going to cost more, from $80 and up to $300. It is best to call the companies for their latest price list and spec sheets.

Sources

Here are just a few of the many companies that manufacture mouse systems. Again, check the ads in the computer magazines listed in chapter 16:

IMCS Mouse-Pen	(805) 239-8976
IMSI Economouse	(415) 454-7101
Key Tronic	(800) 262-6006
Logitech Inc.	(415) 795-8500
Microsoft Mouse	(206) 882-8088
Mouse Systems Corp.	(408) 988-0211
Numonics Cordless Mouse	(800) 654-5449
Summagraphics Corp.	(203) 384-1344

Trackballs

A trackball is a mouse that has been turned upside down. Like the mouse, a trackball must have a voltage from a transformer or other source. It also requires a serial port, or a slot if it is of the bus type.

Instead of moving the mouse to move the ball, you move the ball with your fingers. The trackballs are usually larger than the ball in a mouse, so the possible resolution is better.

Trackballs usually do not require as much desk space as the ordinary mouse. If your desk is as cluttered as mine, then you definitely need a trackball.

The MicroLYNX trackball has a connector that plugs in series with your keyboard connector. This device derives its needed voltage from the same line that feeds your keyboard. The ComLYNX is an identical trackball except that it plugs into a serial port. They both have three buttons and comes with a Pop-Up Menu software program and several drivers. The integral units are $8^{1}/_{2}'' \times 3''$.

Fulcrum Computers has a trackball that has six buttons. The six buttons can be used for certain emulations and control. The Fulcrum is unlike the LYNX in that it uses an optical system.

The MicroSpeed Fasttrap trackball is available in serial or bus versions. It is compatible with Microsoft Mouse programs and comes with several drivers.

Sources

Several other companies manufacture trackballs:

CH RollerMouse	(619) 598-2518
Expert Mouse	(212) 475-5200
Felix PC200	(415) 653-8500
Fulcrum Computer	(707) 433-0202
Honeywell LYNX	(800) 224-3522
Logitech TrackMan	(415) 795-8500
Lynx Trackball	(213) 590-9990
MicroSpeed PC-Trac	(415) 490-1403
Mouse-trak	(214) 494-3073
PC Trackball	(415) 656-1117
TrackerMouse	(508) 226-3008

Digitizers and graphics tablets

Graphics tablets and digitizers are similar to a flat drawing pad or drafting table. Most of them use some sort of pointing device that can translate movement into digitized output to the computer. Some are rather small, some are as large as a standard drafting table. Some cost as little as $150 up to over $1500. Most of them have a very high resolution, are very accurate, and are intended for precision drawing.

Some tablets have programmable overlays and function keys. Some will work with a mouse-like device, a pen light, or a pencil-like stylus. The tablets can be used for designing circuits, for CAD programs, for graphics designs, freehand drawing, and even for text and data input. The most common use is with CAD type software.

Most of the tablets are serial devices, but some of them require their own interface board. Many of them are compatible with the Microsoft and Mouse Systems.

The CalComp WIZ

CalComp Inc., a division of Lockheed Corporation, manufactures several high-end digitizers. They developed the WIZ, which combines many of the mouse functions with those functions found in a high-end digitizing tablet. The highest resolution for a mouse is under 400 dpi; the WIZ is capable of 1000 dpi. The WIZ can be used with several templates such as DOS, Windows, WordPerfect, Lotus 1-2-3, AutoCAD, and others. Figure 10-3 shows the WIZ and the DOS template. To load a command, simply place the WIZ crosshairs over the command listed on the template and click a button. When working with Windows or the other programs, it functions just like a mouse.

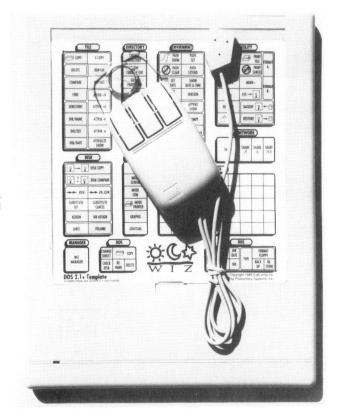

10-3 The CalComp Wiz, a combination mouse and digitizer.

The WIZ has three buttons, or rocker switches, each with two positions for a total of six positions. The positions can be programmed to act like a macro. For instance, I can push one button, and it will change directory, load my WordStar program, then change to the directory where I have my files. It does all of this very fast, almost before I can get my finger off the button.

Sources

Here are some companies that produce digitizers and graphics tablets:

CalComp	(714) 821-2142
Genius	(800) 288-1611
GTCO Corp.	(301) 381-6688
Koala Pad	(408) 438-0946
Kurta Corp.	(602) 276-5533
Pencept Inc.	(617) 893-6390
Summagraphics Corp.	(203) 384-1344

Scanners and optical character readers

Most large companies have mountains of memos, manuals, documents, and files that must be maintained, revised, and updated periodically. If a manual or document is in a loose-leaf form, then only those pages that have changed will need to be retyped. But quite often a whole manual or document will have to be retyped and reissued.

Several companies now manufacture *optical character readers* (OCR) that can scan a line of printed type, recognize each character and input that character into a computer just as if it were typed in from a keyboard. Once the data is in the computer, a word processor can be used to revise or change the data, then print it out again.

Also, the data can be entered into a computer and stored on floppies or a hard disk. If it is a huge amount of data, it could be stored on a write-once read-many (WORM) optical disk or on a CD-ROM so that it takes less space to store.

If copies of the printed matter are also stored in a computer, it can be searched very quickly for any item. Many times I have spent hours going through printed manuals looking for certain items. If the data had been in a computer, I could have found the information in just minutes.

Optical character readers have been around for several years. When they first came out they cost from $6000 to more than $15,000. They were very limited in the character fonts they they could recognize and were not able to handle graphics at all.

Vast improvements have been made in the last few years. Many are now fairly inexpensive, starting at about $900. Some hand-held ones that are very limited are as low as $200. Some very sophisticated commercial models such as the Palantir and Kurzweil can cost as much as $40,000. The more expensive models usually have the ability to recognize a large number of fonts and graphics.

Regent Peripherals manufactures the ScanStation 4000, a scanner that is actually a scanner and computer. It has a built-in 40Mb hard disk and a floppy disk. Optical features can include such things as a VGA port, a tape drive, and a mouse port (Fig. 10-4).

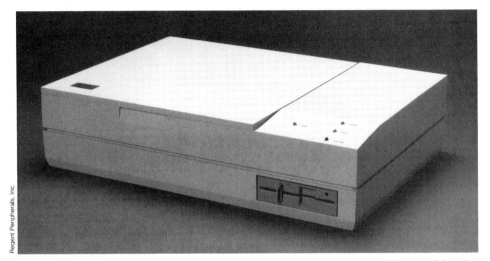

10-4 The Regent ScanStation 4000. It is an unusual scanner in that it has its own 40Mb hard disk and a floppy disk. You could add a keyboard and a monitor for a combination computer and scanner.

An image or OCR text can be scanned onto the hard drive, then copied onto a floppy. The ScanStation 4000 has 400 dpi resolution and supports 256 gray scales as well as line art. It can scan documents up to $8^{1}/_{2}"\times 14"$.

The hand-held models can only scan small portions of text or a graphic. They are not suitable for inputting full pages of text or graphics. At the present time, they are also limited in the number and type of fonts they can recognize.

The Houston Instruments Company specializes in manufacturing plotters. They have developed a scanning head for one of their plotters that can scan a large drawing, digitize the lines and symbols, then input them to a computer. The drawing can then be changed and replotted very easily.

Scanner sources

Several of the companies that manufacture scanning devices are listed here:

AST Research	(714) 863-1480
Canon U.S.A.	(516) 488-6800
CompuScan	(201) 575-0500
Datacopy Corp.	(415) 965-7900
DFI Handy Scanner	(916) 373-1234

GeniScan GS-4000	(714) 590-3940
Houston Instrument	(512) 835-0900
Howtek	(603) 882-5200
Logitech Scanman	(415) 795-8500
Microtek Lab	(213) 321-2121
Regent Peripherals	(206) 772-0613
Saba	(800) 654-5274
Transimage 1000	(408) 733-4111

Other sources for input devices

There are so many manufacturers that I am not going to list the sources. Look in any of the computer magazines listed in chapter 16. You will see many ads for all types of keyboards, scanners, mice, and other input devices.

Some of the magazines such as *PC Sources* and *Computer Shopper* have a separate product listing in the back pages. It is a great help. However, they list only those products that are advertised for that month in their magazine.

Of course, many good products cannot afford the high cost of magazine ads. A larger city will have local computer stores. Larger cities usually have computer swaps, which can be a very good source.

Computers and devices for the handicapped

Several computer devices have been developed that can help the disabled persons. Devices have been developed for the blind, the deaf, the quadraplegic, and other severely disabled persons. Special braille keyboards and keyboards with enlarged keys are available for the blind.

The EyeTyper from the Sentient Systems Technology of Pittsburgh, PA, has an embedded camera on the keyboard that can determine which key the user is looking at. It then enters that key into the computer. Words Plus of Sunnyvale, CA, has a sensitive visor that can understand input from a raised brow, head movement, or eye blinks.

The Speaking Devices Corporation has a telephone that can be trained to recognize an individual's voice. It can then dial up to 100 different numbers when the person tells it to. The same company has a tiny ear phone that also acts as a microphone. These devices would be ideal for a person who can speak, but cannot use their hands.

Devices for the disabled can allow many people to lead more active, useful and productive lives. Some have become artists, programmers, writers, and scientists. These communication devices have allowed them the freedom to use their talents.

Several organizations can help in locating special equipment and lend support. If you know someone who might benefit from the latest technology and devices for the handicapped, contact these organizations:

AbleData	(800) 344-5405
Accent on Information	(309) 378-2961
American Foundation for the Blind	(212) 620-2000
Apple Computer	(408) 996-1010
Closing The Gap, Inc.	(612) 248-3294
Direct Link for the Disabled	(805) 688-1603
Easter Seals Systems Office	(312) 667-8626
IBM National Support Center	(800) 426-2133
National ALS Association	(818) 340-7500
Speaking Devices Corp.	(408) 727-5571
Trace Research and Development Center	(608) 262-6966

Get a tax deduction

Now that you have assembled a new 486, you might be retiring an older computer. You could probably advertise and sell it, but it might be more trouble than it is worth. It might be worth more to you to give it away to an organization like those I have just discussed, or to any legitimate charitable organization. You could then deduct the reasonable value from your income tax.

Most organizations are most happy to get anything that you can give them. And you will be happy by making others happy.

CHAPTER

Telecommunications

About 40 million computers are installed in homes, offices, and businesses. About 20 million of them have a modem or some sort of communications capability. This capability of the computer is one of its most important aspects.

Modems

A *modem* is an electronic device that allows a computer to use an ordinary telephone line to communicate with other computers that are equipped with a modem, Modem is a contraction of the words *modulate* and *demodulate*. The telephone system is analog, computer data is usually in a digital form. The modem modulates the digital data from a computer and turns it into analog voltages for transmission. At the receiving end, a similar modem will demodulate the analog voltage back into a digital form.

A person can use a telephone to communicate with any one of several million persons anywhere in the world. Likewise, a computer with telecommunications capabilities can communicate with several million other computers in the world. A computer with a modem can access over 10,000 bulletin boards in the U.S. It can take advantage of electronic mail, faxes, up-to-the-minute stock market quotations, and a large number of other on-line services such as home shopping, travel agencies, and many other data services and databases. Many of these services and fantastic capabilities are not being utilized fully.

Why modems are not being utilized

Many excellent user friendly software programs and hardware components are available that almost anyone can learn to use. As Peter Norton pointed out in his forward to *Dvorak's Guide to PC Telecommunications*, many people seem to have a "telecommunications phobia." Of the 20 million computers with telecommunication capability, less than one million are being fully utilized. That is a terrible waste of resources.

Believe me, I can understand why a person might have a fear such as this. Years ago when I bought my first modem, I can vividly recall trying to transmit an article to an editor. I tried for some time but could not connect to the editor's modem. I finally gave up and drove 50 miles to hand deliver the article. I felt frustrated and dumb. It was some time before I used the modem again.

If you are one of those persons with a telecommunications phobia, maybe I can help.

CCITT recommended standards

The communications industry is very complex, so there have not been many real standards. The many different manufacturers and software developers all want to differentiate their hardware or software by adding new features, but you might be able to communicate with someone else who is not using the same features.

A United Nations standards committee called the Comite Consultif Internal de Telegraphique et Telephone (CCITT) has helped to establish some standards. This committee has representatives from over 80 countries and several large private manufacturers. The committee makes recommendations only. A company is free to use or ignore them, but more and more companies are now adopting the recommendations.

All CCITT recommendations for small computers have a V or X prefix. The V series is for use with switched telephone networks, which is almost all of them. The X series is for systems that do not use switched phone lines. Revisions or alternate recommendations have bis (second) or ter (third) added. Here are a few CCITT recommendations:

- **V.22**   A 1200 baud standard.
- **V.22 bis**   A 2400 baud standard.
- **V.32**   A 9600 baud standard.
- **V.42**   An error correcting protocol. It includes MNP-4 and LAP M error correction.
- **V.42 bis**   A standard for 4:1 data compression. Under ideal conditions, this standard could permit data transmission speed four times greater than the rated baud rate. With this much compression a 9600 bps modem could transmit 38,400 bps.
- **X.25**   A protocol for packet mode communications on data networks such as Telenet and Tymnet.
- **MNP**   Microcom Networking Protocol, a series of ten different protocols developed by the Microcom Company. Several of their protocols are very similar to the CCITT V series.
- **LAP M & LAP B**   Other protocols that are supported by AT&T and Hayes. They are similar to the CCITT V.42 error correcting standard.

Protocols

Protocols are procedures that have been established for exchanging data, along with the instructions that coordinate the process. Most protocols can sense when the data is corrupted or lost due to noise, static, or a bad connection. It will automatically resend the affected data until it is received correctly.

The most popular protocols are Kermit (named for Kermit the frog), Xmodem, and Ymodem. These protocols transmit a block of data along with an error-checking code, then wait for the receiver to send back an acknowledgement, then send another block and wait to see if it got through okay. If a block does not get through, it is resent immediately. Protocols such as Zmodem and HyperProtocol sends a whole file in a continuous stream of data with error-checking codes inserted at certain intervals. It then waits for confirmation of a successful transmission. If the transmission is unsuccessful, then the whole file must be resent. The sending and receiving modems should both use the same protocol.

Baud rate

Telephone systems were originally designed for voice and have a very narrow bandwidth. They are subject to noise, static, and other electrical disturbances. These problems, and the state of technology at the time, limited the original modems to about 5 characters per second, or a rate of 50 baud.

The term *baud* comes from Emile Baudot (1845-1903), a French inventor. Originally, the baud rate was a measure of the dots and dashes in telegraphy. It is now defined as the actual rate of symbols transmitted per second. For the lower baud rates, it is essentially the same as bits per second. Remember that it takes 8 bits to make a character. Just as periods and spaces separate words, one *start bit* and two *stop bits* separate the on/off bits into characters. A transmission of 300 baud would mean that 300 on/off bits are sent in one second. Counting the start/stop bits, it takes 11 bits for each character. So 300 divided by 11 gives about 27 characters per second (cps).

Some of the newer technologies might actually transmit symbols that represent more than one bit. For baud rates of 1200 and higher, the cps and baud rate can be considerably different. Most modems sold today operate at 2400 baud. Many operate at 4800 and 9600 baud. The 9600 baud rate will eventually become the standard.

When communicating with another modem, both the sending and receiving unit must operate at the same baud rate and use the same protocols. Most of the faster modems are downward compatible and can operate at the slower speeds.

Ordinarily, the higher the baud rate, the less time it will take to download or transmit a file. (This might not always be so because at the higher speeds, more transmission errors might be encountered. In cases of errors, parts of the file, or the whole file, might have to be retransmitted.) If the file is being sent over a long distance line, the length of telephone connect time can be costly. If the modem is used frequently, the telephone bills can be very substantial, especially if you have a slow modem.

How to estimate connect time

You can figure the approximate length of time that it will take to transmit a file. For rough approximations of cps, you can divide the baud rate by 10. For instance a 1200 would be roughly 120 cps, a 2400 would be roughly 240 cps. Look at the directory and determine the number of bytes in the file. Divide the number of bytes in the file by the cps. You then multiply that figure by 1.3 for the start/stop bits to get a final approximation. For instance, with a 1200 baud modem, to figure the time for a 40K file, divide 40K by 120 cps to get 333 seconds times 1.3 to equal about 433 seconds or 7.2 minutes.

If you transmitted the same 40K file with a 2400 baud modem, it would be 40,000 divided by 240 is 167 × 1.3 = 217 seconds or 3.6 minutes. With a 9600 baud modem, the same 40K file could be sent in about 55 seconds.

Considering the telephone rates for long distance, it might be worthwhile to spend a bit more to get a high-speed modem.

Besides the phone line charges you have to pay, the major on-line service companies such as CompuServe, Dataquest, and Dow Jones News/Retrieval charge for connect time to their service. The connect time is much less with some of the high-speed modems. But in order to keep their revenue up, some companies charge more for the higher speed modems.

Sources

I have not listed the names and manufacturers of modems because there are so many. Look in any computer magazine, and you will see dozens of ads. Most of them are fairly close in quality and function.

One company that I do want to mention is USRobotics. They manufacture a large variety of modems, especially the high-end high-speed type. They will send you a free 110 page booklet that explains about all you need to know about modems. To get your free booklet, call (800) 342-5877.

Communications software

In order to use a modem, it must be driven and controlled by software. Dozens of communication programs can be used.

One of the better ones is Relay Silver from VM Personal Computing. They also publish Relay Gold, one of the most versatile of the high-end communications software packages. It has features that allow remote communications, accessing main frames, and dozens of utilities not found on the usual communications programs.

Crosstalk was one of the earlier modem programs. They now have a Crosstalk for Windows version. It works with any Windows version, which makes it very easy to learn and use.

ProComm is one of several low-cost shareware programs. In many areas, it outperforms some of the high-cost commercial programs. The registration cost is $89. Qmodem is another excellent shareware program for a registration cost of only $30. You can get copies of shareware programs from bulletin boards or from any of the several companies who provide public domain software. Shareware is not free. You may try it out and use it, but the developers usually ask that you register the program and send in a nominal sum. For this low cost, they will usually provide a manual and some support.

Here are the phone numbers to contact these companies:

Relay Silver and Relay Gold	(203) 798-3800
Crosstalk	(404) 998-3998
ProComm	(314) 474-8461
QModem	(319) 232-4516

Besides using a faster baud rate, another way to reduce phone charges is to use file compression. Bulletin boards have been using a form of data compression for years. Several public domain programs squeeze and unsqueeze the data.

Basic types of modems

The two basic types of modems are the external desktop and the internal. Each type has some advantages and disadvantages.

The external type requires some of your precious desk space, a voltage source, and a COM port to drive it. The good news is that most external models have LEDs that light up and let you know what is happening during your call.

Both the external and the internal models have speakers that let you hear the phone ringing or if you get a busy signal. Some of the external models have a volume control for the built-in speaker.

The internal modem is built entirely on a board, usually a half or short board. The good news is that it does not use up any of your desk real estate, but the bad news is that it uses one of your precious slots. It does not have the LEDs to let you know the progress of your call. Even if you use an external modem, if your motherboard does not have built-in COM ports, you will need an I/O board and have to use one of your slots for a COM port.

Hayes compatibility

One of the most popular early modems was made by Hayes Microcomputer Products. They have become the IBM of the modem world and have established a *de facto* standard. Of the hundreds of modem manufacturers, with the exception of some of the very inexpensive ones, almost all of them emulate the Hayes standard.

Installing a modem

If you are adding a modem on a board to a system that is already assembled, the first thing to do is to remove the computer cover, find an empty slot, and plug it in.

When the modem board is plugged into the slot on the motherboard, it will have to be set to access either serial port COM1 or COM2. The board will have jumpers or small switches that must be set to enable COM1 or COM2. If you have an I/O board in your system with external COM ports, or built-in COM ports on your motherboard, you must disable whichever port that will be used for the modem. If the modem board is set to use COM1, then COM1 on the I/O board or motherboard, must be disabled.

If you are installing an external modem, you must go through the same procedure to make sure the COM port is accessible and does not conflict. If you have a mouse, a serial printer, or some other serial device, you will have to determine which port they are set to. You cannot have two serial devices set to the same COM port.

It is often difficult to determine which COM port is being used by a device. You can use the AT command to determine if your modem is working. At the DOS prompt C: >, type the following using uppercase:

```
ECHO AT DT12345>COM1:
```

If the modem is set properly, you will hear a dial tone, then the modem will dial 12345. If two devices are set for COM1, there will be a conflict. The computer will try for a while, then give an error message and the familiar Abort, Retry, Ignore, Fail? message.

Plug in the board and hook it up to the telephone line. Unless you expect to do a lot of communicating, you probably will not need a separate dedicated line. The modem might have an automatic answer mode. In this mode, it will always answer the telephone. Unless you have a dedicated line, this mode should be disabled. Check your documentation for a switch or some means to disable it.

Having the modem and telephone on the same line should cause no problems unless someone tries to use the telephone while the modem is using it.

You should have two connectors at the back end of the board. One might be labeled for the line in and the other for the telephone. Unless you have a dedicated telephone line, you should unplug your telephone, plug in the extension to the modem and line, then plug the telephone into the modem. If your computer is not near your telephone line, you might have to go to a hardware store and buy a long telephone extension line.

After you have connected all of the lines, turn on your computer and try the modem before you put the cover back on. Make sure you have software. Call a local bulletin board. Even if you cannot get through or have a wrong number, you should hear the dial tone, then hear it dial the number.

An external modem will be connected to one of the COM ports with a cable. If you did not get a cable with your unit, you will have to buy one. If you have built-in COM ports, it will cost about $5. If you have to use the bus to access the ports, you will need a cable and an I/O board with serial ports.

Bulletin boards

If you have a modem, you have access to several thousand computer bulletin boards. Over 100 are in the San Francisco Bay area, and about twice that many are in the Los Angeles area. Most of them are free of any charge. You only have to pay the phone bill if they are out of your calling area. Some of them charge a nominal fee to join. Some just ask for a tax deductible donation.

Some of the bulletin boards are set up by private individuals, and some by companies and vendors as a service to their customers. Some are set up by users' groups and other special interest organizations. Over 100 boards nationwide have been set up for doctors and lawyers.

Most of the bulletin boards are set up to help individuals. They usually have lots of public domain software and a space where you can leave messages for help, for advertising something for sale, or for just plain old chit-chat.

If you are just getting started, you probably need some software. There are public domain software packages that are equivalent to almost all of the major commercial programs. And the best part is that they are free.

Viruses and Trojan horses

There have been several reports that some individuals have hidden viruses in some public domain and even in some commercial software. This software might appear to work as it should for some time. But eventually, it might contaminate and destroy many of your files.The viruses often cause the files to grow in size and become larger.

Trojan horses usually do not contaminate other files, but they may lie dormant for a certain length of time, or until a program has been run a certain number of times, then it destroys the file. Some commercial software is sold with a system that is somewhat similar to the Trojan horses. The buyer pays to use the program a certain number of times, then it will no longer operate.

If you download bulletin board software, it is probably best to run it from a floppy disk until you are sure that it is not sick.

Several companies have developed software to detect viruses, but it is almost impossible to detect them all. A few years ago when most programs were copy protected, many hackers took great delight in finding ways to defeat the copy protection. It was wrong and the hackers cost the developers money, but they were often considered to be modern-day Robin Hoods by the people who could not afford to pay $700 to $800 for a program.

Those who create viruses and other destructive software get their kicks by indiscriminately hurting people who have done them no wrong. It is a crime that deserves severe punishment, but several who have been caught have been released with little more than probation and a warning.

Antiviral software

Several companies have developed software that can detect most known viruses. Most bulletin board operators are now screening their programs, but it is almost impossible to find some of the viruses. It is advisable to download programs on a floppy diskette and run them for a while before putting them on a hard disk. If a floppy is ruined, you will not be hurt too much.

Fortunately, viruses are not really too common. But even if there is only one, it is still one too many.

Illegal activities

Some of the bulletin boards have also been used for illegal and criminal activities. Stolen credit card numbers and telephone charge numbers have been left on the bulletin boards.

Because of this many of the SYSOPS (the bulletin board system operators) are now carefully checking any software that is uploaded onto their systems. Many of them are now restricting access to their boards. Some of them have had to start charging a fee because of the extra time it takes to monitor the boards.

Where to find the bulletin boards

Several local computer magazines devote a lot of space to bulletin boards and user groups. In California, the *MicroTimes* and *Computer Currents* magazines have several pages of bulletin boards and user groups each month. The *Computer Shopper* has the most comprehensive listing of bulletin boards and user groups of any national magazine. See chapter 16 for the addresses of magazines.

The bulletin board listings in the *Computer Shopper* is compiled by:

Gale Rhoades
P.O. Box 3474
Daly City, CA 94015
(415) 755-2000

She works with an international nonprofit computer user group called FOG. If you know of a bulletin board or user group that should be listed, contact her. She can also supply you with a listing of bulletin boards on a diskette.

CD-ROM

New information is being published and disseminated at an ever increasing rate. The flood of information makes Noah's flood seem like an April shower. I subscribe to over 50 computer magazines, but I have great difficulty just trying to keep up.

I have recently subscribed to the Ziff-Davis Computer Library on CD-ROM. Subscribers get a new CD-ROM filled with articles from over 140 magazines.

One big advantage of having the articles on CD-ROM is that I can search for items that are of interest very quickly. I can also cut and paste items into another file on my hard disk. The subscriptions are rather expensive at over $700, but if you are interested, call (212) 503-3500.

Several other vendors provide hundreds of educational and scientific programs, data, and information on CD-ROM disks. One is the Bureau of Electronic Publishing at (201) 808-2700.

Several companies sell public domain software on CD-ROMs. A CD-ROM can contain over 3000 different programs, just about everything that you would ever need. Call:

Alde Publishing Company	(612) 835-5240
PC-SIG	(800) 245-6717

On-line services

Several large national bulletin boards with information and reference services such as Compuserve, Dataquest, Dow Jones, and Dialog have huge databases of information. As a caller, you can search the databases and download information as easily as pulling the data off your own hard disk. The companies charge a fee for the connect time.

Prodigy is unlike the other on-line services. Prodigy does not charge for connect time. They charge only a very nominal monthly rate. They have phone service to most areas in the larger cities so there is not even a toll charge. They have an impressive list of services including home shopping, home banking, airline schedules and reservations, stock market quotations, and many others. In San Francisco, you can even order your groceries over the line through Prodigy and have them delivered to your door. One of its faults is that it is relatively slow. But because it is so inexpensive (a real bargain), I can live with it. You can contact Prodigy at (800) 759-8000.

E-mail

Many of the national bulletin boards offer electronic mail or *E-mail* along with their other services. These services can be of great value to some individuals and businesses.

E-mail subscribers are usually given a "post office box" at these companies. This is usually a file on one of their large hard disk systems. When a message is received, it is recorded in this file. The next time the subscriber logs on to this service, he or she will be alerted that there is "mail" in their in-box.

E-mail is becoming more popular every day, and there are now several hundred thousand subscribers. The cost for an average message is about one dollar. (The cost for overnight mail from the U.S. Post Office, Federal Express, and UPS is $11 to $13.)

Some of the companies who provide E-mail at the present time:

AT&T Mail	(800) 367-7225
CompuServe	(800) 848-8990
DASnet	(408) 559-7434
MCI Mail	(800) 444-6245
Western Union	(800) 527-5184

LAN E-mail   Most of the larger local area network (LAN) programs also provide an E-mail utility in their software. For those packages that do not provide this utility, there are programs available that work with installed LANs.

The CCITT has recommended that X.400 be the standard for LAN E-mail. This standard provides the *gateway* to installed LANs. Another gateway system supported by Novell and Lotus is the Message Handling System (MHS). For more information about E-mail, contact:

Action Technologies	(800) 624-2162
Inbox Plus	(415) 769-9669
Lotus Express	(800) 345-1043
MS-Mail	(206) 882-8080
PCC Systems	(415) 321-0430
Quickmail	(515) 224-1995

Banking by modem

Many banks offer systems that will let you do all your banking with your computer and a modem from the comforts of your home. You would never again have to drive downtown, hunt for a parking space, then stand in line for a half hour to do your banking.

City services

Several cities have installed networks that allow their citizens who have a computer and a modem to communicate with city offices and departments. Santa Monica, California, has a system that includes a bulletin board, phone numbers of city agencies, access to agendas and staff reports, schedules of coming events, earthquake safety tips, police and crime statistics, information needed to get building permits, licenses, consumer affairs information, city job postings, conferencing, access to the library catalogue, and many other services.

Public domain and shareware

If you do not have a modem yet, or if the local bulletin boards don't have the software you need, several companies will ship you public domain and shareware software on a floppy diskette. These companies have thousands of programs and usually charge from $3 up to $24 for a disk full of programs. Most public domain software companies advertise in the computer magazines listed in chapter 16.

They will send you a catalog listing of their software. Some may charge a small fee for their catalog. Call them for details and latest prices.

New uses for modems

You have probably received one or more of the computerized telephone sales pitches. For years, operations for telephone sales have been people hired to sit at a table with a telephone directory and call everybody in town and give them a sales pitch. But these people have to be paid. They probably even have to have medical coverage for those who suffered digititis on their dialing fingers.

Many of these operators discovered that a computer and modem could do the job much better with several advantages. The computer did not take coffee breaks, it did not have to go to the bathroom, and it seldom made an error by calling a wrong number. The computer was a one-time cost so it did not have to be paid every week. It worked all hours, day in and day out without complaining or asking for overtime. Another advantage, the computer did not have its feelings hurt when someone called it a bad name and slammed the phone down.

Many of the larger department stores and businesses are now using modems for bill collecting. If their computers show that a customer is behind on their payments, the computer automatically calls the customer and requests that a payment be sent in forthwith. It might not be quite as effective as having someone call up and say that someone will come out and break your kneecaps if you do not pay up, but after the initial cost of the computer equipment, it is efficient, automatic, and economical.

Telephone technology advances

Some advances in telephone technology mean that a box can be attached to a telephone that will display the number of the caller. If you know the number of someone you do not want to talk to, you can look at the number and choose whether to answer the phone or not. Certain numbers can be excluded so that the phone will not even ring.

Because the caller's number is displayed by this box, it should help to reduce computerized, unwanted, and obscene calls. It will also be an enormous help to police departments and fire departments and to pizza and fastfood delivery stores.

Some people have objected to the Caller ID system. A court in Pennsylvania has declared it unconstitutional on the grounds that it is an invasion of privacy. It is difficult for me to understand the judge's ruling. How is it violating a person's rights if you want to know who is calling before you answer? If a person comes to your door and puts a hand over the peephole so that you could not see who it was, would you let that person in?

Phonevision is also a new technology that will soon be in all homes. As usual, the phone will probably ring just as you step into the shower, so now you will have to remember to wear your robe.

Laptop modems

Many people are now using laptop computers. Several companies have developed modems so that a person can plug in a laptop anywhere in the world and communicate with the office or wherever.

Many police departments are now using these types of modems in the police cars. Several people have also installed modems for their cellular car phones. Some have even added fax machines to their car phones. This might seem strange to anyone who has never driven on the crowded freeways of Los Angeles and other areas. Some people spend as much as two or more hours commuting each way. Much of this time is just sitting in a bumper-to-bumper traffic jam. So if a bit of business can be transacted, it is not a total waste.

Here is a short list of some of the companies who make miniature modems:

Aproteck Minimodem	(805) 482-3604
Novation Parrot	(714) 841-8791
QIC Research Mimi Modem	(408) 432-8880
Sunhill	(800) 544-1361
Touchbase Worldport	(516) 261-0423

ISDN

ISDN is an acronym for *Integrated Services Digital Network*. Eventually the whole world will have telephone systems that use this concept. It will be a system that will be able to transmit voice, data, video, and graphics in digital form rather than the present analog. When this happens, we can scrap our modems. We will then need only a simple interface to communicate.

ISDN is already installed in several cities. It is scheduled to be fully implemented in the U.S. by 1992. However, do not throw away your modem yet. The new service will be rather expensive and might not be available at all locations for some time.

Facsimile boards and machines

Facsimile (fax) machines have been around for quite a while. Newpapers and businesses have used them for years. They were the forerunners of the scanning machines.

The early machines were similar to the early acoustic modems. Both used foam rubber cups that fit over the telephone receiver/mouthpiece for coupling. They were very slow and subject to noise and interference. Fax machines and modems have come a long way since those early days.

A page of text or a photo is fed into the facsimile machine and scanned. As the scanning beam moves across the page, white and dark areas are digitized as 1s and 0s, then transmitted out over the telephone lines.

Modems and facsimile machines are quite similar and related in many respects. A modem sends and receives bits of data. A fax machine or board usually sends and receives scanned whole page letters, images, signatures, etc. A computer program can be sent over a modem, but not over a fax. A fax sends and receives the information as digitized data. A modem converts the digital information that represents characters into analog voltages, sends it over the line, then converts it back to digital information.

There are times when one or the other is needed. Both units would not be in use at the same time, so the same phone line can be used for both of them.

Millions of facsimile machines are in use today. Most businesses can benefit from the use of a fax. It can be used to send documents, that includes handwriting, signatures, seals, letterheads, graphs, blueprints, photos and other types of data around the world, across the country or across the room to another fax machine.

It costs $11 to $13 to send an overnight letter, but E-mail only costs about $1. A fax machine can deliver the same letter for about 40 cents and do it in less than three minutes. Depending on the type of business, and the amount of critical mail that must be sent out, a fax system can pay for itself in a very short time.

Stand-alone fax units

Some facsimile machines are stand-alone devices that attach to a telephone. They have been vastly improved in the last few years. Most of them are as easy to use as a copy machine. In fact most of them can be used as a copy machine.

Some overseas companies are making stand-alone units that are fairly inexpensive, some for as little as $400. You might not be happy with the low cost ones. You will be better off if you can spend a bit more and get one with a paper cutter, with high resolution, a voice/data switch on the system, a document feeder, automatic dialer, automatic retry, delayed transmission, transmission confirmation, polling, built-in laser printer, and large memory. You might not need, or be able to afford, all of these features but try to get a machine with as many as possible. Of course, the more features, the higher the cost.

Fax computer boards

Several companies have developed fax machines on circuit boards that can be plugged into computers. Many of the newer models have provisions for a modem on the same board. Follow the same procedure to install a fax board as outlined above for an internal modem.

Special software allows the computer to control the fax boards. Using the computer's word processor, letters and memos can be written and sent out over the phone lines. Several letters or other information can be stored or retrieved from the computer hard disk and transmitted. The computer can even be programmed to send the letters out at night when the rates are lower.

The computer fax boards have one disadvantage. They cannot scan information unless a scanner is attached to computer. Without a scanner, the information that can be sent is usually limited to that which can be entered from a keyboard or disk, while stand-alone units scan pages of information, including such things as handwriting, signatures, images, blueprints, and photos. However, the computer can receive and store any fax that is sent. The digitized data and images can be stored on a hard disk, then printed out on a printer.

The fax boards can cost from $195 up to $1500 depending on the extras and goodies installed. Pay close attention to the ads and specifications. I have seen several fax boards advertised for less than $100. The reason for the low cost is that these boards will send fax files, but are unable to receive them. Nowhere in the ad did it mention this fact. Even when I called one company, they were reluctant to admit that their boards only worked in the send mode. The reason they could advertise and sell them for less is because it requires more electronics to receive a fax than it does to send. For a boilerroom type operation that does nothing but send out ads, this board would probably be sufficient.

I have an Intel Connection CoProcessor shown in Fig. 11-1. It is a sophisticated fax board with its own 10 MHz 80188 processor. It has provisions for a small daughter card that contains a 2400 baud modem. Because it has its own processor, it can send and receive fax messages or operate the modem in the background while the computer is busy on other projects.

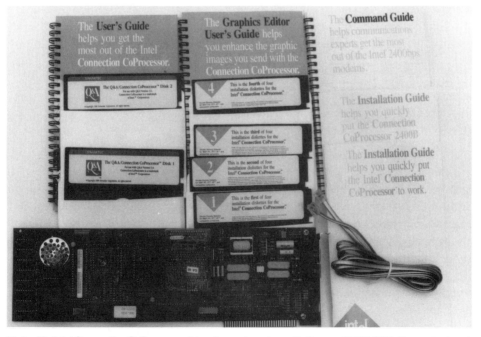

11-1 My Intel Connection CoProcessor. It is a fax and modem with its own 80186 CPU. It can send and receive in the background while you are using your computer for other things.

A discount house lists the Connection CoProcessor for $769 and the modem for $229. For more information, contact Intel Corporation at (800) 538-3373.

The Complete PC company at (408) 434-0145 has several types of special boards. One has a fax, a modem, and a telephone answering machine.

Fax board sources

Here are the phone numbers of just a few fax board manufacturers. Call them for spec sheets and prices:

ADTech SMARTFAX	(818) 578-1339
Advanced Vision MegaFax	(408) 434-1115
Archtek	(818) 912-9800
Asher JT Fax	(800) 334-9339
ATI	(416) 756-0718
Brooktrout Fax-Mail	(617) 235-3026
Carterfone DATAFAX	(214) 634-2424
Chinon	(213) 533-0274
Dash Computer	(408) 734-8879
Datacopy MicroFax	(800) 821-2898
GammaLink GAMMAFAX	(415) 856-7421
KoFax Image Products	(714) 474-1933
Microtek Lab MFAX96	(213) 321-2121
OAZ Communications XAFAX	(714) 259-0909
Panasonic Fax Partner	(201) 348-7000
Pitney-Bowes PATH II & III	(203) 356-5000
Ricoh FB-1	(201) 882-2000
Spectrafax FAXCARD	(813) 775-2737
Touchbase Systems	(516) 261-0423
Zoom Telephonics	(617) 423-1072

Network fax gateways

A large office might have several fax machines. If several computers are in a network in this office, it would be more convenient to have a single fax server in the network. Each person on the network could access the fax from his or her computer. A record could be easily made to the server hard disk. The fax communications would be better utilized by using a fax server.

A fax gateway would be needed to manage the outgoing and incoming fax traffic. Most of the fax gateways also handle E-mail.

Fax gateway sources

Here are a few companies and their product's name who supply fax gateways:

Alcom, Inc.	EasyGate LANFax	(415) 493-3800
Castelle	FaxPress	(800) 359-7654

GammaLink	GammaNet	(415) 856-7421
Interpreter, Inc.	Faxsimile Server	(800) 232-4687
OAZ Communications	NetFax Manager	(408) 745-1750

Scanners

I discussed scanners in chapter 10. They are not absolutely essential to the operation of a PC-based fax, but sometimes it might be necessary to transmit photographs, blueprints, documents, or handwritten signatures on contracts. A scanner is needed to get the most utility from a fax.

In any business that does a lot of communicating, a good fax and modem system would pay for itself in a very short time.

Installing a fax board

Most fax boards are very easy to install and easy to operate. If your computer is already assembled, just remove the five screws that hold the cover on. Check your documentation and set any switches that are necessary. Then plug the board into an empty slot. Replace the computer cover and connect the telephone line.

You should have received some software to control the fax that should be installed on your hard disk. You should be up and ready to send and receive faxes.

If you use a word processing program to create letters or text for a fax transmission, the text must be changed into an ASCII file before it can be sent. Most word processors have this capability.

Telecommuting

One reason I took early retirement from my job at Lockheed was because I hated being stuck in commuter traffic. Of course, another reason was that my books were selling well.

Millions of people risk their lives and fight the traffic every day. Many of these people have jobs that could allow them to stay home, work on a computer, then send the data to the office over a modem or a fax. Even if the person had to buy their own computer, modem, and fax, it still might be worth it. You could save the cost of gasoline, auto maintenance, and lower insurance.

Being able to work at home could be ideal for those who want to stay home with young children, for the handicapped, or for anyone who hates traffic.

12
CHAPTER

Printers

A bit of history   Johann Gutenberg started the printer revolution way back in 1436 when he developed movable type and started printing the first Bible. Though he started printing the first Bible, he did not complete it. He had borrowed money from a man named Johann Fust.   When Gutenberg could not repay the loan, Fust took over the press and types and completed the work started by Gutenberg. So it was Fust who was first to print the Bible, not Gutenberg.

The printing business has improved considerably since 1436.

All you need to know to buy a printer

A short time ago, choosing a printer was a difficult task because there were so many options. There are even more types of printers and manufacturers today, but the task of selecting one is considerably easier. Buy a laser printer. If Gutenberg were around today, you can bet that he would be using a laser printer.

Printer evolution

My first computer was a Morrow Designs with 64K and two 140K disk drives. I bought a 7-pin dot matrix printer to use with it. The printing was terrible. Just as soon as I could afford it, I bought a Brother Daisy Wheel printer. It used a carbon film ribbon and had excellent letter quality output, but it was slower than Heinz's catsup in January. It took two to three minutes to print a single page.

I finally bought a Star NB24-15 dot matrix. It has 24 pins and has fairly good near letter quality printing (NLQ). It is also fairly fast, especially in the draft mode. It will even do some simple graphics, if you have the time to wait. I often receive faxes on my Intel Connection CoProcessor board. It might take five to ten minutes to print a fax with line drawings.

I use several graphics programs that I like to print out occasionally. My Star 24-pin printer is just not able to keep up. Besides, I do a lot of letter writing and am a bit ashamed of the Star output.

I had three printers in my office, all in good working order, so it was difficult justifying the cost of another one. I kept waiting for my Star dot matrix to break down, but after four years of hard work it was still going strong. It was a difficult decision, but I finally retired it and bought a laser.

I decided to buy an HP LaserJet III. I paid a little more than I would have for some of the other laser printers, but I believe that it is well worth it. Figure 12-1 shows my new HP LaserJet III.

12-1 My HP Laserjet III.

Moving up to the LaserJet III from the 24-pin Star is almost like moving up from an XT to a 486. The XT and the dot matrix can both accomplish tasks they were designed for, now there are many other tasks that neither can accomplish. There is no comparison between the dot matrix and the laser as to speed, quality, and added functionality.

Do you need a laser

In many applications, a dot matrix printer is all that is needed to accomplish a task. Clearly, the type of printer needed will depend primarily on what the computer will be used for. The following are some factors that should be considered when shopping for a printer.

If at all possible, before you buy a printer, visit a computer store or a computer show and try it out. Get several spec sheets of printers in your price range and compare them. You should also look for reviews of printers in the computer magazines.

Dot matrix printers

Most of the dot matrix printers sold today are 24 pins. They are fairly reasonable in price and are sturdy and reliable. The 24-pin printer forms characters from a single vertical row of 24 pins in the print head. Small electric solenoids are around each of the wire pins in the head. By pressing various pins as the head moves across the paper, any character can be formed. It is also possible to do some graphics.

Some use a multicolored ribbon to print out color. By mixing the colors on the ribbon, all of the colors of the rainbow can be printed. It is a bit slow, but if you need color to jazz up a presentation, or for accent now and then, they are great.

Some things can be done with a dot matrix that cannot be done with a laser. For instance, a dot matrix can have a wide carriage; the lasers are limited to $8^{1}/_{2}''$ $\times$ 11″. The dot matrix can use continuous sheets or forms; the laser uses cut sheets, fed one at a time. A dot matrix can also print carbons and forms with multiple sheets.

A dot matrix printer can be very noisy. There are enclosures that help to reduce the noise, but they are a bit expensive. I used some packing foam rubber under mine to reduce the noise.

If you can get by with a dot matrix, you should be able to find some at very good prices. The low cost of the lasers are forcing the dot matrix people to lower their prices. In addition to lower prices, many dot matrix companies are also adding features such as more memory and several fonts in order to attract buyers.

Daisy wheel printers

The daisy wheel has excellent letter quality. It has a wheel with all the letters of the alphabet on flexible "petals." If the letter A is pressed, an electric solenoid hammer hits the A as it spins by and presses it against a ribbon onto the paper. The daisy wheel printers are very slow and cannot print graphics. They are also quite noisy. They are practically obsolete.

Hewlett-Packard DeskJet Plus

The DeskJet Plus is a small printer that has quality almost equal to that of a laser. It uses a matrix of small ink jets instead of pins. As the head moves across the paper, the ink is sprayed from the jets to form the letters. Its letter quality approaches that of a laser. It comes with Courier fonts, but it can use several more fonts that are available on plug-in cartridges. It has a speed of 1 to 2 pages per minute (ppm). It is small enough to sit on a desk top and is very quiet. It is relatively inexpensive with a street price of about $600, about the same as a dot matrix.

Laser printers

Lasers have excellent print quality. They are a combination of the copy machine, computer, and laser technology. On the down side, they have lots of moving mechanical parts and are rather expensive.

Laser printers use synchronized, multifaceted mirrors, and sophisticated optics to write the characters or images on a photosensitive rotating drum. The drum is similar to the ones used in repro machines. The laser beam is swept across the spinning drum and is turned on and off to represent white and dark areas. As the drum is spinning, it writes one line across the drum, then rapidly returns and writes another. It is quite similar to the electron beam that sweeps across the face of the monitor one line at a time.

The drum is sensitized by each point of light that hits it. The sensitized areas act like an electromagnet. The drum rotates through the carbon toner. The sensitized areas become covered with the toner. The paper is then pressed against the drum. The toner that was picked up by the drum leaves an imprint of the sensitized areas on the paper. The paper then is sent through a heating element where the toner is heated and fused to the paper.

Except for the writing to the drum, this is the same thing that happens in a copy machine. Instead of using a laser to sensitize the drum, a copy machine takes a photo of the image to be copied. A photographic lens focuses the image onto the rotating drum.

Some companies have developed other systems to write on or sensitize a drum. Some use light emitting diodes (LED), and others use liquid crystal shutters (LCS). Essentially, they do the same thing that a laser beam does. There are some differences. The laser beam is a single beam that is swept across the drum by complex system of rotating mirrors. The LED system has single row of tiny LEDs, at a density of 300 per inch. The LCS system has a strip, or tiny wall, of liquid crystal substance near the drum. Behind the liquid crystal substance is a halogen light. The individual pixels in the liquid crystal can be electronically turned on to let light shine through and sensitize the drum or left off to block the light.

The end result from a laser, an LED, or an LCS machine is all about the same. Many more companies use the laser engine, and it has become the standard. I would recommend the laser type.

Engine   The drum and its associated mechanical attachments is called an engine. Canon, a Japanese company, is one of the foremost makers of engines. They manufacture them for their own laser printers and copy machines, and for dozens of other companies such as Hewlett-Packard and Apple. Several other Japanese companies manufacture laser engines.

Hewlett-Packard LaserJet was one of the first low cost lasers. It was a fantastic success and became the *de facto* standard. Now of the hundreds of laser printers on the market, most of them emulate the LaserJet standard. HP is the IBM of the laser world. Even IBM's laser printer emulates the HP standard.

Low-cost laser printers The competition has been a great benefit to us consumers. It has driven the prices down and forced many new improvements. Several new low-cost models have been introduced that print 4 to 6 pages per minute instead of the 8 to 10 pages of the original models. They are smaller than the originals and can easily sit on a desktop. Most have 512K of memory with an option to add more. The discount price for some of these models is now down to less than $900. The original 8 to 10 page models have dropped from about $3500 down to around $1500. If you can afford to wait a few seconds, the 4 to 6 page models will do almost everything the 8 to 10 pagers will do. The prices will drop even more as the competition increases and the economies of scale in the manufacturing process become greater.

Here are just a few of the low cost 4 to 6 ppm lasers. Call them for the nearest dealer, or check the ads in the local papers and in computer magazines:

Company	Product	ppm	Telephone
Canon	LBP-4	4	(800) 892-0020
Data General	6640	6	(800) 344-3577
Data Products	LZR 650	6	(818) 887-8000
Epson	EPL 6000	6	(800) 922-8911
Facit	P6060	6	(800) 733-2248
Fugitsu (LED)	RX7100	6	(800) 626-4686
Hewlett-Packard	HP IIP	4	(800) 752-0900
Mannesman Tally	MT905	6	(800) 843-1347
Qume (LCS, LED)	Crys.Prt.	6	(800) 223-2479
Rosetta Tech. (LED)	RT3105	5	(800) 937-4224
Texas Inst.	Microlaser	6	(800) 527-3500
Toshiba	Pagelaser	6	(800) 334-3445

Extras for lasers

Do not be surprised if you go into a store to buy a laser printer that was advertised for $1000 and end up paying a lot more than that. The laser printer business is much like the automobile, the computer, and most other businesses. I have seen laser printer ads in the Los Angeles area for a very low price. Then somewhere in the ad, in very small print, they say "without toner cartridge and cables." They might charge up to $150 for the toner cartridge and up to $50 for a $5 cable. Extra fonts, memory, special controller boards, and software will all cost extra. Some printers have small sheet bin feeders. A large size one might cost as much as $200 or more.

Memory   If you plan to do any graphics or desktop publishing (DTP), you will need to have at least one megabyte of memory in the machine. Of course, the more memory, the better. The laser memory chips are usually in SIMM packages. Not all lasers use the same configuration, so check before you buy. Several companies offer laser memories. Here are a couple:

ASP   (800) 445-6190
Elite   (800) 942-0018

Page description languages   If you plan to do any complex desktop publishing you might need a *page-description language* (PDL) of some kind. Text characters and graphics images are two different species of animals. Monitor controller boards usually have all of the alphabetical and numerical characters stored in ROM. When you press the letter A from the keyboard, it dives into the ROM chip, drags out the A and displays it in a precise block of pixels wherever the cursor happens to be. These are called *bit-mapped* characters. If you wanted to display an A that was twice as large, you would have to have a complete font set of that type in the computer.

Printers are very much like the monitors and have the same limitations. They have a library of stored discrete characters for each font that they can print. My dot matrix Star printer has an internal font and two cartridge slots. Several different font cartridges can be plugged into these slots, but they are limited to those fonts that happen to be plugged in.

With a good PDL, the printer can take one of the stored fonts and change it or scale it to any size you want. These are *scalable fonts*. With a bitmapped font, you have one typeface and one size. With scalable fonts, you might have one typeface with an infinite number of sizes. Most of the laser printers will accept ROM cartridges with as many as 35 or more fonts. You can print almost anything that you want with these fonts if your system can scale them.

Speed   Laser printers can print from 6 to over 10 pages per minute depending on the model and what they are printing. Some very expensive high-end printers can print over 30 pages per minute.

A dot matrix printer is concerned with a single character at a time. The laser printers compose, then print, a whole page at a time. With a PDL, many different fonts, sizes of type and graphics can be printed. But the laser must determine where every dot that makes up a character, or image is to be placed on the paper before it is printed. This composition is done in memory before the page is printed. The more complex the page, the more memory it will require, and the more time needed to compose the page. It may take several minutes to compose a complex graphics. Once composed, it will print out very quickly.

A PDL controls and tells the laser where to place the dots on the sheet. Adobe's PostScript is the best known PDL. Several companies have developed their own PDLs. Of course, none of them are compatible with the others. This has caused a major problem for software developers because they must try to include drivers for each one of these PDLs. Several companies are attempting to clone PostScript, but it is doubtful that they can achieve 100% compatibility. Unless you need to move your files from a machine that does not have PostScript to one that does, you might not need to be compatible.

Hewlett-Packard includes their Printer Control Language 5 (PCL), a scalable system, on their LaserJet IIIs. They are working on kits that will upgrade the earlier LaserJets to the PCL 5 system.

PostScript printers   Printers sold with PostScript installed, such as the Apple LaserWriter, can cost as much as $3000 more than one without PostScript. Hewlett-Packard is offering a PostScript option for their LaserJet IID (the IID duplexes print on both sides of the paper) for a list price of $995. The PostScript option for the IIP and III printers is $695. The street prices should be less.

PostScript on disk   Several software companies have developed PostScript software emulation. One of the better ones is LaserGo's GoScript (619) 450-4600. QMS offers UltraScript and the Custom Applications Company has Freedom of Press.

Resolution   Almost all of the lasers have a 300 × 300 dots per inch resolution (dpi), which is very good, but not nearly as good as 1200 × 1200 dpi typeset used for standard publications. Several companies have developed systems to increase the number of dots to 600 × 600 dpi or more.

At 300 × 300 dpi, it is possible to print 90,000 dots in one square inch. On an $8^{1}/_{2}$″ × 11″ page of paper, if you deduct a one inch margin from the top, the bottom and both sides, then you would have $58^{1}/_{2}$ square inches × 90,000 dots or 5,265,000 possible dots.

Paper size   Most laser printers are limited to $8^{1}/_{2}$ × 11 paper (A size). The QMS PS-2200 and the Unisys AP 9230 can print 11 × 17 (B size) as well as the A size:

QMS PS-2200   (800) 631-2692
Unisys AP 9230   (215) 542-2240

Maintenance   Most of the lasers use a toner cartridge that is good for 3000 to 5000 pages. The original cost of the cartridge is about $100. Several small companies are now refilling the spent cartridges for about $50 each.

Of course there are other maintenance costs. Because these machines are very similar to the repro copy machines, they have a lot of moving parts that can wear out and jam up. Most of the larger companies give a *mean time between failures* (MTBF) of 30,000 up to 100,000 pages. Remember that these are only average figures and not a guarantee.

The true cost of a laser is not just the original price. Most of the lasers are expected to have a lifetime of 300,000 pages. According to figures quoted by Winn L. Rosch in *PC Week* (Feb. 26, 1990), an HP LaserJet IIP would require about $8,130 to print 300,000 pages. This works out to about 2.71 cents per page. The Epson EPL-6000 will use about $10,260 to print 300,000 pages, or about 3.42 cents per page. These two printers sell for about the same price, around $900, but the Epson could cost more than $2000 more for consumables during its lifetime. Many vendors provide a spec sheet with the expected cost per page.

Paper   There are many different types and weights of paper. Almost any paper will work in your laser. If you use a cheap paper in your laser, it could leave lint inside the machine and cause problems in print quality. Generally speaking, any bond paper or a good paper made for copiers will work fine. Colored paper made for copiers will also work fine. Some companies are marking copy papers with the word "laser" and charging more for it.

Many of the laser printers are equipped with trays to print envelopes. Hewlett-Packard recommends envelopes with diagonal seams and gummed flaps. Make certain that the leading edge of the envelope has a sharp crease.

Some companies make address labels that can withstand the heat of the fusing mechanism of the laser. Other specialty supplies can be used with your laser. The Integraphix Company carries several different items that you might find useful. Call them at (800) 421-2515 for a catalog.

Sources

There are just too many laser companies to list them all. Look for ads in the local papers and in any computer magazine for the nearest dealer.

Color

A few color printers are available, at a cost of $7000 and up to $15,000. These printers are often referred to as laser color printers, but they do not actually use the laser technology. They use a variety of thermal transfer technologies using a wax or rolls of plastic polymer. The wax or plastic is brought into contact with the paper, then heat is applied. The melted wax or plastic material then adheres to the paper. Very precise points, up to 300 dots per inch, can be heated. By overlaying three or four colors, all of the colors of the rainbow can be created.

The cost of color prints ranges from about 5 cents a sheet for the Howtek Pixelmaster, which uses wax material similar to crayons, up to about 83 cents apiece for the large 11 × 17 inch sheets from the QMS ColorScript 30. The *PC Magazine* said that they save about $750,000 a year by using a color printer for corporate use rather than a photographic process. Another big plus is that the results from a color printer are available almost immediately. Any errors or corrections can be easily made.

Most of the color printers have PostScript, or they emulate PostScript. The Tektronix Phaser CP can also use the Hewlett-Packard Graphics Language (HPGL) to emulate a plotter. These color printers can print out a page much faster than a plotter.

Several other color printers will be on the market soon. There is lots of competition, so the prices should come down. Here are just a few of the companies who have color printers:

CalComp	(800) 225-2627
Howtek Pixelmaster	(603) 882-5200
NEC Technologies	(508) 264-8000
QMS ColorScript	(800) 631-2692
Seiko Instruments	(408) 922-5800
Tektronix	(800) 835-6100

Plotters

Plotters are devices that can draw almost any shape or design under the control of a computer. A plotter can have from one up to eight or more different colored pens. There are several different types of pens for various applications such as writing on different types of paper or on film or transparencies. Some pens are quite similar to ball point pens, others have a fiber type point. The points are usually made to a very close tolerance and can be very small so that the thickness of the lines can be controlled. The line thicknesses can be very critical in some precise design drawings.

The plotter arm can be directed to choose any one of the various pens. This arm is attached to a sliding rail and can be moved from one side of the paper to the other. A solenoid can lower the pen at any predetermined spot on the paper for it to write.

While the motor is moving the arm horizontally from side to side, a second motor moves the paper vertically up and down beneath the arm. This motor can move the paper to any predetermined spot and the pen can be lowered to write on that spot. The motors are controlled by predefined X-Y coordinates. They can move the pen and paper in very small increments so that almost any design can be traced out.

Values could be assigned of perhaps 1 to 1000 for the Y elements and the same values for the X or horizontal elements. The computer could then direct the plotter to move the pen to any point or coordinate on the sheet.

Plotters are ideal for such things as printing out circuit board designs, for architectural drawings, for making transparencies for overhead presentations, for graphs, charts, and many CAD/CAM drawings. All of this can be done in as many as seven different colors.

Plotters come in several different sizes. Some desktop units are limited to only A and B sized plots. Large floor-standing models can accept paper as wide as four feet and several feet long.

A desk model can cost as little as $200 and up to $2000. A floor-standing large model can cost from $4000 up to $10,000. If you are doing very precise work, for instance designing a transparency that will be photographed and used to make a circuit board, you will want one of the more accurate and more expensive machines.

Many good graphics programs are available that can use plotters, but there are several manufacturers of plotters. Again, there are no standards. Just like the printers, each company has developed its own drivers. Again, this is very frustrating for software developers who must try to include drivers in their programs for all of the various brands.

Hewlett-Packard has been one of the major plotter manufacturers. Many of the other manufacturers now emulate the HP drivers. Almost all of the software that requires plotters include a driver for HP. If you are in the market for a plotter, try to make sure that it can emulate the HP.

Houston Instruments is also a major manufacturer of plotters. Their plotters are somewhat less expensive than the Hewlett-Packard.

One of the disadvantages of plotters is that they are rather slow. Some software programs allow laser printers to act as plotters. Of course, they are much faster than a plotter, but except for the colored printers, they are limited to black and white.

Plotter sources

Here is a list of some of the plotter manufacturers. Call them for a product list and latest prices:

Alpha Merics	(818) 999-5580
Bruning Computer Graphics	(415) 372-7568
CalComp	(800) 225-2667
Hewlett-Packard	(800) 367-4772
Houston Instrument	(512) 835-0900
Ioline Corp.	(206) 775-7861
Roland DG	(213) 685-5141

Plotter supplies

It is important that a good supply of plotter pens, special paper, film, and other supplies be kept on hand. Plotter supplies are not as widely available as printer supplies. A very high priced plotter might have to sit idle for some time if the supplies are not on hand. Most of the plotter vendors provide supplies for their equipment. Here is the name of one company that specializes in plotter pens, plotter media, accessories and supplies:

Plotpro
P.O. Box 800370
Houston, TX 77280
(800) 223-7568

Installing a printer or plotter

Most IBM compatible computers allow for four ports, two serial and two parallel. No matter whether it is a plotter, or a dot matrix, daisy wheel, or laser printer, it will require one of these ports. If you have a 286 or 386 computer, these ports might be built into the motherboard. (See the previous chapter and the discussion for installing modems.)

If you have built-in ports, you will still need a short cable from the motherboard to the outside. You will then need a longer cable to your printer. If you do not have built-in ports, you will have to buy interface boards.

Almost all laser and dot matrix printers use the parallel ports. Some of them have both serial and parallel. Many of the daisy wheel printers and most of the plotters use serial ports. For the serial printers, you will need a board with an RS232C connector. The parallel printers use a Centronics type connector. When you buy your printer, buy a cable from the vendor that is configured for your printer and your computer.

Printer sharing

Ordinarily a printer will sit idle most of the time. Some days I do not even turn my printer on. Most large offices and businesses have several computers. Almost all of them are connected to a printer in some fashion because it would be a waste of money if each one had a separate printer that was only used occasionally. It is fairly simple to make arrangements so that a printer or plotter can be used by several computers. If there are only two or three computers and they are fairly close together, it is not much of a problem.

Manual switch boxes that cost from $25 to $150 can allow any one of two or three computers to be switched on line to a printer. With a simple switch box, if the computers use the standard parallel ports, the cables from the computers to the printer should be no more than 10 feet long. Parallel signals will begin to degrade if the cable is longer than 10 feet and could cause some loss of data. A serial cable can be as long as 50 feet.

If an office or business is fairly complex, then several electronic switching devices are available. Some of them are very sophisticated and can allow a large number of different types of computers to be attached to a single printer or plotter.

Many of them have built-in buffers and can allow cable lengths up to 250 feet or more. The costs range from $160 up to $1400.

Of course there are several networks that are available to connect computers and printers together. Many of them can be very expensive to install.

One of the least expensive methods of sharing a printer is for the person to generate the text to be printed out on one computer, record it on a floppy diskette, then walk over to a computer that is connected to a printer. If it is in a large office, a single low cost XT clone could be dedicated to a high-priced printer.

Printer sharing device sources

Here are the names and phone numbers of some of these companies that provide switch systems. Call them for their product specs and current price list:

Altek Corp.	(301) 572-2555
Arnet Corp.	(615) 834-8000
Belkin Components	(213) 515-7585
Black Box Corp.	(412) 746-5530
Buffalo Products, Buffalo XL-256	(800) 345-2356
Crosspoint Systems	(800) 232-7729
Digital Products, PrintDirector	(800) 243-2333
Extended Systems, ShareSpool	(208) 322-7163
Fifth Generation, Logical Connection	(800) 225-2775
Quadram, Microfazer VI	(404) 564-5566
Rose Electronics	(713) 933-7673
Server Technology, Easy Print	(800) 835-1515
Western Telematic	(800) 854-7226

If Gutenberg were around today, I am sure that he would be quite pleased with the progress that has been made in the printer business.

13
CHAPTER

Using your computer in business

The 486 computer is an excellent business tool. Many businesses can be operated from a home office. Several advantages in having a home office are no commuting, no high office rent, possibly taking care of young children at same time, and setting your own hours.

A home office

If you have a home office for a business, you might be able to deduct part of the cost of your computer from your income taxes. You might even be able to deduct a portion of your rent, telephone bills, and other legitimate business expenses.

I cannot give you all of the IRS rules for a home office, but the book, *J.K. Laser's Your Income Tax* has a few details. I cannot list all of the IRS rules and regulations for a home office, so before you go deducting expenses, I would recommend that you buy the latest tax books and consult with the IRS or a tax expert. There are many, many rules and regulations, and they change frequently. For more information, call the IRS and ask for publication #587, *Business Use of Your Home*. Look in your telephone directory for the local or 800 number for the IRS.

Other tools of the trade

I mentioned that the 486 was an excellent business tool. The following items are some other tools that go very well with the 486 in business uses.

Point of sale terminals

Point of sale terminals (POS) are usually a combination of a cash drawer, a computer, and special software. It provides a fast customer checkout, credit card handling, audit and security, reduces paperwork, and provides efficient accounting. By keying in codes for the various items, the computer can keep a running inventory of everything that is sold. The store owner can immediately know when to reorder certain goods. A POS system can provide instant sales analysis data as to which items sell best, buying trends, and of course, the cost and the profit or loss.

A simple cash drawer with a built-in 40-column receipt printer might cost as little as $500. More complex systems might cost $1500 and more. Software can cost from $175 up to $1000, but it might replace a bookkeeper and an accountant. In most successful businesses that sells goods, a POS system can easily pay for itself. Here are a few of the POS hardware and software companies:

Alpha Data Systems	(404) 499-9247
Computer Time	(800) 456-1159
Datacap Systems	(215) 699-7051
Kimtron	(408) 436-6550
Merit Digital Systems	(604) 985-1391
NCR Corp.	(800) 544-3333
Printer Products	(617) 254-1200
Softpoint	(408) 253-5700
Synchronics	(901) 761-1166

Bar codes

Bar codes are a system of black and white lines that are arranged in a system much like the Morse code of dots and dashes. By using combinations of wide and narrow bars and wide and narrow spaces, any numeral or letter of the alphabet can be represented.

Bar codes were first adopted by the grocery industry. They set up a central office that assigned a unique number, a Universal Product Code (UPC), for just about every manufactured and prepackaged product sold in grocery stores. Different sizes of the same product have a different and unique number assigned to them. The same type products from different manufacturers will also have unique numbers.

When the clerk runs an item across the scanner, the dark bars absorb light and the white bars reflect the light. The scanner decodes this number and sends it to the main computer. The computer then matches the input number to the number stored on its hard disk. Linked to the number on the hard disk is the price of the item, the description, the amount in inventory, and several other pieces of information about the item. The computer sends back the price and the description of the part to the cash register where it is printed out. The computer then deducts that item from the overall inventory and adds the price to the overall cash received for the day.

A store might have several thousand items with different sizes and prices. Without a bar code system the clerk must know most of the prices, then enter them in the cash register by hand. Many errors can occur. With bar codes, the human factor is eliminated. The transactions are performed much faster and with almost total accuracy.

At the end of the day, the manager can look at the computer output and immediately know such things as how much business was done, what inventories need to be replenished, and what items were the biggest sellers. With the push of a button on the computer, he or she can change any or all of the prices of the items in the store.

Bar codes can be used in many other ways to increase productivity, to keep track of time charged to a particular job, track inventory, and many other benefits. Many businesses, large or small, benefit from the use of bar codes.

Some bar code readers or scanners are actually small portable computers that can store data, then be downloaded into a larger computer. Some systems require their own interface card that must be plugged into one of the slots on the computer motherboard. Some companies have devised systems that can be inserted in series with the keyboard so that no slot or other interface is needed. Key Tronic has a keyboard with a bar code reader as an integral part of the keyboard.

Special printers have been designed for printing bar code labels. Labels can also be printed on the better dot matrix and on laser printers. Several companies specialize in printing up labels to your specifications. Bar codes can be very accurate. Several companies make Point of Sale (POS) systems that have a bar code reader, a computer, and a cash drawer all integrated into a single system. Some of these POS systems can be tied together in a local area network for a larger type store that might have several cash registers. A bar code scanner can read data into a computer at about 1700 characters per minute with absolute accuracy.

Whole books have been written about the bar code and other means of identification. Hundreds of vendors and companies offer service in this area. If you are interested in the bar code and automatic identification technology, two magazines sent free to qualified subscribers are:

ID Systems
174 Concord St.
Peterborough, NH 03458
(603) 924-9631

Automatic I.D. News
P.O. Box 6158
Duluth, MN 55806-9858

Call or write for subscription qualification forms.

Radio frequency I.D.

Another system of identification is the use of small tags on materials that can be read by a RFID system. These systems can be used on production lines and many places that are difficult to access.

One RFID system is being used in California for toll bridge collection. A person buys a small tag that is good for a month of tolls.The tag is placed in the window of the auto and is automatically read as the driver passes through the toll gate. You do not even have to slow down for the tag to be read and fed to the computer.

RFID type systems can also be used in stores, libraries, and other places. Many clothing stores use a system that has detectors at the exits. If someone tries to walk through with an item that has not had the tag removed, it will set off an alarm.

Computerized voice output

Computer synthesized voice systems have been developed to do hundreds of tasks. Sensors can be set up so that when a beam is broken, it sends a signal to a computer to alert a person of danger. The Atlanta airport has an underground shuttle to move people to the various airline gates. It has several sensors that feed into a computer. If a person is standing in the doorway, it will ask the person to move and the train will not move until it is safe to do so.

Many automated banking systems will allow you to dial a number over the telephone into a computer. A computerized voice asks questions and lets you pay your bills, move money from one account to another and do almost all of your banking by telephone.

The telephone system has computerized voices for the time and for giving out numbers.

New software and devices for synthesizesd voice are being developed every day. Some systems will allow a computer to act as a burglar detector and deterrent, an audible fire alarm detector, for interactive tutoring and training systems, or one of many other tasks.

Voice data input

Another way to input data into a computer is to talk to it with a microphone. You need electronics that can take the signal created by the microphone, detect the spoken words, and turn them into a form of digital information that the computer can use.

The early voice data input systems were very expensive and limited. One reason was that the voice technology required lots of memory. The cost of memory has dropped considerably in the last few years, and the technology has improved in many other ways.

Voice technology involves "training" a computer to recognize a word spoken by a person. When you speak into a microphone, the sound waves cause a diaphragm, or some other device, to move back and forth in a magnetic field and create a voltage that is analogous to the sound wave. If this voltage is recorded and played through a good audio system, the loudspeaker will respond to the amplified voltages and reproduce a sound that is identical to the one input to the microphone.

When a person speaks a word into a microphone, it creates a unique voltage for that word and that particular person's voice. This voltage is fed into an electronic circuit and the pattern is digitized and stored in the computer. If several words are spoken, the circuit will digitize each one of them and store them. Each one of them will have a distinct and unique pattern. Just as no two leaves from a tree are the same, no two patterns will be the same. Later when the computer hears a word, it will search through the patterns that it has stored to see if the input word matches any one of its stored words.

Of course, once the computer is able to recognize a word, you can have it perform some useful work. You could command it to load and run a program or perform any of several other tasks.

Because every person's voice is different, the computer would not recognize the voice of anyone who had not trained it. Training the computer might involve saying the same word several times so that the computer can store several patterns of the person's voice.

Voice data input is very useful whenever you must use both hands for doing a job but still need a computer to perform certain tasks. Voice data is also useful on production lines where the person does not have time to enter data manually. It can also be used in a laboratory where a scientist is looking through a microscope and cannot take his eyes off the subject to write down the findings or data. In other instances, the person might have to be several feet from the computer and still need to input data through the microphone lines. The person might even be miles away and be able to input data over a telephone line.

In most of the systems in use today, the computer must be trained to recognize a specific word so the vocabulary is limited. However, every word that can be spoken can be derived from just 42 phonemes. Several companies are working on systems that will take a small sample of a person's voice that contains these phonemes. Using the phonemes from this sample, the computer could then recognize any word that the person speaks.

Local area networks

If you have a small business where there are several other computers, you might consider connecting them together into a network. The 486 is excellent as a server for *local area networks* (LANs). You can attach several terminals or smaller computers to your 486. This would give the less expensive computers most of the benefits of the 486. The 486 could have very large databases, files, information, and software that could be accessed and shared by these terminals. A LAN can allow multitasking, multiusers, security, centralized backup, and shared resources such as printers, modems, fax machines, and other peripherals.

A good network system can support as many as 100 or more terminals or stations. Those terminals could be very inexpensive PCs, or a combination of PCs, 286s, and 386s. On a good system, the terminals will have almost all of the benefits that the powerful 486 has. A good network can multiply by several times the power and utility of a server.

Of course, the larger and more complex the network, the more expensive. If you have a small business, you might not need a large network or one that is very sophisticated. Many types of LANs have many levels of complexity. A LAN can be two or more computers tied together so that they can share and process the same files. This would be called a *shared CPU* system since all the terminals share the same CPU. This can work well if there are only a few terminals on line, but if several are vying for attention at the same time, there will usually be some delay.

Some systems use diskless terminals. One reason would be for security reasons to prevent the copying of the data and software. These terminals are usually low-cost PCs with a monitor. Earth Computer at (714) 964-5784 has designed a keyboard with built-in ports, a network interface, a video adapter and memory. Only a monitor is needed to make the keyboard a diskless terminal.

Equipment needed for LANs

Besides the terminals, other types of equipment needed to form a LAN are plug-in boards, cables, and software. Most systems require a plug-in board in each terminal and a master board in the server. The boards may cost from $125 up to $1000 each or more. Several types of cable can be used such as the inexpensive standard telephone cables, twisted pair telephone cables, coaxial shielded cables, and fiberoptic cables. The type of system installed would dictate the type of cable needed. A simple system might require only standard telephone cables. A fast sophisticated system might need the shielded coaxial or the fiberoptic.

Besides the plug-in boards, the system will need special drivers and LAN software to control and manage the network. Some companies supply special software to match their hardware. Many companies such as Novell develop network software for several types of network hardware. They have software for both large and small systems. Here are a few LAN software companies:

Banyan Systems	(800) 828-2404
Corvus Systems	(800) 426-7887
IBM	(900) 426-2468

Novell	(408) 747-4000
Simple-NET Systems	(714) 996-5088
3COM Corp.	(408) 562-6400

Most software is sold with the explicit understanding and agreement that it will be used on a single computer by a single user. If it is to be used on a network, they usually charge more. So you might need to pay more for the word processors, spreadsheets, databases, and other commercial programs.

Low-cost switches and LANs

You might have just a couple of computers and want them to share a printer or switch from a laser printer to a dot matrix. This can be done very easily with mechanical switch boxes. Some switch boxes can handle the switching needs for as many as four or five systems. These boxes can cost from $50 up to $500 or more. Here are some vendors of mechanical switchers:

Black Box Corporation	(412) 746-5530
Global Computer Supplies	(800) 845-6225
Inmac Supplies	(408) 727-1970
Lyben Computer Systems	(313) 589-3440
MISCO	(800) 876-4726
R + R Direct	(800) 654-7587

Electronic switch boxes can be a bit more sophisticated and have more capabilities and functions. Some offer buffers and spooling. Computone Products has an ATCC Cluster Controller that can control up to 64 terminals. See Fig. 13-1. Here are a few vendors:

Aten Research	(714) 992-2836
Computone Products	(800) 241-3946
Data Spec	(818) 772-9977
Interex Computer Products	(316) 524-4747
Protec Microsystems	(800) 363-8156
Rose Electronics	(713) 933-7673
Total Technology	(714) 241-0406
Western Telematic	(714) 586-9950

Several companies provide low-cost LANs that use the RS232 serial port. One that I have used and can recommend is the NetLine ManyLink. I have used it to tie three computers together in my office. Some other low-cost RS232 systems are:

Applied Knowledge	(408) 739-3000
DeskLink	(800) 662-2652
LanLink 5X	(800) 451-5465
LANtastic	(602) 293-6363
NetLine ManyLink	(801) 373-6000

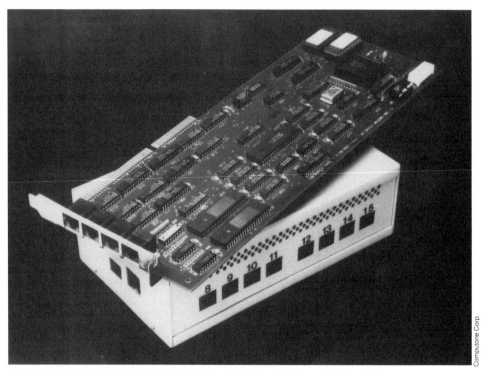

Computone Corp.

13-1 The Computone ATCC Cluster Controller which can control up to 64 terminals.

LANs that use interface cards or plug-in boards are usually more sophisticated and powerful. One low-cost interface card that I have used and can recommend is from the Invisible Software Company and another is MultiTech Systems.

Invisible Software Company	(415) 570-5967
MultiTech Systems	(800) 328-9717

LAN magazines

Most of the computer magazines carry articles on networking from time to time. The Novell Corporation is the leading manufacturer of network products, and they publish a free magazine to qualified subscribers called *LAN Times*. If you need a network system, I would suggest that you contact Novell and ask for a subscription form. Here is the address:

LAN Times
151 East 1700 So., Suite 100
Provo, UT 84606

Books on LAN

Many books have been published on networking. These are some from Windcrest:

> *TOPS: The IBM/Macintosh Connection*, S. Cobb and M. Jost, #3210
> *Networking with the IBM Token-Ring*, C. Townsend, #2829
> *Networking with Novell NetWare: A LAN Manager's Handbook*, P.
>   Christiansen, S. King, and M. Munger, #3283
> *Networking with 3 + Open*, S. Schatt, #3437

You can order them from:

TAB BOOKS
Blue Ridge Summit, PA 17294-0850
(800) 822-8138

Call TAB and McGraw-Hill for catalogs.

Desktop publishing

Desktop publishing (DTP) can cover a lot of territory. A system could be just a PC with a word processor and a dot matrix printer, or it could be a full blown system that used laser printers with PostScript and lots of memory, scanners, 286 or 386 computers with many, many megabytes of hard disk space, sophisticated software, and other goodies.

As always, the type of system needed will depend on what you want it to do. (And of course, how much money you want to spend.)

DTP can be used for newsletters, ads, flyers, brochures, sales proposals, sophisticated manuals, and all sorts of printed documents. I have a friend who has written and published several books with a fairly simple and relatively inexpensive DTP system.

Desktop publishing software

If your project is not too complex, you can probably do a fairly good job with a good laser printer and a good word processing program. WordStar 6.0 has page preview, scalable fonts, and several other functions that could be used in DTP. Microsoft Word, WordPerfect 5.0, AMI, and several others could also be used. Most of the more sophisticated word processors will let you add graphics and flow the text around them.

If you are doing a more complicated and professional type of DTP, with a lot of graphics and different types and fonts, then you should use the higher level software packages. The premier high-end packages are Ventura from Xerox and Page-Maker from Aldus. GEM Desktop Publisher from DRI and Inte Graphics from

IMSI are much less expensive and will do almost everything one would need to do for a lot less money. Many, many other software packages range from $89 up to $15,000. Here are just a few companies who supply page-layout software:

Acorn Plus	Easy Laser	(213) 876-5237
Aldus Corp.	PageMaker	(206) 622-5500
Ashton-Tate	Byline	(800) 437-4327
CSI Publishing	Pagebuilder	(800) 842-2486
Data Transforms	Fontrix	(303) 832-1501
Digital Research	GEM DTP	(800) 443-4200
Haba/Arrays	Front Page	(818) 994-1899
IMSI	Inte Graphics	(415) 454-8901
LTI Softfonts	Laser-Set	(714) 739-1453
Savtek	ETG Plus	(800) 548-7173
Timeworks	Publish It	(800) 535-9497
Xerox Corp.	Ventura	(800) 832-6979

Clip art

Some software packages have images that you can import and place in your page layout. The software will let you move them around, rotate, size, or revise them. The images are of humans, animals, business, technical, industrial, borders, enhancements, etc. Most of the companies have the images set up in modules on floppies. Most have several modules with hundreds and even thousands of images. Micrografx has the most comprehensive modules. The cost of each of the modules ranges from $15 up to $200. Contact the companies for more information:

Antic	(800) 234-7001
Artware Sys.	(800) 426-3858
CD Designs	(800) 326-5326
EMS Shareware	(301) 924-3594
Kinetic Corp.	(502) 583-1679
Metro ImageBase	(800) 525-1552
Micrografx	(800) 272-3729
Micrograph	(206) 838-4677
PCsoftware	(619) 571-0981
Springboard	(800) 445-4780
Studio Ad Art	(800) 453-1860

Printers for DTP

If you are primarily going to be doing text, then you might be able to get by with a good 24-pin dot matrix printer. You will need a laser printer if you expect to be doing a lot of graphics and using different style types and fonts.

For a high-level DTP system, you will need a laser with a good page description language (PDL). The Adobe PostScript is the original and most popular PDL. A PDL laser can be rather expensive if it is configured with sufficient memory, fonts, and type styles. Refer back to chapter 12 for further discussion of laser printers.

Books for DTP

If you are serious about DTP, there are several books on the subject. Here are a few that Windcrest publishes:

Mastering PageMaker, G. K. Gurganus, #3176
Ventura Publisher, E. McClure, #3012
The Print Shop Companion, P. Seyer and H. Leitch, #3218
IBM Desktop Publishing, G. Lanyi and J. Barrett, #3109
The Illustrated Handbook of Desktop Publishing and Typesetting, 2nd
    Edition, M.L. Kleper, #3350

You can order these books from:

TAB BOOKS
Blue Ridge Summit, PA 17294-0850
(800) 822-8138

DTP magazines

Also devoted to DTP are several magazines. Here are three of them:

Publish!
P.O. Box 51966
Boulder, CO 80321-1966

PC Publishing
P.O. Box 5050
Des Plaines, IL 60017

EP&P
650 S. Clark St.
Chicago, IL 60605-9960

PC Publishing and *EP&P* are free if you qualify. Send for qualification form. Most of the other magazines listed in chapter 16 quite often have DTP articles.

14 CHAPTER

Adjuncts

Once you have your computer and peripherals set up, a few other items can make using it more enjoyable.

UPS

UPS in this case means *uninterruptible power supply*. You probably know that if the power to a computer is interrupted, even for a fraction of a second, any data that is being worked on can be lost forever. UPS systems are designed to prevent losses due to power interruptions.

If you live in an area where there are lots of lightning storms, you are probably familiar with the UPS systems. A lot of people have found out the hard way that there are other causes of power failure besides lightning. Drivers knock over power poles, helium-filled metallic balloons short out power lines, and the power company itself has unexpected failures occasionally.

Power failures can have many other causes. Once my three-year-old granddaughter walked into the room where I was working. I did not pay too much attention to her, so she walked over to the wall and unplugged my computer. I lost about two hours of hard work. I love my granddaughter, but I put a lock on the door.

Later I also got a copy of WordStar 5.0. This version, and all versions since then, have an option that automatically saves your files to disk at specified intervals as do several other software packages. If there is a specified length of time when no typing is detected from the keyboard, it automatically saves a backup of the file. It has saved me hours of work.

I worked in a large office at one time. Most of us had popcorn on our coffee breaks. It is surprising how much power is consumed by the electric popcorn poppers and coffee makers. If somebody turned on both machines at the same time, it would cause the circuit breaker to drop out. If anyone happened to be working on a computer, all data was lost. The boss could have made us take out all the popcorn and coffee machines, but because he was a good guy (and he also liked the popcorn), he called maintenance and had a new electric circuit installed.

Not all power problems are as easy to solve as these two. That is why several large companies manufacture UPS systems.

How the power supply operates

Your system probably has a power supply in a chrome-plated enclosure. It is supplied with 110 volt alternating current (AC) at 60 Hz. The power supply must convert the 110 volts AC to 5 volts and 12 volts direct current (DC) needed by the computer. The power supply rectifies the 60 Hz AC voltage and turns it into DC. This direct current is then chopped up by switching power transistors at a rate of 50,000 Hz to 100,000 Hz. It is effectively turned back into a high frequency AC voltage. This AC voltage is then fed into a transformer which reduces the voltage. At this point, it is still AC voltage. It is then rectified again and the final output is 5 volts and 12 volts DC.

The UPS system takes the 110 volts AC, then sends it through a transformer to reduce it to 12 volts. It then rectifies this voltage and uses it to charge and maintain a charge on a 12 volt battery.

Two main systems in use today are the *on-line* and the *standby* systems. Both systems invert the 12 volts DC from the battery and changes it to 110 volts AC. Transistors chop up the 12 volts DC from the battery, then send it through a transformer to step it up to 110 volts AC for the computer power supply.

On-line UPS

The on-line systems are in series with the voltage to the computer. The 110 volts is used to charge the battery which feeds the computer at all times. If there is a power failure, or a brownout where the voltage drops very low, the battery will continue to supply voltage. But because it is no longer being charged up, it will eventually become discharged.

Standby UPS

The standby system is in parallel with the 110 volts to the computer. It also uses a 12 volt battery which is continuously charged up. The standby system switches on-line only in the event of a power failure. Its sensors detect power failures and immediately switch over. It takes two or more milliseconds for the system to switch.

Advantages and disadvantages

Both systems have advantages and disadvantages. The on-line system operates all the time, which could reduce the life of the battery. Because it is on-line all of the time, it offers the best protection.

The standby is less expensive, and the battery might last a bit longer. However, some people worry that the switching times may allow the loss of data.

The cost of these systems depends primarily on the amount of power that you want from them. A single computer should require no more than 300 or 400 watts. This would provide power from 5 to 20 minutes so the system could be shut down. Some systems can provide power for up to an hour or more for a single computer, or provide power for three or four computers long enough to save any open files, then shut them down. The cost of these systems ranges from $500 up to $1500 or more.

Plug-in board UPS

Depending on the wattage required, some of the UPS systems can be very large and heavy. The Emerson Company has developed a plug-in board with a battery on it. They call it the AccuCard. The small half-card size board plugs into any slot on the motherboard. The small 12 volt battery is kept charged up by the bus voltage. In the event of a power outage, the 12 volt battery can supply voltage to the bus long enough to shut the system down. It will even remember which file you were working on and will automatically reload it when the power comes back. It costs only $249. Other than having to give up a slot, it is a fantastic idea. Emerson also manufactures several other large UPS systems up to several kilovolt amps (KVA).

Dakota Microsystems also manufactures a UPS on a plug-in full size card. It lists for $299.

Emerson Company   (800) 222-5877
Dakota Microsystems   (800) 999-6288

A built-in UPS

If you remove the cover of your power supply, you will find a lot of empty space in it. The PC Power & Cooling Company has taken advantage of the extra space and developed a power supply with a built-in UPS. They have installed a battery inside the power supply. It is a standby type and provides DC power for the computer and 110 volts for a monitor for as long as 8 minutes.

UPS sources

Call these companies for more information about their UPS products:

Alpha Technologies   (206) 647-2360
American Power Conversion (401) 789-5735
Best Power Technology   (800) 356-5794
Clary Corp.   (818) 287-6111
Dynatech Computer Power   (800) 638-9098

PC Power and Cooling Co.	(619) 723-9513
SL Waber	(800) 634-1485
Taesung	(800) 874-3160
Unison	(714) 855-8700

Power panel

Your system will probably have five or six power cords to be plugged in. If you have a single power source, it will be a lot neater, and there will be less chance of having grounding problems. Many people use a power strip with five or six outlets. These power strips are available at most hardware and discount stores.

I have a power panel that is about 12″ wide, 13″ deep, and 2″ high. It has five power outlets in the back for the computer, the monitor, the printer, and two auxiliary devices. It has lighted switches in the front so that I can switch any device on or off. The panel sits on top of my computer and the monitor sits on top of the panel. It is very handy. They cost from $15 up to $30 or more. Most of them claim to have surge protection, but it is only minimal. They are available at most computer supply stores and from several mail order stores. Check the mail order catalogues listed in chapter 16.

Furniture and office supplies

If you are setting up your computer at home or in a business, you will probably need a desk, chairs, filing cabinets, shelves, furniture, and supplies. Most of the mail order catalogues listed in chapter 16 carry everything that you might need in an office. They have air purifiers, coffee makers, cables, furniture, paper, work stations, and lots more. The catalogues are free, and most of them have a toll-free number. You should be aware that most of the items from the catalogue stores are very expensive. Everything is sold at list or above. Most of them have no discount prices.

Several discount computer supply stores advertise in the *Computer Shopper* and other computer magazines. The prices are considerably less at these stores.

If you live near a large city, check out the nearby discount stores. Most of them carry some computer supplies.

Most of the larger cities have stores that sell used office furniture, such as desks, chairs, tables, filing cabinets, and other supplies. They usually have some very good bargains.

Lighting in your office can be very important. Improper lighting can cause reflection and glare from the screen. Anti-glare products are listed in the computer supply catalogues. Some of them even claim to reduce or eliminate Video Display Terminal (VDT) radiation. The amounts of radiation emitted by a VDT is very small. Several studies have been done on VDT radiation, but absolute evidence of health damage has not yet been found. The shields do help eliminate the glare, and they can help eliminate some VDT radiation.

Supply sources

Here is a list of mail order firms who send out their catalogs that cover office supplies, paper, ribbons, diskettes, cartridges, toner, pens, hardware, software, and electronic supplies:

Altex Electronics
300 Breesport
San Antonio, TX 78216
(800) 531-5369

Businessland Direct
P.O. Box 610955
San Jose, CA 95161-0955
(800) 551-2468

Damark
6707 Shingle Creek Pkwy.
Minneapolis, MN 55430
(800) 729-9000

Data Dynamics
2750 Gundry Ave.
Signal Hill, CA 90806
(800) 999-1172

Dartek
949 Larch Ave.
Elmhurst, IL 60126
(800) 832-7835

Devoke
1500 Martin Ave.
Santa Clara, CA 95052-8051
(800) 822-3132

Digi-Key
P.O. Box 677
Thief River Falls, MN 56701-0677
(800) 344-4539

800-SOFTWARE
940 Dwight Wy. #14
Berkeley, CA 94710
(800) 227-4587

Fidelity Graphics Arts Catalog
P.O. Box 155
Minneapolis, MN 55440
(800) 328-3034

Global
2318 E. Del Amo Blvd.
Compton, CA 90220
(800) 227-1246

Inmac
2465 Augustine Dr.
Santa Clara, CA 95054
(800) 547-5444

Jameco Electronics
1355 Shoreway Rd.
Belmont, CA 94002
(415) 592-8097

Jade Computer
4901 W. Rosecrans Av.
Hawthorne, CA
(213) 973-7707

JDR Microdevices
2223 Branham Lane
San Jose, CA 95124
(800) 538-5000

Jensen
P.O. Box 50020
Phoenix, AZ 85076-0020
(602) 968-6231

MISCO
One Misco Plaza
Holmdel, NJ 07733
(800) 876-4726

Moore
P.O. Box 5000
Vernon Hills, IL 60061
(800) 323-6230

Priority One
21622 Plummer St.
Chatsworth, CA
(818) 709-5464

National Computer Accessories
1510 McCormick St.
Sacramento, CA 95814
(916) 441-1568

Selective Software
903 Pacific Ave.
Santa Cruz, CA 95060
(800) 423-3556

Nebs Computer Forms
500 Main St.
Groton, MA 01470
(800) 225-9550

Tenex
P.O. Box 6578
South Bend, IN 46660-6578
(800) 776-6781

Power Up!
2929 Campus Dr.
San Mateo, CA 94403
(800) 851-2917

This is not a complete listing, but it will give you an idea of what is available. Thumbing through these magazines is a great way to be aware of what is available and do some price comparisons without leaving home. You should be aware that some of the magazines listed are not discount houses. They might have slightly higher prices than those you may see advertised in some of the computer magazines.

15
CHAPTER

Essential software

Software is never as easy to learn and use as they say it is. Learning software should be similar to learning to drive. If you know how to drive an automobile, you can drive almost any car without any special training. It should be the same for computer software programs, especially for such basic programs as word processing, databases, and spreadsheets. Just because people know how to drive an automobile does not necessarily mean that they could handle an 18-wheel semi without a bit of training. Likewise, just because they know a word processing program would not necessarily mean that they should be able to run complex programs such as Ventura or AutoCAD without a bit of training. But it would sure help if there was a bit more standardization as to the operation of software.

One thing that has prevented standardization has been the "look and feel" issue brought about by the Lotus lawsuit against Paperback Software. Lotus claimed that Paperback Software's VP-Planner was too similar to their 1-2-3. They didn't claim that it violated any of their code, but that VP-Planner had screens and keyboard commands that were very similar to 1-2-3, so it had the "look and feel" of Lotus.

The fact that anyone who knew 1-2-3 could also use VP-Planner is great from the consumer standpoint. VP-Planner does everything that 1-2-3 does and sells for less than half the cost of 1-2-3. So you can understand why Lotus did not like the idea.

The suit was instituted by Lotus in January of 1987. It was finally decided in mid-1990 that Paperback Software had indeed violated the Lotus copyright. Paperback has said that they will appeal, but it is doubtful that they will.

Lotus is now suing Borland because their Quattro screen has the same look as 1-2-3.

Windows 3.0

Microsoft introduced Windows 3.0 on May 22, 1990. By May of 1991, they expect to sell over five million copies. This is one of the fastest selling of any software package. One reason is that it makes the PC easier to learn and to use.

Windows 3.0 is a *graphical user interface* (GUI, pronounced gooey). It is a shell that allows other programs and applications to run from within it.

One reason the Apple Macintosh is so easy to use is that most of the software it uses operates with icons and a mouse. You need only point at an icon and click. There is no need to learn a lot of arcane commands. Apple developed the icon system from research that was done by Xerox at their Palo Alto Research Center (PARC) in the late 1970s. It was a technology that was years ahead of its time, so Xerox did not pursue it.

Windows 3.0 from Microsoft brings the Macintosh icon ease-of-use features to the DOS world. Hewlett-Packard has also developed New Wave, a program that uses icons and mice. Now Apple claims that both Microsoft and Hewlett-Packard are infringing on their product by using icons and a pointing system. Like Lotus, they have taken their case to court.

The lawsuit has caused some concern among software developers, but I do not expect that it will cause much damage to either company.

Ironically, Xerox, and not Apple, did the original research on icons and mice. Xerox recently brought suit against Apple, but it was thrown out because they had waited too long before acting.

Requirements It is possible to run Windows 3.0 on an XT in real mode, but it will be very slow. It runs fairly well on a 286 with a minimum of 1Mb. It will run best on a 386 or 486 with 2Mb to 3Mb of RAM.

Automatic setup and installation Windows 3.0 has many features that make it easy to learn and to use. Even the installation is easy and automatic. The Setup program detects the users hardware configuration and installs Windows to take full advantage of it.

On-line help Windows has over 1Mb of hypertext help available from the many applications it runs and from the user shell. Pressing the F1 key brings up a screenful of help. Help is indexed so that you can quickly find what you need. It also features simple error messages if you make a mistake, sometimes offering solutions to the error.

Breaking the 640K barrier Many applications written for Windows will let you break the 640K barrier. These applications will take advantage of the protected mode of the 486, enabling it to use all of the extended memory that you have. It also speeds up programs and improves handling of high resolution bit-mapped graphics. It allows multitasking by letting you run several application programs at the same time.

Additional accessories   Windows 3.0 comes with the following accessories and applications:

- *Calculator*. The calculator is both a standard and a scientific calculator. Calculations can be stored in memory.
- *Calendar*. This calendar is a combined month-long calendar and daily appointment book. Appointments can be set up so that an alarm can flash or a beep can alert you.
- *Cardfile*. Cardfile is like a set of index cards that can be used to keep track of names, addresses, phone numbers, directions, or other things that you might want. It can sort itself.
- *Clock*. The clock can be placed in a window and can be displayed as a digital or an old fashioned analog with hands.
- *Notepad*. The notepad is a text editor for jotting down notes and short memos. It can also be used to create batch files.
- *Recorder*. The recorder allows you to record a sequence of keystrokes and mouse actions to create macros. You can record up to several hundred keystrokes or mouse clicks, then have them played back, or inserted in a file, by using only two or three keystrokes.
- *Clipboard*. Clipboard is a temporary storage location that is always available for transferring information or data from one window or application to another. Information is cut or copied from one application then pasted into another location or window.
- *Write*. Write is a basic word processor that can be used to create, save, and print documents. It is not as full-featured as a stand-alone word processor, but can be quite handy for many small tasks.
- *Paintbrush*. With Paintbursh, you can create simple drawings or elaborate color art. It has several icons that represent tools that can help you create your drawings.
- *Terminal*. Terminal is an application that allows you to connect to another computer over a serial cable or it can be the operating software for a modem.
- *Reversi and Solitaire*. Reversi and Solitaire are two games. If you have a good boss, you may be able to convince him that playing these games are necessary to learn the basics of Windows. If he is not all that understanding, you can still play them when he is not around. If you should see him coming, they can be quickly removed from the screen and replaced with a legitimate job that you had loaded and running in the background.

Windows vs. OS/2   Windows 3.0 has almost all of the features found in OS/2. It costs less and will work on clones. It has a very broad installation base so lots of software will be available for it. Without a doubt, Windows 3.0 will be the GUI standard for years to come.

Third-party applications for Windows

Many third-party application programs have been developed to run in the Windows environment. They take advantage of the windows and pull-down menus of this vital tool.

One application program for Windows 3.0 is called Yourway from Prisma Software at (619) 259-1400. It acts as a core and allows users to build their own personal productivity workstation. When Windows is called up, Yourway comes up and is used as a control center for other programs. It allows you to launch into other programs such as spreadsheets, databases, or word processors. It allows data exchange through the Windows Clipboard and by traditional file import. It provides the user a direct data tie with other Windows applications that support *dynamic data exchange* (DDE). With DDE, if a spreadsheet file is changed, and a second file has similar data, the second file is updated automatically.

In the past, people bought Macintosh because it was easier to use, even though it cost more than a clone.

For more about Windows, contact:

Microsoft Windows
16011 N.E. 36th Way
Redmond, WA 98073
(206) 882-8080

Off-the-shelf and ready-to-use software

You will probably never have to do any programming. Ready-made software for almost every application you can dream of is available. More software is already written and immediately available than you can use in a lifetime. Off-the-shelf programs can do almost everything that you could ever want to do with a computer. Yet thousands and thousands of software developers are working overtime to design new programs. It is almost like the soap business, they constantly issue new and improved versions. Quite often, the old version can still do all you need to do.

For most general applications, you will need certain basic programs. (Speaking of basic, BASIC is one that is needed. GW-BASIC from Microsoft is more or less the standard. Many applications still use BASIC. Even if you are not a programmer, it is simple enough that you can design a few special applications yourself with it.) The categories of programs that you will need to do productive work with your computer are disk operating systems (DOS), word processors, databases, spreadsheets, utilities, shells, communications, Windows, graphics, and computer-aided design (CAD). Depending on what you intend to use your computer for, hundreds of others meet special needs.

Software can be more expensive than the hardware. The prices can also vary from vendor to vendor. Few people pay the list price. It will pay to shop around. I have seen software with a list price of $700 advertised by a discount house for as little as $350. Also remember that excellent free public domain programs can do almost everything that the high-cost commercial programs can do. Check your local bulletin board, user group, or the ads for public domain software in most computer magazines.

I cannot possibly list all of the thousands of software packages available. Again, subscribe to the magazines listed later. Most of them have detailed reviews of software in every issue. Briefly, here are some of the essential software packages that you will need.

Operating systems software

MS-DOS   DOS to a computer is like gasoline to an automobile. Without it, it will not operate. DOS is an acronym for *disk operating system*. But it does much more than just operate the disks. In recognition of this, the new OS/2 has dropped the D.

You can use any version of DOS on your 486. I do not know why anyone would want to, but you can even use version 1.0. Of course, you would be severely limited in what you could do. I would recommend that you buy MS-DOS 4.01, 5.0, or DR DOS 5.0.

With DOS Version 4.01 you are still limited to 640K. To break the 640K barrier, you can use Windows 3.0, OS/2, or Presentation Manager if you do not mind spending a bit more.

Many good commands are in DOS, but some, if not used properly, can be disastrous. Be very careful when using commands such as FORMAT, DEL, ERASE, COPY, and RECOVER. When invoked, RECOVER renames and turns all of the files into FILE0001.REC, FILE0002.REC, etc. The disk will no longer be bootable and critical files might be garbled. Many experts say that you should erase the RECOVER command from your disk files and leave it only on your original diskettes. It should only be used as a last resort. The Norton Utilities, Mace Utilities, PC Tools, or one of the other utilities would be much better to unerase or restore a damaged file. Even COPY can wipe out a file if copied to a file with the same name.

DR DOS 5.0   Digital Research has beaten Microsoft to the punch. They have released DR DOS 5.0 which allows you to move the operating system, TSRs, buffers, drivers and others, out of conventional memory up to memory above 640K. It has FileLINK that allows you to connect and transfer files over a serial cable. It has ViewMAX to view, organize, and execute files and commands using only one or two keystrokes or a mouse. It has comprehensive on-line help, supports disk partitions up to 512Mb, has disk cache, a full-screen text editor, password protection, and many other features not found in DOS. It can be easily installed over any version of DOS and is fully compatible with all of the DOS commands. There is no need to learn new commands.

OS/2   Up until the end of 1989, only 150,000 copies of OS/2 had been sold. OS/2 is designed specifically for PS/2 machines. Its ROM BIOS functions might not be compatible with most clones. Companies such as Compaq, Dell, Zenith, and others have designed versions for their clones. Unless you have some special need for multitasking or multiusing, you might not need OS/2. You can probably get by with DOS and Windows 3.0. Besides, not much software is available yet to take advantage of OS/2. Cost can be another factor in staying with DOS. It will also take some time to learn OS/2.

DESQview   This is an excellent alternative to OS/2. It allows multitasking and multiusers. You can have up to 50 programs running at the same time and have as many as 250 windows open. It runs all DOS software. It is simple to learn and use. It is also very inexpensive.

Concurrent DOS 386   This is another excellent alternative to OS/2. It is a multitasking and multiuser operating system. It takes advantage of the 80486 virtual 8086 mode and allows simultaneous processing of DOS applications. It is easy to install and operates with familiar DOS commands. Call them at (800) 443-4200.

Unix   Unix has several advantages over DOS for high-end design and workstations. It is not limited to the 640K memory barrier, but it is rather difficult to learn.

Word processors

The most used of all software is word processing. Literally hundreds of word processor packages are available, each one slightly different than the others. It amazes me that they can find so many different ways to do the same thing. Most of the word processor programs come with a spelling checker. Some of them come with a thesaurus which can be very handy. They usually also include several other utilities for such things as communications programs for your modem, outlines, desktop publishing, print merging, and many others.

WordStar   There are probably more copies of WordStar (in all its versions) in existence than any other word processor. Many magazine and book editors expect their writers to send manuscripts to them on a diskette in WordStar.

I have version 6.0 of WordStar. It came to me on 21 360K diskettes. (Six of those diskettes are filled with software for different printer drivers. Standardization would eliminate the need for these several hundred printer drivers.) My original WordStar for the little Morrow came on a single 140K diskette, and the entire program was less that 130K. The basic WordStar still is not much more than that, but they keep adding extra programs and utilities to it.

WordPerfect   WordPerfect is one of the hottest-selling word processors. They give free unlimited toll-free support. WordPerfect has the ability to select fonts by a proper name, has simplified printer installation, the ability to do most desktop publishing functions, columns, and many other useful functions and utilities.

Microsoft Word   This package of course was developed by the same people who gave us MS-DOS. It has lots of features and utilities. It is about number three among the best sellers in the country. Microsoft also has Word for Windows.

PC-Write   This shareware word processor is free if copied from an existing user. They ask for a $16 donation. Full registration with manual and technical support is $89. It is easy to learn and is an excellent personal word processor.

If you want to learn more about word processors, subscribe to almost any computer magazine. Most of them will have a review of a different package almost every issue.

Database programs

Database packages are very useful for managing large amounts of information. Most programs allow you to store information, search it, sort it, do calculations, and make up reports, and several other very useful features.

At the present time, there are almost as many database programs as there are word processors. Few of them are compatible with others, but a strong effort in the industry is to establish some standards under the Structured Query Language (SQL) standard. Several of the larger companies have announced their support for this standard.

The average price for the better known database packages is almost twice that of word processors.

dBASE IV   Ashton-Tate with their dBASE II was one of the first with a database program for the personal computer. It is a very powerful program and has hundreds of features. It is a highly structured program and can be a bit difficult to learn. dBASE IV is much faster than dBASE III, has built-in compiler, SQL, and an upgraded user interface along with several other enhancements.

askSam   The name is an acronym for *Access Knowledge via Stored Access Method*. It is a free-form, text-oriented database management system, almost like a word processor. Data can be typed in randomly, then sorted and accessed. Data can also be entered in a structured format for greater organization. It is not quite as powerful as dBASE IV, but it is much easier to use. It is also much less expensive. It is ideal for personal use and for the majority of business needs. They also have a discount program for students.

R:base 3.0   R:base has been around for a long time. It has recently been revised and updated. It now has pull-down menus, has mouse support, is fully relational for multi-table tasks, and has an English-like procedural language. It is one of the more powerful and more versatile of the present-day database pro-grams. Microrim is so sure that you will like the program that they offer an unlim-ited, no-questions-asked, money-back, 90-day guarantee.

Spreadsheets

Spreadsheets are primarily number crunchers. They have a matrix of cells in which data can be entered. Data in a particular cell can be acted on by formulas and mathematical equations. If the data in the cell that is acted on affects other cells, recalculations are done on them. Several of the tax software programs use a simple form of spreadsheet. The income and all the deductions can be entered. If an additional deduction is discovered, it can be entered and all the calculations will be done over automatically.

Spreadsheets are essential in business for inventory, for expenses, for accounting purposes, for forecasting, for making charts, and for dozens of other vital business uses. A large number of spreadsheet programs are available, so I only list a few of them.

Microsoft Excel   For years, Lotus 1-2-3 has been the premier spreadsheet but it appears that Excel is taking the top spot and honors. It is a very powerful program, with pull-down menus, windows, and dozens of features, including per-formance as a database.

Quattro   The Quattro spreadsheet looks very much like Lotus 1-2-3, but it has better graphics capabilities for charts, calculates faster, has pull-down menus, can print sideways, and has several other features not found in Lotus 1-2-3. One of the better features is the suggested list price.

SuperCalc5   SuperCalc was one of the pioneer spreadsheets. It was intro-duced in 1981, but it has never enjoyed the popularilty of Lotus, although it has features not found in Lotus. It is an excellent spreadsheet compatible with Lotus 1-2-3 files and can link to dBASE and several other files. Computer Associates has also developed several excellent account packages.

VP-Planner Plus   Adam Osborne started the Paperback Software Company after his Osborne Computer Company went bankrupt. He developed several low-cost software clones. Lotus sued him because his VP-Planner had the "Look and feel" of their Lotus 1-2-3. VP-Planner has most of the features found in Lotus 1-2-3, yet its price is less than one-half the cost of Lotus. It has pull-down menus, supports a mouse, has an Undo command, macro library, and others.

Lotus 1-2-3   Lotus verison 3.0 requires an enormous amount of memory. It runs best on 386s and 486s. Release 2.2 can be run on machines with 640K. Ver-sion 3.0 can link between several spreadsheets, has a macro "learn" keystroke capture feature, a library of reusable macros, a single operation for Undo, search and replace, and several macro commands.

Utilities

Utilities are essential tools that can unerase a file, detect bad sectors on a hard disk, diagnose problems, unfragment a disk or file, sort, and do many other things. Norton Utilities was the first, and is still foremost, in the utility department. Mace Utilities has several functions not found in Norton. Mace Gold is an integrated package of utilities that includes POP, a power out protection program, a backup utility, TextFix and dbFix for data retrieval. PC Tools has even more utilities than the Norton or Mace Utilities.

Steve Gibson's SpinRite, Prime Solution's Disk Technician, and Gazelle's OPTune are excellent hard disk tools for low-level formatting, for defragmenting, and for detecting potential bad sectors on a hard disk.

Disk Manager   Ontrack, the people who have sold several million copies of Disk Manager for hard disks, also has a utility program called DOSUTILS. It provides tools to display and modify any physical sector of a hard disk, to scan for bad sectors, and the diagnose and analyze the disk.

Norton Utilities   Norton also has Norton Commander, a shell program. Norton has recently released Norton Backup, a fantastic new hard disk backup program.

Mace Utilities   Mace Utilities developed by Paul Mace was recently acquired by Fifth Generation Systems, the people who developed FastBack, the leading backup program.

PC Tools   This is an excellent program that just about does it all. It has data recovery utilities, hard disk backup, a DOS shell, a disk manager, and more.

SpinRite II   SpinRite can perform low-level formatting on hard disks. This software can check the interleave and reset it for the optimum factor. It can do this without destroying your data. It can defragment a disk, test a hard drive, and detect any marginal areas. SpinRite can maximize hard disk performance and prevent hard disk problems before they happen. (Steve Gibson, the developer of SpinRite, writes a weekly column for *InfoWorld*.)

Disk Technician   From Prime Solutions, Disk Technician does essentially the same thing that SpinRite does, and a bit more.

OPTune   Optune is another hard disk utility that can maximize its performance. It is similar to SpinRite and Disk Technician. Gazelle Systems also developed QDOS II, an excellent shell program and Back-It, a very good hard disk backup program.

CheckIt   From TouchStone Software, this program quickly checks and reports on your computers configuration, the type of CPU it has, the amount of memory, the installed drives, and peripherals. It runs diagnostic tests of the installed items and can do performance benchmark tests.

Directory and disk management programs

Dozens of disk management programs can help you keep track of your files and data on the hard disk, find, rename, view, sort, copy, delete, and perform many other useful tasks with your files. These programs can save an enormous amount of time and make life a lot simpler.

XTreePro Gold Executive Systems XTree was one of the first and still one of the best disk management programs. It has recently been revised and it is now much faster and has several new features.

QDOS II QDOS II is a disk management program that is similar to XTree. It is not quite as sophisticated, but it is less expensive.

Tree86 3.0 Tree86 is another low cost disk management program that is similar to XTree.

Wonder Plus 3.08 Wonder, or 1DIR, was one of the early disk management shells. It has recently been revised and updated.

Other utilities

If you have a lot of files in several subdirectories, you can sometimes forget in which subdirectory you filed something. A couple of programs can go through all of your directories and look for a file by name, but because you are only allowed eight characters for a file name, it can be difficult to remember what is in each file. Several programs can search through all your files and find almost anything that you tell them to. You do not even have to know the full name that you are looking for. You can use wildcards and find matches.

Magellan 2.0 Magellan 2.0 is a very sophisticated program that can navigate and do global searches through files and across directories. It finds text and lets you view it in a window. It will let you compress files, do backup, compare, undelete, and use several other excellent utilities.

Three other search programs are very similar. Text Collector is a bit faster than Gofer and has a few more features. Dragnet works under the Windows environment. They are not nearly as sophisticated as Magellan and are somewhat limited.

Sidekick Plus Sidekick is in a class by itself. It was first released in 1984 and has been the most popular pop-up program ever since. It has recently been revised and enlarged so that it does much more than the simple calculator, notepad, calendar, and other utilities it had originally. It now has all of the original utilities plus scientific, programmer, and business calculators; an automatic phone dialer; a sophisticated script language; and much more. Sidekick loads into memory and pops up whenever you need it, no matter what program you happen to be running at the time.

Windows Graph   Windows Graph is a presentation graphics program that uses Windows. Data from spreadsheets and other files can be ported to the program to make all sorts of graphs. Micrografx also has several other graphics programs and graphics aids such as ClipArt, Draw Plus, Designer, and Graph Plus.

ClickStart   The hDC Computer Corp. has developed ClickStart, an applications organizer for Windows. It allows you to customize Windows and your applications, design your own icons and help screens, password protect confidential files, and many more useful utilities.

HyperPAD   The Brightbill-Roberts Company has developed HyperPAD, which makes the PC look more and more like the Macintosh. HyperPAD is quite similar to HyperCard. HyperPAD can be used with or without a mouse. It can be used to create, modify, and run personal applications from a pad. The pads are similar to a menu. It comes with several pads which can be modified and customized. You need only point and click, or use an arrow key to run an application.

Computer-aided design (CAD)

AutoCAD   A high-end cost design program. It is quite complex with an abundance of capabilities and functions, but it is also rather expensive at about $3000. It is the IBM of the CAD world and has more or less established the standard for the many clones that have followed.

DesignCAD 2D and DesignCAD 3D   These CAD programs will do just about everything that AutoCAD will do at about one-tenth of the cost. Design-CAD 3D allows you to make three-dimensional drawings. The list price for 2D is $299 and for 3D it is $399. The discount houses are advertising them for as little as $142 and $188.

Other programs

Many other programs for accounting, statistics, finance, and many other applications exist. Some are very expensive, some are very reasonable.

I cannot possibly mention all of the fantastic software that is available. Thousands and thousands of ready-made software programs will allow you to do almost anything with your computer. Look through any computer magazine for the reviews and ads. You should be able to find programs for almost any application.

16
CHAPTER

Mail order
and magazines

I have tried to list a few vendors when I mentioned a product, but it is not possible to list all of the sellers and sources for the products that you might need. There are thousands of vendors and many more thousands of products.

One of the best ways to find what you need is through the magazine advertisements. The magazines also usually have a few informative articles scattered among the ads.

If you live near a large city, you can also visit the computer stores in town. You can actually see and touch the merchandise, maybe even try it out before you buy it.

Again, if you live near a large city, there will probably be a few swap meets every now and then. In the San Francisco Bay Area and in the Los Angeles Area, there is one almost every weekend. Going to a swap meet is usually better than going to a computer store. You can look at lots of items and compare prices and features. Often several booths or vendors are selling the same thing. You can take a pad and pencil, go to each vendor, get his best price, then make your best deal. Sometimes you can even haggle a bit with the vendors. Some will try to meet the price of their competition. The best time to haggle is when it gets near closing time. Some of them would rather sell at a reduced price rather than pack the goods up and take them back to their store.

Mail order

Shopping at a local computer store can be a hassle time-wise and traffic-wise. Or you can look through a magazine, find an ad for what you need, pick up your phone, order the components, and have them delivered to your door. An extra plus is that it might cost you 40% less than what you would pay at the local store. On the down side, you might have to wait three or four weeks before you get your goodies. Of course, you can usually pay extra and have them shipped by an express service in which case you could probably get them overnight or within a couple of days. Another big minus is that you are buying the components sight unseen. You have only the word of the advertiser that he will send them. But if you use a bit of common sense and follow a few basic rules, you should not have to worry.

Ten rules for ordering by mail

Because of mail fraud, the publishers and the advertisers got together and formed the *Microcomputer Marketing Council* (MMC) of the Direct Marketing Association.

They now police the advertisers fairly closely. But just to be on the safe side, here are a few rules that you should follow when ordering through the mail:

1. Make sure the advertiser has a street address. In some ads, they give only a phone number. If you decide to buy from this vendor, call and verify that a live person on the other end has a street number. Before you send any money, do a bit more investigation. If possible, look through past issues of the same magazine for previous ads. If he has been advertising for several months, then he is probably okay.
2. Check through the magazines for other vendors prices for this product. The prices should be fairly close. If it appears to be a bargain that is too good to be true, then (you know the rest).
3. Buy from a vendor who is a member of the Microcomputer Marketing Council (MMC), of the Direct Marketing Association (DMA), or some other recognized association. The members of marketing associations have agreed to abide by the ethical guidelines and rules of the associations. Except for friendly persuasion and the threat of expulsion, the associations have little power over the members. But most members realize what is at stake and put a great value on their membership. Most who advertise in the major computer magazines are members. The Post Office, the Federal Trade Commission, the magazines and the legitimate businessmen who advertise have taken steps to try to stop the fraud and scams.
4. Do your homework. Know exactly what you want, state precisely the model, make, size, component, and any other pertinent information. Tell them which ad you are ordering from, ask them if the price is the same, if the item is in stock, and when you can expect delivery. If the item is not in stock, indicate whether you will accept a substitute or want

your money refunded. Ask for an invoice or order number. Ask the person's name. Write down all of the information, the time, the date, the company's address and phone number, description of the item, and promised delivery date. Save any and all correspondence.

5. Ask if the advertised item comes with all the necessary cables, parts, accessories, software, etc. Ask what the warranties are. Ask what is the seller's return or refund policies and with whom should you correspond if there is a problem.

6. Do not send cash. You will have no record of it. If possible, use a credit card. If you have a problem, you can possibly have the bank refuse to pay the amount. A personal check can cause a delay of three to four weeks while the vendor waits for it to clear. A money order or credit card order should be filled and shipped immediately. Keep a copy of the money order.

7. If you have not received your order by the promised delivery date, notify the seller.

8. Try the item out when you receive it. If you have a problem, notify the seller immediately by phone, then in writing. Give all details. Do not return the merchandise unless the dealer gives you authorization. Make sure to keep a copy of the shipper's receipt or packing slip or evidence that it was returned.

9. If you believe the product is defective or you have a problem, reread your warranties and guarantees. Reread the manual and any documentation. It is very easy to make an error or misunderstand how an item operates if you are unfamiliar with it. Before you go to a lot of trouble, try to get some help from someone else. At least get someone to verify that you do have a problem. Many times a problem can disappear, and the vendor will not be able to duplicate it.

10. Try to work out your problem with the vendor. If you cannot, then write to the consumer complaint agency in the seller's state. You should also write to the magazine and to the DMA at 6 E. 43rd St., New York, NY 10017.

Federal Trade Commission Rules

If these rules are not followed by the company you ordered from, you can notify the Federal Trade Commission. Here is a brief summary of the FTC rules:

1. The seller must ship your order within 30 days unless the ad clearly states that it will take longer.

2. If it appears that the seller cannot ship when promised, he must notify you and give a new date. He must give you the opportunity to cancel the order and refund your money if you desire.

3. If the seller notifies you that he cannot fill your order on time, he must include a stamped self-addressed envelope or card so that you can respond to his notice. If you do not respond, he may assume that you agree to the delay. He still must ship within 30 days of the end of the original 30 days or cancel your order and refund your money.

4. Even if you consent to a delay, you still have the right to cancel at any time.

5. If you cancel an order that has been paid for by check or money order, he must refund the money. If you paid by credit card, your account must be credited within one billing cycle. Store credits or vouchers in place of a refund are not acceptable.

6. If the item you ordered is not available, the seller may not send you a substitute without your express consent.

Magazines

Here are some of the magazines that you should subscribe to if you want to keep up:

Byte
P.O. Box 558
Highstown, NJ 08520-9409

Compute!
P.O. Box 3244
Harlan, IA 51593-2424

Computer Currents
5720 Hollis St.
Emeryville, CA 94608

Computer Monthly
P.O. Box 7062
Atlanta, GA 30357-0062

Computer Graphics World
P.O. Box 122
Tulsa, OK 74101-9966

Computer Shopper
P.O. Box 51020
Boulder, CO 80321-1020

Data Based Advisor
P.O. Box 3735
Escondido, CA 92025-9895

Home Office Computing
P.O. Box 51344
Boulder, CO 80321-1344

LAN Magazine
Miller Freeman Publications
P.O. Box 50047
Boulder, CO 80321-0047

MicroTimes
5951 Canning St.
Oakland, CA 94609

PC Computing
P.O. Box 50253
Boulder, CO 80321-0253

PC World
P.O. Box 51833
Boulder, CO 80321-1833

PC Magazine
P.O. Box 51524
Boulder, CO 80321-1524

PC Resource
P.O. Box 50302
Boulder, CO 80321-0302

PC Sources
P.O. Box 50237
Boulder, CO 80321-0237

Publish!
P.O. Box 51966
Boulder, CO 80321-1966

Personal Workstation
P.O. Box 51615
Boulder, CO 80321-1615

Unix World
P.O. Box 1929
Marion, OH 43306

Free magazines to qualified subscribers

The magazines listed in this section as free are sent only to qualified subscribers. The subscription price of a magazine usually does not come anywhere near covering the costs of publication, mailing, distribution and other costs. Most magazines depend almost entirely on advertisers for their existence. The more subscribers that a magazine has, the more it can charge for its ads. Naturally, the magazine can attract a lot more subscribers if the magazine is free.

PC Week and *InfoWorld* are excellent magazines. They are so popular that the publishers have to limit the number of subscribers. They cannot possibly accommodate all the people who have applied. They have set standards which have to be met in order to qualify. They do not publish the standards, so even if you answer all of the questions on the application, you still might not qualify.

To get a free subscription, you must write to the magazine for a qualifying application form. The form will ask several questions such as how you are involved with computers, the company you work for, whether you have any influence in purchasing the computer products listed in the magazines, and several other questions that give them a very good profile of their readers.

The list of magazines is not nearly complete. Hundreds of trade magazines are sent free to qualified subscribers. Many of the trade magazines are highly technical and narrowly specialized.

PC Week
P.O. Box 5920
Cherry Hill, NJ 08034

Computer Systems News
600 Community Dr.
Manhasset, NY 11030

InfoWorld
1060 Marsh Rd.
Menlo Park, CA 94025

Communications Week
P.O. Box 2070
Manhasset, NY 11030

PC Today
P.O. Box 85380
Lincoln, NE 68501-9815

Computer Reseller News
P.O. Box 2040
Manhasset, NY 11030

Computer Design
Circulation Dept.
Box 3466
Tulsa, OK 74101-3466

Computer Products
P.O. Box 14000
Dover, NJ 07801-9990

Computer Technology Review
924 Westwood Blvd. Suite 650
Los Angeles, CA 90024-2910

California Business
Subscription Dept.
P.O. Box 70735
Pasadena, CA 91117-9947

Designfax
P.O. Box 1151
Skokie, IL 60076-9917

Discount Merchandiser
215 Lexington Ave.
New York, NY 10157

EE Product News
P.O. Box 12982
Overland Park, KS 66212-9817

Electronics
A Penton Publication
P.O. Box 985061
Cleveland, OH 44198-5061

Electronic Manufacturing
Lake Publishing
P.O. Box 159
Libertyville, IL 60048-9989

Electronic Publishing & Printing
650 S. Clark St.
Chicago, IL 60605-9960

Federal Computer Week
P.O. Box 602
Winchester, MA 01890-9948

Identification Journal
2640 N. Halsted St.
Chicago, IL 60614-9962

ID Systems
174 Concord St.
P.O. Box 874
Peterborough, NH 03458-0874

Automatic I.D. News
P.O. Box 6170
Duluth, MN 55806-9870

LAN Times
122 East, 1700 South
Provo, UT 84606

Lasers & Optronics
301 Gibraltar Dr.
P.O. Box 601
Morris Plains, NJ 07950-9827

Machine Design
Penton Publishing
P.O. Box 985015
Cleveland, OH 44198-5015

Modern Office Technology
Penton Publishing
1100 Superior Ave.
Cleveland, OH 44197

Manufacturing Systems
P.O. Box 3008
Wheaton, IL 60189-9972

Medical Equipment Designer
Huebcore Communications
29100 Aurora Rd., #200
Cleveland, OH 44139

Mini-Micro Systems
P.O. Box 5051
Denver, CO 80217-9872

Modern Office Technology
1100 Superior Ave.
Cleveland, OH 44197-8032

Office Systems 90
P.O. Box 3116
Woburn, MA 01888-9878

Office Systems Dealer 90
P.O. Box 2281
Woburn, MA 01888-9873

Photo Business
1515 Broadway
New York, NY 10036

The Programmer's Shop
5 Pond Park Rd.
Hingham, MA 02043-9845

Quality
P.O. Box 3002
Wheaton, IL 60189-9929

Reseller Management
301 Gibraltar
Box 601
Morris Plains, NJ 07950-9811

Robotics World
6255 Barfield Rd.
Atlanta, GA 30328-9988

Unix Review
Circulation Dept.
P.O. Box 7439
San Francisco, CA 94120-7439

Scientific Computing & Automation
301 Gibraltar Dr.
Morris Plains, NJ 07950-0608

Surface Mount Technology
Lake Publishing Corp.
P.O. Box 159
Libertyville, IL 60048-9989

Public domain software

Here is a short list of companies that provide public domain, shareware and low cost software:

PC-Sig
1030D East Duane Ave.
Sunnyvale, CA 94086
(800) 245-6717

MicroCom Systems
3673 Enochs St.
Santa Clara, CA 95051
(408) 737-9000

Public Brand Software
Box 51315
Indianapolis, IN 46251
(800) 426-3475

Software Express/Direct
Box 2288
Merrifield, VA 22116
(800) 331-8192

Selective Software
903 Pacific Ave. Suite 301
Santa Cruz, CA 95060
(800) 423-3556

The Computer Room
P.O. Box 1596
Gordonsville, VA 22942
(703) 832-3341

Computers International
P.O. Box 6085
Oceanside, CA 92056
(619) 630-0055

PC Plus Consulting
14536 Roscoe Blvd. #201
Panorama City, CA 91402
(818) 891-7930

Micro Star
P.O. Box 4078
Leucadia, CA 92024-0996
(800) 443-6103

International Software Library
511 Encinitas Blvd. Suite 104
Encinitas, CA 92024
(800) 992-1992

National PD Library
1533 Avohill
Vista, CA 92083
(619) 941-0925

Shareware Express
27601 Forbes Rd., #37
Laguna Niguel, CA 92677
(714) 367-0080

Most of the companies listed above can provide a catalog listing of their software. Some of them charge a small fee for their catalog. Write to them or call them for details and latest prices.

This list is not complete. You may find several other companies advertised in some of the magazines listed earlier.

Books

One of the better ways to learn about computers is through books. Many bookstores will ship computer books to you. Several companies publish computer books. One of the companies is Windcrest. For a catalog, write to the address in the front of this book. You can find many books at your local bookstore or library. If they do not have exactly what you want, write the publisher (the address can often be found on the copyright page) for a catalog.

17
CHAPTER

Troubleshooting

Not too many books have been written on the subject of troubleshooting. Some that you find might be obsolete and out of date. Even if you find one that is current and up to date, chances are rather slim that it will address your particular problem.

I do not want to discourage anyone, but thousands of things can go wrong. It is very easy to plug a cable in backwards or forget to set a switch. Sometimes it is difficult to determine if it is a hardware problem caused by software, or vice versa. Not every problem can be addressed here, but you can do several common-sense things to solve many of your problems.

One of the best ways to find answers is to ask someone who has had the same problem. One of the best places to find those people is at a user's group. If at all possible, join one.

You can also get help from local bulletin boards. Your computer is not complete without a modem so that you can contact them.

Several local computer magazines list user groups and bulletin boards as a service to their readers. The nationally published *Computer Shopper* prints a very comprehensive list each month.

Is it worth it

If you find a problem on a board, a disk drive, or some component, you might try to find out what it would cost before having it repaired. With the low-cost clone hardware that is available, it is often less expensive to scrap a defective part and buy a new one.

Write it down

The chances are if your computer is going to break down, it will do it at the most inopportune time. If it breaks down, try not to panic. Ranting, cussing, and crying might make you feel better, but it will not solve the problem. Under no circumstances should you beat on your computer with a chair or baseball bat.

Instead get out a pad and pencil and write down everything as it happens. It is very easy to forget. Write down all the particulars, how the cables were plugged in, the software that you were running, and anything that might be pertinent. If you have error messages on your screen, use the PrtSc (Print Screen) key to print out the messages.

If you cannot solve the problem, you might have to call a friend or your vendor for help. If you have all the written information before you, it will help. Try to call from your computer, if possible, while it is acting up.

Power-on self-test (POST)

Everytime you turn your computer on, it does a power-on self-test or POST. It checks the RAM, the floppy drives, the hard disk drives, the monitor, the printer, the keyboard, and other peripherals that you have installed.

If it does not find a unit, or if the unit is not functioning correctly, it will beep and display an error code. The codes start with 100 and may go up to 2500. Ordinarily, the codes are not displayed if there is no problem. If there is a problem, the last two digits of the code will be something other than 00s. Here are some of the codes that you might encounter:

- 101 Motherboard failure.
- 109 Direct Memory Access test error.
- 121 Unexpected hardware interrupt occurred.
- 163 Time and date not set.
- 199 User indicated configuration not correct.
- 201 Memory test failure.
- 301 Keyboard test failure or a stuck key.
- 401 Monochrome display and/or adapter test failure.
- 432 Parallel printer not turned on.
- 501 Color Graphics display and/or adapter test failure.
- 601 Diskette drives and/or adapter test failure.
- 701 Math coprocessor test error.
- 901 Parallel printer adapter test failure.
- 1101 Asynchronous Communications adapter test failure.
- 1301 Game control adapter test failure.
- 1302 Joystick test failure.
- 1401 Printer test failure.
- 1701 Fixed disk drive and/or adapter test failure.

2401 Enhanced Graphics display and/or adapter test failure.

2501 Enhanced Graphics display and/or adapter test failure.

DOS has several other error messages if you try to make the computer do something it cannot do. Many of the messages are not very clear. The DOS manual explains some of them, but it does not give very much detail.

Electrostatic discharge (ESD)

Before you touch any of the components or handle them, you should ground yourself and discharge any static voltage that you might have built up. You can discharge yourself by touching an unpainted metal part of the case of a computer or other device that is plugged in. A person can build up a charge of 4000 volts or more of electrostatic voltage. If you walk across some carpets and then touch a brass doorknob, you can often get a shock and sometimes see a spark fly. Most electronic assembly lines have the workers wear a ground strap whenever they are working with any electrostatic discharge sensitive components.

When I am installing memory chips, or handling other ICs, I often use a clip lead to ground myself. I clip one end to my metal watchband and the other end to the computer case.

Power supply

Most of the components in your computer are fairly low power and low voltage. The only high voltage in your system is in the power supply, and it is pretty well enclosed. So there is no danger of shock if you open your computer and put your hand inside it. But you should NEVER connect or disconnect a board or cable while the power is on. Fragile semiconductors can be destroyed if you do so.

Most of the power supplies have short-circuit protection. If too much of a load is placed on them, they will drop out and shut down, similar to what happens when a circuit breaker is overloaded. Most of the power supplies are designed to operate only with a load. If you take one out of the system and turn it on without a load, most of them will not work. You can plug in a floppy drive to act as a load if you want to check the voltages out of the system.

The fan in the power supply should provide all the cooling that is normally needed. But if you have stuffed it into a corner and piled things around it to shut off all its circulation, it could possibly overheat. Heat is an enemy of semiconductors, so try to give it plenty of breathing room.

The semiconductors in your computer have no moving parts. If they were designed properly, they should last indefinitely. Heat is the enemy that can cause semiconductor failure. The fan in the power supply should provide adequate cooling. All of the openings on the back panel that correspond to the slots on the motherboard should have blank fillers. Even the holes on the bottom of the chassis should be covered with tape. This forces the fan to draw air in from the front of the computer, pull it over the boards and exhaust it through the opening in the power supply case. Nothing should be placed in front of or behind the computer that would restrict air flow.

If the fan is not running (you should be able to hear it), then the power supply might be defective.

Here are the pin connections and wire colors from the power supply:

Disk drive power supply connections

Pin	Color	Function
1	Yellow	+12 VDC
3	Black	Ground
4	Red	+5 VDC

Power supply connections to the motherboard

	Pin	Color	Function
P8	1	White	Power Good
	2	No connection	
	3	Yellow	+12 VDC
	4	Brown	−12 VDC
	5	Black	Ground
	6	Black	Ground
P9	1	Black	Ground
	2	Black	Ground
	3	Blue	−5 VDC
	4	Red	+5 VDC
	5	Red	+5 VDC
	6	Red	+5 VDC

The eight slotted connectors on the motherboard have 62 contacts, 31 on the A side and 31 on the B side. The black ground wires connect to B1 of each of the eight slots. B3 and B29 have +5 VDC, B5 −5 VDC, B7 −12 VDC, and B9 has +12 VDC. These voltages go to the listed pins on each of the eight plug-in slots.

Levels of troubleshooting

There are many levels of troubleshooting. To do a thorough analysis of a system requires some rather sophisticated and expensive instruments. This advanced level of troubleshooting would require tools such as a good high-frequency oscilloscope, a ditigal analyzer, a logic probe, signal generators, a voltohmmeter, some clip leads, a pair of side cutter dikes, a pair of long-nose pliers, various screwdrivers, nut drivers, a soldering iron and solder, different-sized screws and bolts, and a test bench with a power supply, disk drives, and a computer with some empty slots so that you could plug in the suspect boards and test them. You would also need plenty of light over the bench and a flashlight or a small light to light up the dark places in the case.

And most importantly, you would need quite a lot of training and experience. You probably will not need all that equipment and training. Most problems that you encounter will be rather minor problems, where just a little common sense and some investigation will tell you what is wrong.

Recommended tools

Here are some tools that you should have around the house for troubleshooting:

- You should have several sizes of screwdrivers. A couple of them should be magnetic for picking up and starting small screws. You can buy magnetic screwdrivers, or you can make one yourself. Just take a strong magnet and rub it on the blade of the screwdriver a few times. The magnets on cabinet doors will do, as will the voice coil magnet of a loudspeaker. Remember to be very careful with any magnet around your floppy disks, because it can erase them.
- You should also have a small screwdriver with a bent tip that can be used to pry up ICs. Some of the larger ICs are very difficult to remove. One of the blank fillers for the slots on the back panel also makes a good prying tool.
- You should have a couple pairs of pliers. You should have at least one pair of long-nose pliers.
- You will need a pair of side cutter dikes for clipping leads of components and cutting wire. You might buy a pair of cutters that also have wire strippers.
- You should not have to do any soldering but you never know when you might need to. A soldering iron might come in handy. And, of course, some solder.
- No home should be without a voltohmmeter. A voltohmmeter can be used to check for the correct wiring in house wall sockets (the wide slot should be ground), and it can be used to check switches and wiring continuity in your computer, house, phone lines, etc. The only four voltages to check for are $+12$ volts, -12 volts, $+5$ volts, and -5 volts. Voltohmmeters are relatively inexpensive.
- You might also want to have several clip leads. You can buy them at the local electronic store.
- You will need a flashlight for looking into the dark places inside the computer.

Fewer bugs

In the early days, the clone computers had lots of bugs and errors. Some manufacturers did not spend a lot of money on quality control and testing. Most of the computer manufacturers have been making the parts long enough now that the designs have been firmed up and most bugs have been eliminated.

The number one cause of problems

If you assembled your computer properly, it should work perfectly. But there is always the possibility that something was not plugged in correctly or some minor error was made.

By far the greatest problem in assembling a unit, or adding something to a computer, is not following the instructions. Quite often it is not necessarily the fault of the person trying to follow the instructions. I have worked in the electronic industry for many years, but sometimes I have great difficulty in trying to decipher and follow certain manuals and instructions. Sometimes a very critical instruction or piece of information might be inconspicuously buried on page 300 of a 450-page manual.

If you have just assembled your computer or added something to it, turn it on and check it out before you put the cover on. If something is wrong, it is usually easier to find the problem.

Before you turn it on, though, recheck all the cables and any boards or chips. Make sure that they are seated properly and in the right place. Read the instructions again, then turn on the power. If it works, then put the cover on and button it up.

Common problems

For most of the common problems, you will not need a lot of test gear. Most of my problems were due to my stupid errors. Many problems are caused by not taking the time to read the manual or instructions, or not being able to understand them.

If you look closely, you might see a cable that is not plugged in properly, a board that is not completely seated, or a switch that is not set right. And many other obvious things.

You can listen for any unusual sounds. The only sound from your computer should be the noise of your drive motors and the fan in the power supply.

If you have ever smelled a burned resistor or a capacitor, you will never forget it. If you smell something very unusual, try to locate where the smell originates.

If you touch the components and some seem to be unusually hot, it could be the cause of your problem. It is always best to be cautious. Except for the insides of your power supply, the voltage should not be more than 12 volts in your computer, so it should be safe to touch the components.

How to find the problem

If it seems to be a problem on the motherboard or a plug-in board, look for chips that have the same number. Try swapping them to see if the problem goes away or worsens. If you suspect a board and you have a spare or can borrow one, swap it.

Also, if you suspect a board, but do not know which one, take the boards out to the barest minimum. Then add them back until the problem develops. CAUTION! Always turn off the power when plugging in or unplugging a board or cable.

Wiggle the boards and cables to see if it is an intermittent problem. Many times a wire can be broken and still make contact until it is moved. Next, check the ICs and connectors for bent pins. If you have installed memory ICs and get errors, check to make sure that they are seated properly and all the pins are in the sockets. If you swap an IC, make a note of how it is oriented before removing it. A small dot of white paint or a U-shaped indentation should be at the end that has pin 1. If you forgot to note the orientation, look at the other ICs. Most of the boards are laid out so that all of the ICs are oriented the same way. The chrome fillers that are used to cover the unused slots in the back of the case make very good tools for prying up ICs.

You might also try unplugging a cable or a board and plugging it back in. Sometimes the pins may be slightly corroded or not seated properly. Before unplugging a cable, you might put a stripe on the connectors with a marking pen or nail polish so that you can easily see how they should be plugged back in.

The problem could be in a dip switch. You might try turning it on and off a few times. CAUTION! Again, always write down the positions before touching the switches.

Remember, always make a diagram of the wires, cables, and switch settings before you disturb them. It is easy to forget how they were plugged in or set before you moved them. You could end up making things worse. Make a pencil mark before turning a knob or variable coil or capacitor so that it can be returned to the same setting when you find out that it did not help. Better yet, resist the temptation to reset these types of components. Most were set up using highly sophisticated instruments. They do not usually change enough to cause a problem.

If you are having monitor problems, check the switch settings on the motherboard. Some motherboards have dip switches or shorting bars that must be set to configure the system for monochrome, CGA, EGA, or VGA. Most monitors also have fuses. You might check them. Also check the cables for proper connections.

Printer problems, especially the serial printers, are so many that I will not even attempt to list them here. Many printers today have parallel and serial. The IBM defaults to the parallel system. If at all possible, use the parallel port. Parallel printers have very few problems as compared to serial printers.

Most printers have a self-test. It might run this test fine, but then completely ignore any efforts to get it to respond to the computer if the cables, parity, and baud rate are not properly set.

Sometimes the computer will hang up. You might have told it to do something that it could not do. You can usually do a warm reboot of the computer by pressing the Ctrl, Alt, and Del keys simultaneously. Of course, this would wipe out any file in memory that you might have been working on. Occasionally, the computer might not respond to a warm boot. (You could pound on the keyboard all day long, and it would ignore you.) In that case, you will have to switch off the main power, let it sit for a few seconds, then power up again.

Diagnostic and utility software

When IBM came out with the XT, they developed a diagnostic or set-up disk that was included with every machine. It checked the keyboard, the disk drives, the monitor, peripherals, and performed several other tests. When the AT was released, the diagnostic disk was revised a bit to include even more tests. You had to have the disk to set the time, date, and all of the other on-board CMOS system configuration.

Most of the newer BIOS chips now have many of the diagnostic routines built in. These routines allow you to set the time and date, tell the computer what type of hard drive and floppies that are installed, the amount of memory, the wait states, and several other functions. The AMI BIOS has a very comprehensive set of built-in diagnostics that allows hard and floppy disk formatting, checks speed of rotation of disk drives, does performance testing of hard drives, and several other tests.

I mentioned these utility software programs in chapter 16. Many of them have a few diagnostics among the utilities:

- *Norton Utilities*—It also includes several diagnostic and test programs such as disk doctor, disk test, format recover, directory sort, system information, and many others.
- *Mace Utilities*—It does about everything that Norton does and a few other things. It has recover, defragment, diagnose, remedy, and several other very useful programs primarily for the hard disk.
- *PC Tools*—From Central Point Software, PC Tools has several utilities much like the Norton and Mace Utilities. It has a utility that can recover data from a disk that has been erased or reformatted. It has several other data recovery and DOS utilities. It can be used for hard disk backup and has several utilities such as those found in SideKick.
- *SpinRite, Disk Technician, OPTune, and DOSUTILS*—These are utilities that allow you to diagnose, analyze, and optimize your hard disk.
- *CheckIt*—From TouchStone Software, CheckIt checks and reports on your computer configuration by letting "you look inside your PC without taking off the cover." It reports on the type of processor, amount of memory, video adapter, hard and floppy drives, clock/calendar, ports, keyboard, and mouse, if present. It also tests the motherboard, hard and floppy disks, RAM, ports, keyboard, mouse, joystick, and other tests. It can also run a few benchmark speed tests.
- *Interrogator*—Dysan, a branch of Xidex Corporation, has developed the Interrogator software. It can check a floppy disk drive for head alignment and performance and do several other diagnostic tests. If you are having

17-1   The Blue-Magic diagnostic board. It can be used to find and diagnose problems on the mother-board and the peripherals.

trouble reading software on a certain drive, a quick test with this software will tell you whether it is the drive or the software.

One of the best diagnostic tools that I have seen is Blue-Magic from Paramount Electronics at (408) 298-9915 (Fig. 17-1). This unit is a small half size board that can be plugged into a slot of a PC, XT, 286, 386, or 486 motherboard. Even if the computer is completely inoperative, as long as the power supply and monitor are still good, Blue-Magic can check out all of the circuits and pinpoint the defective areas. Once the tests are initiated, they will continue to run unattended until stopped. If there is an intermittent failure in the system, it will find it. It keeps track of the passes and failures of the chips as it continuously loops through the tests. Blue-Magic is also an ideal tool for doing burn-in on units.

Again, if at all possible, join a user's group and get to know the members. They can be one of your best sources of troubleshooting. Most of them have had similar problems and are glad to help.

Glossary

access time   The amount of time it takes the computer to find and read data from a disk or from memory. The average access time for a hard disk is based on the time it takes the head to seek and find the specified track, for the head to lock on to it, and for the head to spin around until the desired sector is beneath the head.

active partition   The partition on a hard disk that contains the boot and operating system. A single hard disk can be partitioned into several logical disks such as drive C, drive D, and drive E. This can be done at the initial formatting of the disk. Only one partition, usually drive C, can contain the active partition.

adapter boards or cards   The plug-in boards needed to drive monitors. Most monitor boards are monochrome graphic adapters (MGA), color graphic adapters (CGA), or enhanced graphic adapters (EGA). The EGA boards give a higher resolution than the CGA when used with a high-resolution monitor. The video graphics adapters (VGA) can give an even higher resolution than the EGA.

algorithm   A step-by-step procedure, scheme, formula, or method used to solve a problem or accomplish a task. May be a subroutine in a software program.

alphanumeric   Having both numerals and letters.

analyst   A person who determines the computer's needs to accomplish a given task. The job of an analyst is similar to that of a consultant. Note that there are no standard qualifications requirements for either of these jobs. Anyone can call themselves an analyst or a consultant. They should be experts in their field, but might not be.

ANSI   American National Standards Institute. A standard adopted by MS-DOS for cursor positioning used in the ANSI.SYS file for device drivers.

ASCII   American Standard Code for Information Interchange. Binary numbers from 0 to 127 that represent the upper- and lowercase letters of the alphabet, the numbers 0-9, and the several symbols found on a keyboard. A block of eight 0s and 1s are used to represent all of these characters. The first 32 characters, 0-31, are reserved for noncharacter functions of a keyboard, modem, printer, or other device. Number 32, or 0010 0000, represents the space, which is a character. The numeral 1 is represented by the binary number for 49, which is 0011 0001. Text written in ASCII is displayed on the computer screen as standard text. Text written in other systems, such as WordStar, has several other characters added and is very difficult to read. Another 128-character representation has been added to the original 128 for graphics and programming purposes.

ASIC   Application Specific Integrated Circuit.

assembly language   A low-level machine language made up of 0s and 1s.

asynchronous   A serial type of communication where one bit at a time is transmitted. The bits are usually sent in blocks of eight 0s and 1s.

autoexec.bat   If present, this file is run automatically by DOS after it boots up. You can configure this file to suit your own needs; it can load and run certain programs or configure your system.

.BAK files   Anytime that you edit or change a file in certain applications the program will save the original file as a backup and append the extension .BAK to it.

BASIC   Beginners All-Purpose Symbolic Instruction Code. A high-level language that was once very popular. Many programs and games still use it. It comes with DOS as GW BASIC.

batch   The batch command can be used to link commands and run them automatically. The batch commands can be made up easily by the user. They all have the extension .BAT.

baud   Bits per second. A measurement of the speed or data transfer rate of a communications line between the computer and printer, modem, or another computer. Most present-day modems operate at 2400 baud or higher.

benchmark   A standard type program against which similar programs can be compared.

bidirectional   Both directions. Most printers print in both directions, thereby saving the time it takes to return to the other end of a line.

binary   Binary numbers are 0s and 1s.

BIOS   Basic Input-Output System. The BIOS is responsible for handling the input output operations.

bits   Binary digits. A contraction of Binary and digITs.

boot or bootstrap   When a computer is turned on, all the memory and other internal operators have to be set or configured. The IBM takes quite a while to boot up because it checks all the memory parity and most of the peripherals. A small amount of the program to do this is stored in ROM. Using this, the computer pulls itself up by its bootstraps. A warm boot is sometimes necessary to get the computer out of an endless loop, of it it is hung up for some reason. A warm boot can be done by pressing Ctrl, Alt, and Del.

bubble memory   A nonvolatile type memory that is created by the magnetization of small bits of ferrous material. It held a lot of promise at one time, but it is rather expensive to make and is slower than semiconductor memory.

buffer   Usually some discrete amount of memory that is used to hold data. A computer can send data thousands of times faster than a printer or modem can utilize it. But, in many cases, the computer can do nothing else until all of the data has been transferred. The data can be input to a buffer, which can then feed the data into the printer as needed. The computer is then freed to do other tasks.

bug, debug The early computers were made with high-voltage vacuum tubes. It took rooms full of hot tubes to do the job that a credit card calculator can do today. One of the large systems went down one day. After several hours of troubleshooting, the technicians found a large bug had crawled into the high-voltage wiring and been electrocuted, but it had shorted out the whole system. Since that time, any type of trouble in a piece of software or hardware is called a *bug*. To *debug* it, of course, is to try to find the errors or defects.

bulletin boards Usually a computer with a hard disk that can be accessed with modem. Software and programs can be uploaded or left on the bulletin board by a caller, or a caller can scan the software that has been left there by others and download any that he or she likes. The bulletin boards often have help and message services—a great source of help for a beginner.

burst mode Means that the bus is taken over and a packet of data is sent as a single unit. During this time, the bus cannot be accessed by other requests until the burst operation is completed. This allows as much as 33 Mb per second or more to be transmitted over the bus.

bus Wires or circuits that connect a number of devices together. It can also be a system. The IBM PC bus is the configuration of the circuits that connect the 62 pins of the 8 slots together on the motherboard. It has become the *de facto* standard for the clones and compatibles.

byte A byte is 8 bits or a block of 8 0s and 1s. These 8 bits can be arranged in 256 different ways (2^8). Therefore, one byte can be made to represent any one of the 256 characters in the ASCII character set. It takes one byte to make a single character. Because the word "byte" has four characters, it requires 4 bytes, or 32 bits.

cache memory A high-speed buffer set up in memory to hold data that is being read from RAM or hard disks. Often a program will request the same data over and over again. This can be quite time consuming, depending on the access speed of the disk drive or the location of the data in RAM. If the requested data is cached in high-speed memory, it can be accessed almost immediately.

carriage width The width of a typewriter or printer. The two standard widths are 80 columns and 132 columns.

cell A place for a single unit of data in memory, or an address in a spreadsheet.

Centronics parallel port A system of 8-bit parallel transmission first used by the Centronics Company. It has become a standard and is the default method of printer output on the IBM.

character A letter, a number, or an 8-bit piece of data.

chip An integrated circuit, usually made from a silicon wafer. It can be microscopically etched and have thousands of transistors and semiconductors in a very small area. The 80286 CPU used in the AT has an internal main surface of about a half inch. It has 120,000 transistors on it, the 386 has 275,000, the 486 has 1.2 million.

CISC Complex Instruction Set Computing. This is the standard type of computer design as opposed to the RISC or reduced instruction set computers used in larger systems. It can require as many as six steps for a CISC system to carry out a command. The RISC system might need only two steps to perform a similar function.

clock The operations of a computer are based on very critical timing, so they use a crystal to control their internal clocks. The standard frequency for the PC and XT is 4.77 million cycles per second, or million hertz. The turbo systems operate at 6 to 8 MHz. The 486 operates at 25 MHz to 33 MHz.

cluster Two or more sectors on a track of a disk. Each track of a floppy or hard disk is divided into sectors.

COM Usually refers to serial ports COM1 or COM2. These ports are used for serial printers, modems, a mouse or other pointing device, or plotters and other serial devices.

.COM A .COM or .EXE extension on the end of a file name indicates that it is program that can run commands to execute programs.

COMDEX The nation's largest computer exposition and show, usually held once in the spring in Atlanta and in the fall in Las Vegas.

COMMAND.COM An essential command that must be present in order to boot and start the computer.

composite video A less expensive monitor that combines all the colors in a single input line.

console In the early days, a monitor and keyboard were usually set up at a desk-like console. The term has stuck. A console is a computer. The command COPY CON allows you to use the keyboard as a typewriter. Type COPY CON PRN or COPY CON LPT1, and everything you type will be sent to the printer. At the end of your file, or letter, type Ctrl-Z or F6 to stop sending.

consultant Someone who is supposed to be an expert who can advice and help you determine what your computer needs are (similar to an analyst). No standard requirements or qualifications must be met, so anyone can take the title analyst or consultant.

conventional memory The first 640K of RAM memory, the memory that DOS handles. The PC actually has 1Mb of memory, but the 384K above the 640K is reserved for system use.

coprocessor Usually an 8087, 80287, or 80387 that works in conjunction with the CPU and vastly speeds up some operations.

copy protection A system that prevents a disk from being copied.

CPS Characters Per Second. When referring to a printer, the speed that it can print.

CPU Central Processing Unit such as the 8088, 80286, 80386 or 80486.

CSMA/CD   Carrier Sense Multiple Access with Collision Detection. A network system that controls the transmissions from several nodes. It detects if two stations try to send at the same time. It notifies the senders to try again at random times.

CRT   Cathode ray tube. The large tube that is the screen of computer monitors and televisions.

current directory   The directory that is in use at the time.

cursor   The blinking spot on the screen that indicates where next character will be input.

daisy wheel   A round printer or typewriter wheel with flexible fingers that have the alphabet and other formed characters.

database   A collection of data, usually related in some way.

DATE command   Date will be displayed anytime DATE is typed at the prompt sign.

DES   Data Encryption Standard. First developed by IBM, it can be used to encrypt data so that it is almost impossible to decode it unless you have the code.

DIP   Dual Inline Pins. A DIP refers to the two rows of pins on the sides of most integrated circuit chips.

disk controller   A plug-in board that is used to control the hard and/or floppy disk drives. All of the read and write signals go through the controller.

DMA   Direct Memory Access. Some parts of the computer such as the disk drives can exchange data directly with the RAM without having to go through the CPU.

documentation   Manuals, instructions, or specifications for a system whether it is hardware or software.

DOS   Disk Operating System. Software that allows programs to interact and run on a computer.

dot matrix   A type of printer that uses a matrix of thin wires or pins to make up the print head. Electronic solenoids pushed the pins out to form letters out of dots that were made when the pins pushed against the ribbon and paper. Older printers used seven pins which gave rather poor quality print. Newer 24-pin heads can print in near-letter-quality (NLQ) type.

double density   At one time, most disks were single-sided and had a capacity of 80 to 100K. Then the capacity was increased and technology was advanced so that the disks could be recorded on both sides with up to 200K per side double-sided, double-density. Then quad density was soon introduced with 400K per side. Then of course, the newer 1.6Mb high-density disks. All of the above figures are before formatting. Most double-density is the common 360K formatted. The quad ends up with 720K formatted and the high density is 1.2Mb. The $3^1/2''$ disks standard format is 720K. The high-density $3^1/2''$ disks hold 1.44MB.

DPMI   DOS Protected Mode Interface. A proposed specification to govern the interaction of large applications with each other, DOS, and OS/2.

DRAM   Dynamic Random Access Memory. This is the usual type of memory found in personal computers. It is the least expensive of memory types.

DTP   Desktop Publishing. A rather loose term that can be applied to a small personal computer and a printer as well as to high-powered sophisticated systems.

dumb terminal   A terminal that is tied to a mainframe or one that does not have its own microprocessor.

duplex   A characteristic of a communications channel which enables data to be transmitted in both directions. Full duplex allows the information to be transmitted in both directions simultaneously. In a half duplex, it can be transmitted in both directions, but not at the same time.

EATA   Enhanced AT Attachment. A standard proposed by the Common Access Method (CAM) committee. Their proposal would define a standard interface for connecting controllers to PCs. It would define a standard software protocol and hardware interface for disk controllers, SCSI host adapters, and for other intelligent chip embedded controllers.

ECHO   A command that can cause information to be displayed on the screen from a BAT or other file. ECHO can be turned on or off.

EEPROM   An Electrically-Erasable Programmable Read-Only Memory chip.

EGA   Enhanced Graphics Adapter. Board used for high-resolution monitors.

EISA   Extended Industry Standard Architecture, a clone bus system for the 386 or 486.

E-mail   Electronic mail. A system that allows messages to be sent through LANs (local area networks) or by modem over telephone lines.

EMS   Expanded Memory Specification. A specification for adding expanded memory put forth by Lotus, Intel, and Microsoft (LIM EMS).

EPROM   An Erasable Programmable Read-Only Memory chip.

ergonomics   The study and science of how the human body can be the most productive in working with machinery. This would include the study of the effects of things like the type of monitor, the type of chair, lighting, and other environmental and physical factors.

errors   DOS displays several error messages if it receives bad commands or there are problems of some sort.

ESDI   Enhanced Small Disk Interface. A hard disk interface that allows data to be transferred to and from the disk at a rate of 10 megabits per second. The older standard ST506 allowed only 5 megabits per second.

.EXE   A file with this extension indicates that it is an executable file that can run and execute the program. It is similar to the .COM files.

expanded memory   Memory that can be added to a PC above 640K. It can only be accessed through special software.

expansion boards   Boards that can be plugged into one of the 8 slots on the motherboard to add memory or other functions.

extended memory   Memory that can be added to an 80286, 80386, or 80486. It can be addressed with Windows 3.0.

external commands   DOS commands that are not loaded into memory when the computer is booted.

FAT   File Allocation Table. This is a table on the disk that DOS uses to keep track of all the parts of a file. A file can be placed in sector 3 of track one, sectors 5 and 6 of track 10 and sector 4 of track 20. The FAT would keep track of where they are and will direct the read or record head to those areas.

fax   A shortened form of the word *facsimile* and *X* for transmission. A fax machine scans an image or textual document and digitizes it in a graphical form. As it scans an image, a 0 or 1 is generated depending on the presence or absence of darkness, or ink. The 0s and 1s are transmitted over the telephone line as voltages (see *modem*).

fonts   The different types of print letters such as Gothic, Courier, Times Roman, Helvetica, and others.

format   The process of preparing a disk so that it can be recorded. The format process lays down tracks and sectors so that data can be written anywhere on the disk and recovered easily.

fragmentation   If a disk has several records that have been changed several times, there are bits of the files on several different tracks and sectors. This slows down writing and reading of the files because the head has to move back and forth to the various tracks. If these files are copied to a newly formatted disk, each file will be written to clean tracks that are contiguous. This will decrease the access time to the floppy disk or hard disk.

friction feed   A printer that uses a roller or platen to pull the paper through.

game port   An Input/Output (I/O) port for joysticks, trackballs, paddles, and other devices.

gigabyte   One billion bytes. This will probably be a common-size memory in a very short time.

glitch   An unexpected electrical spike or static disturbance that can cause loss of data.

global   A character or something that appears throughout an entire document or program.

googol   A very large figure, 1 followed by 100 zeros.

GUI   Graphical user interface. It usually makes use of a mouse, icons, and windows such as those used by the Macintosh.

handshaking   A protocol or routine between systems, usually the printer and the computer, to indicate readiness to communicate with each other.

hard disk   A disk drive that can usually store a large amount of data. It has one or more magnetically coated platters that spin at 3600 RPM in a sealed casing.

hardware   The physical parts that make up a computer system such as disk drives, keyboards, monitors, etc.

Hayes-compatible Hayes was one of the first modem manufacturers. Like IBM, they created a set of standards that most others have adopted.

hexadecimal A system that uses the base 16. The binary system is based on 2, the decimal system is based on 10. The hexadecimal goes from 0, 1, 2, 3, 4, 5, 6, 7, 8, 9, A, B, C, D, E, F. 10 would be 16 in the hexadecimal system, and it starts over so that 20 would be 32 in hexadecimal. Most of the memory locations are in hexadecimal notation.

hidden files The files that do not show up in a normal directory display.

high-level language A language such as BASIC, Pascal, or C. These program languages are fairly easy to read and understand.

ICs Integrated Circuits. The first integrated circuit was the placing of two transistors in a single can early in the 1960s. Then ways were found to put several semiconductors in a package. It was called SSI, or Small-Scale Integration. Then LSI, or Large-Scale Integration, then VLSI or Very-Large-Scale Integration were developed. Today we have VHSIC or Very-High-Scale Integrated Circuits.

IDE Integrated Disk Electronics. Western Digital and other companies are manufacturing hard drives with most of the controller circuitry on the disk assembly, but they still need an interface of some sort to connect to the computer. The hard drives are somewhat similar to SCSI and ESDI.

interface A piece of hardware or a set of rules that allows communications between two systems.

internal commands Those commands that are loaded into memory when DOS boots up.

interpreter A program that translates a high-level language into machine-readable code.

ISDN Integrated Services Network. A standard for telephone communications for transmission of voice, data, and images.

kilobyte Roughly 1000 bytes, also known as 1K or more exactly, 1024 bytes. This is 2^{10}.

LAN Local Area Network. Where several computers might be tied together or to a central server.

laser printer A type of printer that uses the same type of "engine" used in copy machines. A laser beam electronically controlled sweeps across a drum. It charges the drum with an image of the letters or graphics that is to be printed. The charged drum then picks up toner particles and deposits them on the page so that a whole page is printed at once.

LIM-EMS Lotus-Intel-Microsoft Expanded Memory Specification.

low-level format Most hard disks must have a preliminary low-level format performed on them before then can be formatted for DOS. Low-level formatting is also sometimes called *initializing*.

low-level language A machine level language. Usually in binary digits that would be very difficult for most people to understand.

LQ Letter Quality. The type from a daisy wheel or formed type printers.

macro A series of keystrokes that can be recorded, somewhat like a batch file, then be typed back when one or more keys is pressed. For instance, I can type my entire return address with just two keystrokes.

mainframe A large computer that can serve several users.

megabyte Roughly 1,000,000 bytes, also known as 1Mb. More precisely, it is 2^{20} or 1,048,576 bytes. It takes a minimum of 20 data lines to address 1Mb, a minimum of 24 lines (2^{24}) to address 16Mb, and a minimum of 25 lines (2^{25}) to address 32Mb.

menu A list of choices or options. A menu-driven system makes it very easy for beginners to choose what they want to run or do.

MFM Modified Frequency Modulation. The scheme for the standard method of recording on hard disks. See RLL.

MHz Megahertz, a million cycles per second. Some older technicians still call it CPS. A few years ago, a committee decided to honor Heinrich Rudolf Hertz (1857-1894) for his early work in electromagnetism. So they changed the cycles per second, CPS, to Hertz or Hz.

mode A DOS command that must be invoked to direct the computer output to a serial printer.

modem A contraction of modulator-demodulator. A device that allows data to be sent over telephone lines.

modes The 80286 and 80386 will operate in three different modes, the real, the protected, and the virtual. For more details, see chapter 9.

mouse A small pointing device that can control the cursor and move it anywhere on the screen. It usually has one to three buttons that can be assigned various functions.

MTBF Mean Time Before Failure. An average of the time between failures, usually used in describing a hard disk or other component.

multitasking The ability of the computer to perform more than one task at a time. Many of the newer computers have this capability when used with the proper software.

multiuser A computer that is capable of providing service to more than one user such as a server for a local area network (LAN).

NEAT chipset New Enhanced AT chipset from Chips and Technology. Chips and Technology combined the functions of several chips found on the original IBM motherboard into just a few very large scale integrated circuits (VLSI). These chips are used on the vast majority of clone boards.

NLQ Near Letter Quality. The better formed characters from a dot matrix printer.

null modem cable A cable with certain pairs of wires crossed over. If the computer sends data from pin 2, the modem might receive it on pin 3. The modem would send data back to the computer from its pin 2 and be received by the computer on pin 3. Several other wires would also be crossed.

OOP   Object Oriented Programs. A type of programming that utilizes parts of existing programs to provide new applications.

OS/2   An operating system that allows the 80286, 80386, and 80486 machines to directly address huge amounts of memory. It removes many of the limitations that DOS imposes. OS/2 does not benefit the PCs or XTs to any great degree.

parallel   A system that uses 8 lines to send 8 bits at a time, or one whole byte.

parity checking   In the computer memory system, parity checking is an error detection technique that verifies the integrity of the RAM memory contents. This is the function of the ninth chip in a memory bank. Parity checking systems are also used in other areas such as verifying the integrity of data transmitted by modem.

PIF   Program Information File. Files used by Windows that supply information about how an application uses the screen, memory, and other, computer resources. These programs have a .pif extension.

plotter   An X-Y writing device that can be used for charts, graphics, and many other functions that most printers can't do.

prompt   The > sign that shows that DOS is waiting for an entry.

protocol   The rules and methods by which computers and modems can communicate with each other.

QIC   Quarter-Inch Cartridge tape. A width of tape used in tape backup systems. Some standards using this size tape have been developed, but still several non-standard systems are in use.

RAM   Random Access Memory. This is computer memory that is used to temporarily hold files and data as they are being worked on, changed or altered. This volatile memory can be written to and read from. Any data stored in it is lost when the power is turned off.

RGB   Red, Green, and Blue. The three primary colors that are used in color monitors and TVs. Each color has its own electron gun that shoots streams of electrons to the back of the monitor display and causes it to light up in the various colors.

RISC   Reduced Instruction Set Computing. A design that allows a computer to operate with fewer instructions allows it to run much faster.

RLL   Run Length Limited. A scheme of hard disk recording that allows 50 percent more data to be recorded on a hard disk than the standard MFM scheme. ARLL or ERLL, for Advanced or Enhanced RLL, will allow twice as much data to be recorded on a hard disk. The older MFM system divided each track into 17 sectors of 512 bytes each. The RLL format divides the tracks into 26 sectors with 512 bytes each. The ARLL and ERLL divides them into 34 sectors per track.

ROM   Read-Only Memory. This memory is not lost when the power is turned off. The primary use of ROM is in the system BIOS and on some plug-in boards.

scalable typeface Unlike bitmapped systems where each font has one size and characteristic, scalable systems allow typeface to be shrunk or enlarged to different sizes to meet specific needs. Once a font has been scaled, it is then stored as bitmapped. This allows much more flexibility and uses less memory. There are also scalable graphic systems.

SCSI Small Computer System Interface, pronounced scuzzy. A fast parallel hard disk interface system developed by Shugart Associates and adopted by the American National Standards Institute (ANSI), the SCSI system allows multiple drives to be connected. It supports a transfer rate of 1.2 megabytes per second. Because a byte is 8 bits, this is about the same as the ESDI 10 megabit per second rate.

sector A section of a track on a floppy or hard disk. A sector ordinarily holds 512 bytes. A 360K disk has 40 tracks per side. Each track is divided into 9 sectors.

serial The transmission of one bit at a time over a single line.

SIMM Single Inline Memory Module.

SIP Single Inline Pins. Many small resistor packs and integrated circuits have a single line of pins.

source The origin, or the disk to be copied from.

SPARC Scalable Processor Architecture. A RISC system developed by Sun Microsystems for workstations.

spool Simultaneous Peripheral Operations On Line. A spooler acts as a storage buffer for data which is then fed out to a printer or other device. In the meantime, the computer can be used for other tasks.

SRAM Static RAM. A type of RAM that can be much faster than DRAM. SRAM is made up of actual transistors that are turned on or off and will maintain their state without constant refreshing such as needed in DRAM. SRAM is considerably more expensive and requires more space than DRAM.

target The disk to be copied to.

time stamp The record of the time and date that is recorded in the directory when a file is created or changed.

tractor A printer device with sprockets or spikes that pulls the computer paper with the holes in the margins through the printer at a very precise feed rate. A friction feed platen might allow the paper to slip, move to one side or the other, and not be precise in the spacing between the lines.

Trojan horse A harmful piece of code or software that is usually hidden in a software package that will later cause destruction. It is unlike a virus in that it does not grow and spread.

TSR Terminate and Stay Resident. When a program such as SideKick is loaded in memory, it will normally stay there until the computer is booted up again. If several TSR programs are loaded in memory, there might not be enough left to run some programs.

turbo Usually means a computer with a faster-than-normal speed.

user-friendly Usually means bigger and more expensive. It should make using the computer easier.

user groups Usually a club or a group of people who use computers. Often the club will be devoted to users of a certain type of computer, but in most clubs anyone is welcome to join.

vaporware Products that are announced, usually with great fanfare, but are not yet ready for market.

VCPI Virtual Control Program Interface. A plug-in board that allows a computer to address memory above 640K.

virtual Something that might be essentially present, but not in actual fact. If you have a single disk drive, it will be drive A, but you also have a virtual drive B if you want to copy from A to B.

virus Destructive code that is placed or embedded in a computer program. The virus is usually self-replicating and will often copy itself onto other programs. It might lie dormant for some time, then completely erase a person's hard disk or cause other problems.

volatile Refers to memory units that lose stored information when power is lost. Nonvolatile memory would be that of a hard disk or tape.

VRAM Video RAM. A type of special RAM used on video or monitor adapters. The better adapters have more memory so that they can retain full-screen high-resolution images.

windows Many new software packages are now loaded into memory where they stay in the background until they are called. When called, the program will pop up on the screen in a window. The Microsoft company has a software package called *Windows 3.0* that provides a GUI operating environment for many DOS programs.

Index